W9-AEY-061

Modern Critical Views

ELIZABETH BISHOP

Modern Critical Views

Continued at back of book

Modern Critical Views

ELIZABETH BISHOP

Edited with an introduction by

Harold Bloom

Sterling Professor of the Humanities
Yale University

1985
CHELSEA HOUSE PUBLISHERS
New York

THE COVER:
The poet Elizabeth Bishop, some of whose most remarkable poems concern confrontations with the sea, as in "At the Fishhouses" and "The End of March," is shown reflecting upon the characteristic scene of her dramatic meditations.—H.B.

Cover illustration by Robin Peterson

Copyright © 1985 by Chelsea House Publishers,
a division of Chelsea House Educational Communications, Inc.

   345 Whitney Avenue, New Haven, CT 06511
   95 Madison Avenue, New York, NY 10016
   5068B West Chester Pike, Edgemont, PA 19028

Printed and bound in the United States of America

10 9 8 7 6 5 4 3

Library of Congress Cataloging in Publication Data

Elizabeth Bishop.
    (Modern critical views)
    Bibliography: p.
    Includes index.
    1. Bishop, Elizabeth, 1911-   —Criticism and
interpretation—Addresses, essays, lectures.   I. Bloom,
Harold.   II. Series.
PS3503.I785Z64   1985   811'.54   85–5965
ISBN 0–87754–624–X

Contents

Editor's Note

This volume gathers together the best literary criticism devoted to the late Elizabeth Bishop. I have arranged these reviews, critical essays, and readings of individual poems in the order of their publication. My own introduction briefly traces Miss Bishop in the traditions of American poetry, while analyzing two poems, the early "The Unbeliever" and the late "The End of March." The poet John Ashbery's review is an illuminating tribute by a great poet of the generation after Bishop and with the introduction helps to locate some of the larger contours of her achievement.

Jan B. Gordon's pioneering essay on the cartographic element in Bishop's imagination is followed by the poet Richard Howard's reading of "In the Waiting Room," with its emphasis upon a very different aspect of her creativity. The essay by Jerome Mazzaro, and the long excerpt from David Kalstone's study of Bishop, examine fundamental issues of memory and deliberate self-limitation in her art.

Larger dimensions of Bishop's lifework are explored in the subsequent studies by John Hollander, Helen Vendler, and Willard Spiegelman, all of which center upon different perspectives in her singular moral vision. The study of her prosody by Penelope Laurans is then followed by David Lehman's juxtaposition of the poet's fictional prose with her verse.

Brief readings of three crucial poems, by the poets Sandra McPherson and J. D. McClatchy and the critic David Walker, provide a transition to the two most recent essays. David Bromwich achieves a retrospective synoptic view of a crucial unifying element in Bishop, while Joanne Feit Diehl relates the poet to her largest tradition, the American Sublime, thus bringing the volume back full circle to its introduction. Future studies of Bishop doubtless will give us a larger and more detailed sense of her continuity with the great sequence that goes from Emerson and Dickinson on through Stevens and Marianne Moore, a sequence in which Elizabeth Bishop is both a legitimate heir and now also a strong ancestor.

Introduction

The principal poets of Elizabeth Bishop's generation included Roethke, Lowell, Berryman, Jarrell, and, in a different mode, Olson. Whether any of these articulated an individual rhetorical stance with a skill as sure as hers may be questioned. Her way of writing was closer to that of Stevens and Marianne Moore, in the generation just beyond, than to any of her exact contemporaries. Despite the differences in scale, her best poems rival the Stevens of the shorter works, rather than the perhaps stronger Stevens of the sequences.

Bishop stands, then, securely in a tradition of American poetry that began with Emerson, Very, and Dickinson, and culminated in aspects of Frost as well as of Stevens and Moore. This tradition is marked by firm rhetorical control, overt moral authority, and sometimes by a fairly strict economy of means. The closing lines in *Geography III* epitomize the tradition's self-recognition:

> He and the bird know everything is answered,
> all taken care of,
> no need to ask again.
> —Yesterday brought to today so lightly!
> (A yesterday I find almost impossible to lift.)

These poignant lines have more overt pathos than the poet ever allowed herself elsewhere. But there is a paradox always in the contrast between a poetry of deep subjectivity, like Wordsworth's or Stevens's or Bishop's, and a confessional poetry, like Coleridge's or that of Bishop's principal contemporaries. When I read, say, "The Poems of Our Climate," by Stevens, or "The End of March," by Bishop, I encounter eventually the overwhelming self-revelation of a profoundly subjective consciousness. When I read, say, "Skunk Hour" by Lowell or one of Berryman's sonnets, I confront finally an opacity, for that is all the confessional mode can yield. It is the strength of Bishop's tradition that its clarity is more than a surface phenomenon. Such strength is cognitive, even analytical, and surpasses philosophy and psychoanalysis in its power to expose human truth.

There are grander poems by Bishop than the relatively early "The

Unbeliever," but I center upon it here because I love it best of all her poems. It does not compare in scope and power to "The Monument," "Roosters," "The Fish," "The Bight," "At the Fishhouses," "Brazil, January 1, 1502," "First Death in Nova Scotia," or the extraordinary late triad of "Crusoe in England," "The Moose," and "The End of March." Those ten poems have an authority and a possible wisdom that transcend "The Unbeliever." But I walk around, certain days, chanting "The Unbeliever" to myself, it being one of those rare poems you never evade again, once you know it (and it knows you). Its five stanzas essentially are variations upon its epigraph, from Bunyan: "He sleeps on the top of a mast." Bunyan's trope concerns the condition of unbelief; Bishop's does not. Think of the personae of Bishop's poem as exemplifying three rhetorical stances, and so as being three kinds of poet, or even three poets: cloud, gull, unbeliever. The cloud is Wordsworth or Stevens. The gull is Shelley or Hart Crane. The unbeliever is Dickinson or Bishop. None of them has the advantage; the spangled sea wants to destroy them all. The cloud, powerful in introspection, regards not the sea but his own subjectivity. The gull, more visionary still, beholds neither sea nor air but his own aspiration. The unbeliever observes nothing, but the sea is truly observed in his dream:

> which was, "I must not fall.
> The spangled sea below wants me to fall.
> It is hard as diamonds; it wants to destroy us all."

I think that is the reality of Bishop's famous eye. Like Dickinson's, its truest precursor, it confronts the truth, which is that what is most worth seeing is impossible to see, at least with open eyes. A poetry informed by that mode of observation will station itself at the edge where what is most worth saying is all but impossible to say. I will conclude here by contrasting Bishop's wonderful trope of the lion, in "The End of March," to Stevens's incessant use of the same figure. In Stevens, the lion tends to represent poetry as a destructive force, as the imposition of the poet's will-to-power over reality. This image culminates in "An Ordinary Evening in New Haven":

> Say of each lion of the spirit
>
> It is a cat of a sleek transparency
> That shines with a nocturnal shine alone.
> The great cat must stand potent in the sun.

Against that destructive night in which all cats are black, even the transparent ones, Stevens sets himself as a possible lion, potent in the light of the idea-of-ideas. Here, I take it, Bishop's affectionate riposte:

> They could have been teasing the lion sun,
> except that now he was behind them
> —a sun who'd walked the beach the last low tide,
> making those big, majestic paw-prints,
> who perhaps had batted a kite out of the sky to play with.

A somewhat Stevensian lion sun, clearly, but with something better to do than standing potent in itself. The path away from poetry as a destructive force can only be through play, the play of trope. Within her tradition so securely, Bishop profoundly plays at trope. Dickinson, Moore, and Bishop resemble Emerson, Frost, and Stevens in that tradition, with a difference due not to mere nature or mere ideology but to superb art.

JOHN ASHBERY

"The Complete Poems"

One hopes that the title of Elizabeth Bishop's new book is an error and that there will be more poems and at least another *Complete Poems*. The present volume runs to a little more than 200 pages, and although the proportion of pure poetry in it outweighs many a chunky, collected volume from our established poets (Miss Bishop is somehow an establishment poet herself, and the establishment ought to give thanks; she is proof that it can't be all bad), it is still not enough for an addict of her work. For, like other addicting substances, this work creates a hunger for itself; the more one tastes it, the less of it there seems to be.

From the moment Miss Bishop appeared on the scene it was apparent to everybody that she was a poet of strange, even mysterious, but undeniable and great gifts. Her first volume, *North & South* (1946), was the unanimous choice of the judges in a publisher's contest to which 800 manuscripts were submitted. Her second won the Pulitzer Prize. One of her poems is enough to convince you that you are in expert hands and can relax and enjoy the ride; in the words of Marianne Moore reviewing *North & South*, "At last we have someone who knows, who is not didactic." Few contemporary poets can claim both virtues.

Her concerns at first glance seem special. The life of dreams, always regarded with suspicion as too "French" in American poetry; the little mysteries of falling asleep and the oddness of waking up in the morning; the sea, especially its edge, and the look of the creatures who live in it; then diversions and reflections on French clocks and mechanical

From *The New York Times Book Review* (June 1, 1969). Copyright © 1969 by *The New York Times*.

toys that recall Marianne Moore (though the two poets couldn't be more different; Miss Moore's synthesizing, collector's approach is far from Miss Bishop's linear, exploring one).

And yet, what more natural, more universal experiences are there than sleep, dreaming and waking; waking, as she says in one of her most beautiful poems, "Anaphora," to: "the fiery event/of every day in endless/endless assent." And her preoccupation with wildlife and civilized artifacts comes through as an exemplar of the way we as subject feel about the objects, living or inert, that encircle us. We live in a quandary, but it is not a dualistic conflict between inner and outer reality, it is rather a question of deciding how much the outer reality is our reality, how far we can advance into it and still keep a toe-hold on the inner, private one, "For neither is clearer/nor a different color/than the other," as Miss Bishop says.

This strange divided singleness of our experience is a theme that is echoed and alluded to throughout Miss Bishop's work, but never more beautifully than in a short prose poem called "Rainy Season; Sub-Tropics," here collected for the first time. It consists of three monologues spoken by a giant toad, a crab and a giant snail, respectively, somewhat along the lines of Jules Renard's *Histoires Naturelles*, yet Miss Bishop's poems are actually brief, mordant essays on the nature of being. Conceivably these are thoughts that could occur to the creatures in question, yet at the same time they are types, and not metaphors, of thoughts that occur to an intellectually curious person. "I live, I breathe, by swallowing," confides the toad, who also mentions "the almost unused poison that I bear, my burden and my great responsibility." And the snail, frank but bemused, observes: "I give the impression of mysterious ease, but it is only with the greatest effort of my will that I can rise above the smallest stones and sticks."

One can smile at the way these creatures imperfectly perceive their habitat, but their dilemma is ours too, for we too confusedly feel ourselves to be part thing and part thought. And "we'd rather have the iceberg than the ship,/although it meant the end of travel." Our inert thingness pleases us, and though we would prefer not to give up "travel" or intellectual voyaging, in a showdown we would doubtless choose the iceberg, or object, because it mysteriously includes the soul: "Icebergs behoove the soul/(both being self-made from elements least visible)/to see them so: fleshed, fair, erected indivisible."

This quality which one can only call "thingness" is with her throughout, sometimes shaping a whole poem, sometimes disappearing right after the beginning, sometimes appearing only at the end to add a decisive fillip. In "Over 2000 Illustrations and a Complete Concordance," which is possibly her masterpiece, she plies continually between the steel-engraved vignettes of a gazetteer and the distressingly unclassified events of a real voyage. A nightmarish little prose tale called "The Hanging of the Mouse" concludes with a description so fantastically accurate that it shoots currents of meaning backward into the enigmatic story. "His whiskers rowed hopelessly round and round in the air a few times and his feet flew up and curled into little balls like young fern-plants."

As one who read, reread, studied and absorbed Miss Bishop's first book and waited impatiently for her second one, I felt slightly disappointed when it finally did arrive nine years later. *A Cold Spring* (1955) contained only sixteen new poems, and the publishers had seen fit to augment it by reprinting *North & South* in the same volume. Moreover, some of the new poems were not, for me, up to the perhaps impossibly high standard set by the first book. Several seemed content with picture-making: they made marvelous pictures, it is true, but not like those in *North & South* which managed to create a *trompe-l'oeil* that conquered not just the eye and the ear but the mind as well. And in several, the poet's life threatened to intrude on the poetry in a way that didn't suit it. One accepted without question the neutral "we" in earlier poems as the necessary plural of "I," but a couple of the new ones veered dangerously close to the sentimental ballad of the Millay-Teasdale-Wylie school, to one's considerable surprise, notably "Varick Street" with its refrain: *"And I shall sell you sell you/sell you of course, my dear, and you'll sell me."*

A Cold Spring does, however, contain the marvelous "Over 2000 Illustrations" which epitomizes Miss Bishop's work at its best; it is itself "an undisturbed, unbreathing flame," which is a line of the poem. Description and meaning, text and ornament, subject and object, the visible world and the poet's consciousness fuse together to form a substance that is undescribable and a continuing joy, and one returns to it again and again, ravished and unsatisfied. After twenty years (the poem first appeared in *Partisan Review* in 1948) I am unable to exhaust the meaning and mysteries of its concluding line: "And looked and looked our infant sight away," and I suspect that its secret has very much to do with the nature of Miss Bishop's poetry. Looking, or attention, will absorb the object with its meaning. Henry James advises us to "be one of those on whom nothing is lost," without specifying how this is to be accomplished. Miss Bishop, at the end of her poem "The Monument," which describes a curious and apparently insignificant monument made of wooden boxes, is a little more specific: "Watch it closely," she tells us. The power of vision, "our infant sight," is both our torment and our salvation.

Her next book, *Questions of Travel* (1965), completely erased the doubts that *A Cold Spring* had aroused in one reader. The distance between Varick Street and Brazil may account for the difference not just in thematic material but in tone as well. We are introduced to the country in the opening poem, "Arrival at Santos," with its engagingly casual rhymes ("seen" rhymes with "Miss Breen," a fellow passenger) and rhythms; its prosy, travel-diary style, its form so perfectly adapted to its content that there isn't a bulge or a wrinkle. After telling us about the ocean voyage and the port where it has ended, she terminates as only she can with a brief statement of fact that seems momentous: "We leave Santos at once;/we are driving to the interior."

Her years in the *la-bas* of Brazil brought Miss Bishop's gifts to maturity. Both more relaxed and more ambitious, she now can do almost anything she pleases, from a rhymed passage "From Trollope's Journal" to a Walker Evansish study of a "Filling Station"; and from a funny snapshot of a bakery in Rio at night ("The gooey tarts are red and sore") to "The Burglar of Babylon," a ballad about the death of a Brazilian bandit in which emotionally charged ellipses build up a tragic grandeur as in Godard's *Pierrot le Fou*.

Perhaps some of the urgency of the *North & South* poems has gone, but this is more than compensated by the calm control she now commands. Where she sometimes seemed nervous (as anyone engaged in a task of such precision has a right to be) and (in *A Cold Spring*) even querulous, she now is easy in a way that increased knowledge and stature allow. Her mirror-image "Gentleman of Shalott" in *North & South* was perhaps echoing the poet's sentiments when he said, "Half is enough." But the classical richness of her last poems proves that frugality need not exclude totality; the resulting feast is, for once, even better than "enough."

JAN B. GORDON

Days and Distances:
The Cartographic Imagination
of Elizabeth Bishop

My house, my fairy
palace, is
of perishable
clapboards with
three rooms in all,
my grey wasps' nest
of chewed-up paper
glued with spit.

from "Jeronimo's House"

Elizabeth Bishop's abodes are always "fairy palaces" of incredible interiority where child-like inhabitants construct rooms within rooms—all of which reflect a delicate fragility at the locus of intersection. If not real children, the figures who populate her poems are epistemological primitives whose approach to ordinary existence is never ordinary. *The Diary of 'Helena Morley,'* the first book translated from the Portuguese after Elizabeth Bishop moved to Brazil, is ostensibly the diary of a real "Helena," whose life in a Brazilian mining town must have resembled Miss Bishop's early existence, replete with bronchitis, in rural Nova Scotia. When the volume was published in Portuguese in 1942, the then grown "Helena" contributed an introduction:

From *Salmagundi* (1973). Copyright © 1973 by Skidmore College.

And now a word to my granddaughters: you who were born in comfort-able circumstances and who feel sorry when you read the stories of my childhood, you do not need to pity poor little girls just because they are poor. We were so happy! Happiness does not consist in worldly goods but in a peaceful home, in family affection, in a simple life without ambition—things that fortune cannot bring and often takes away.

Her world is happy as a direct function of its containment; self-enclosed, the child experiences evanescence as a corollary to freedom. It is only when the delicate fragility breaks down that the child's world falls apart. In a short story, "In the Village," Miss Bishop has described in vivid detail the child's experience of loss, but once again the perspective is that of adult reminiscence. The story itself is suspended between two sharp sounds: the scream of the now deceased mother and the metallic clang of the village blacksmith's anvil. Death appears merely as an absence surrounded by a world punctuated with the commerce of grief: a fire in a sympathetic neighbor's house; the arrival of parcels of cakes; and cartons of musty personal effects. Her memory thematically resembles those paintings of Brueghel; although the child regards time as having stopped, the country-side moves through all the phases appropriate to the Nova Scotia summer. There is an harmonious balance between the silence of personal grief and the noise of a world that pays little heed to the artificial egocentricity induced by the departure of a loved one. Cows continue to lose their way on the path home; house repairs must be completed before winter sets in; and the blacksmith's hammer continues to serve as a village timepiece. The story exhibits the same tension in its mode of composition, for the progress of chronological time is always interrupted by the circuitous nature of the adult narrator's dramatization of the crisis of childhood loss. Lines of narration proceed only to be broken off with large patches of white space—the spaces of nature struggling with the spaces of absence.

Such a conflict is almost always at the heart of Elizabeth Bishop's craft and is nowhere better illustrated than in a story, written while she was still at Vassar, which appeared in *Partisan Review* in March, 1938. Like so much of Elizabeth Bishop's art, "In Prison" begins with a question about the nature of perception only to eventually move into ontological issues. The result is often deceptive, since the poems, like so many of the short stories, begin as if they were puzzles or riddles while simultaneously demanding that the "pieces" be taken seriously. Yet, precisely because they always begin with a question or series of questions, a number of the poems appear as epistemological exercises. This particular story is a mono-logue wherein a narrator who seeks some principle of order in a universe which he imagines to be chaotic, comes to the conviction that his imprisonment is part of nature's design. Willing to substitute the paranoia of determinism for what most men define as freedom, Miss Bishop's prisoner recognizes that only incarceration transforms acts of conscience into arenas of potentiality. He focuses upon the details of interiority so that his willed criminality becomes part of the aesthete's intentionality: the hues of sunlight refracted upon the walls of his cell; the harlequinage of nuance in personal dress; the fascination with the traces that food leaves upon a tin plate. For his leisure reading, the narrator devotes himself to a naturalistic tome, an objective catalogue of pseudo-events to which is added layer upon layer of literary criticism. At a certain point in the process, the reader is unable to distinguish the prisoner's criticism of the book from the book itself. There is no authorial intent against which one might commit the *crime* of the intentional fallacy; the book provides the *basis* for a literary criticism, but because of the infinite regress of multiple layering, the critic-criminal never knows where he is, but only what he has lost. Taste has become a substitute for freedom. In this world her solitary speaker extends Hegelian philosophy to its logical limits—freedom is the knowledge of Necessity. His dilemma is that of the man who can live in the universe only to the extent that he remains ignorant of its presence, and the baroque constructions of his imagination resemble that city described from a window in one of Elizabeth Bishop's poems:

> . . . carefully revealed,
> made delicate by over-workmanship,
>   detail upon detail,
>   cornice upon facade,
>
> reaching so languidly up into
> a weak white sky, it seems to waver there.
>   ("Love Lies Sleeping")

On another level, the most acute loss faced by the protagonist of "In Prison" is the absence of the historical. In the environment where every intersection is a corner, there is virtually no lineage. His critical exercise is virtually indistinguishable from the book which serves as its object, and questions of priority and succession pale beneath the metaphysics of the layer. Since time has virtually disappeared, there is no meaning, save in the shade or the nuance—the projection of the inadequacy of taste to make circumscription a synonym for appropriation. The predominant metaphor for this activity is map-making—a sort of charting of poetic voyages which is in part, at least, autobiographical. In her craft, as in her life, geography always triumphs over history. Following her graduation from Vassar in 1934 and a brief sojourn in New York, Elizabeth Bishop went to Paris in 1935, only to return to the United States in 1936

to winter on Florida's West Coast. Obviously enchanted by a fishing trip
to Key West, she later elected to live there in 1938 after excursions to
Ireland, London, and Italy. Until she went to Mexico in 1943, Elizabeth
Bishop lived off and on in the Florida Keys. In 1951 she elected to use the
money awarded to her from a number of literary prizes to sail to the Straits
of Magellan. En route, she stopped off to visit friends in Rio de Janeiro
only to be afflicted by one of her childhood allergies. Forced to remain in
Rio for treatment, she settled in nearby Petropolis where she now lives
with her friend, Lota de Macedo Soares. She continues, however, to visit
the United States, usually for brief visits, serving most recently as writer-
in-residence at Harvard.

   The course of her life's wanderings has a peculiar pattern. Nova
Scotia, the Straits of Magellan, interior journeys into the Amazon estuary—
all of these places demarcate geographical boundaries between land and
sea. Whether consciously or not, Elizabeth Bishop seems fascinated by
geographical *extremities*—fingers of water or land that are the sensory
receptors of a larger mass. Straits, peninsulas, icebergs, radio antennas
("The Unbeliever"), wharfs and quais, capes ("Cape Breton"), and promon-
tories are the structures of her world. These are spaces which all share the
quality of near isolation; they are almost, but not quite, geologically
severed as if, like Miss Bishop herself, they were being constantly pulled
back to their origin. And the first poem of her 1945 volume, *North &
South*, engages us in the dilemma of that layered struggle between land
and sea:

> Land lies in water; it is shadowed green.
> Shadows, or are they shallows, at its edges
> showing the line of long sea-weeded ledges
> where weeds hang to the simple blue from green.
> Or does the land lean down to lift the sea from under,
> drawing it unperturbed around itself?
> Along the fine tan sandy shelf
> is the land tugging at the sea from under?
>
> ("The Map")

The poem itself is a mere study of a map and of the art of carto-
graphy. Musing over the color gradations that separate charted from
uncharted areas, Elizabeth Bishop's introductory poem is itself a kind of
map to the volume. Although the poem commences with one kind of
question—does the land lie on the water or does the water lie on the
land?—its conclusion involves the necessary transcendence of the
epistemological:

Are they assigned, or can the countries pick their colors?
—What suits the characters or the native waters best.
Topography displays no favorites; North's as near as West,
More delicate than the historians' are the map-makers' colors.
("The Map")

The historical precedence of land or water has nothing whatsoever to do with the aesthetics of the "picture" beneath the glass. Maps pose the question of freedom originally encountered in the early story, "In Prison": the existence of voluntary acts would imply the possibility of choices, and to the contrary, these countries cannot elect their colors. Topography is helpless to accommodate the third dimension and hence reduces all to the flat objectivity of *necessary direction*, itself a paradox. The map which purports to guide us to a location is, from an aesthetic perspective, a neutral space where we lose rather than gain our way. Like Elizabeth Bishop herself, we are wanderers rather than travelers and the "map" is an intermediary surface between those two states of being. She has taken an object known primarily for its utility in getting us from one place to another and restored it to an existence purged of history. In the process, the aesthetic preferences of "character" or "native waters" is sacrificed to the delicacy of the map-maker. Neither land nor water lends shape, but rather the artificial profiles of the cartographer. So obsessed with geographical boundaries, and the precise calibration of latitude and longitude, the printer nonetheless allows "the names of seashore towns [to] run out to sea." Words, whether on maps or in poems, always exceed the intersections to which they point.

But the poetic vision which imagines the most innocuous of events as "marking out maps like Rand McNally's" ("Roosters") surely embodies intriguing premises. It is a world where the poet charts—which is to say, that scale and perspective become primary considerations. Although the genre would seem to be that of the landscape, map-making is really a pseudo-landscape, enacting, to borrow from the vocabulary of Claude Lévi-Strauss, *bricolage*. She is fascinated with this activity, as the poem "Large Bad Picture" testifies:

Remembering the Strait of Belle Isle or
some northerly harbor of Labrador,
before he became a schoolteacher
a great-uncle painted a big picture.

Receding for miles on either side
into a flushed, still sky
are overhanging pale blue cliffs
hundreds of feet high,

> their bases fretted by little arches,
> the entrances to caves
> running in along the level of a bay
> masked by perfect waves.

The subject of the poem is an amateur's attempt to construct a coastal scene on canvas. As the painter becomes involved with the process of "remembering" so in the second stanza the coast line is "receding for miles on either side." There is the characteristic interiorization, followed by the quest for a sterile perfection: the "perfect waves" and later, the black birds "hanging in n's in banks." His feeble landscape lacks grandeur precisely because the painter of the "Large Bad Picture" has substituted *reconstruction* for imaginative construction: the spars of the vessels are like "burnt match-sticks" and the glassy sea resembles the middle of some "quiet floor." In order to capture that tone of the painting, Miss Bishop herself consciously resorts to the same gimmick as her great-uncle:

> In the pink light
> the small red sun goes rolling, rolling,
> round and round and round at the same height
> in perpetual sunset, comprehensive, consoling,
>
> while the ships consider it.
> Apparently they have reached their destination.
> It would be hard to say what brought them there,
> commerce or contemplation.

Her stanzas are artificially linked with "while" and "as" in order to establish simultaneity where none exists in the same way that the schoolteacher-painter has several objects—birds, ships, sun, and an aquatic animal—within an association which appears as a suspension. The conflict in the painting is one between "commerce or contemplation," since some objects move, while others remain static or "perpetual" in their motionlessness. Everything in the poem, like the painting, is strung together with some technique, or word, like "apparently." The terrible painting is simultaneously part cheap commercial oil painting and part the authentic product of an old man's contemplation; like its very lines, this landscape is hung between "receding" and "remembering" in stanzas one and two. And those trapped birds in "n's" above some cliff are "hanging" in Elizabeth Bishop's poem in such a way that we almost hear the "n" trapped between hard "g's." Again, like the world of her travels, everything in Miss Bishop's poetic universe is nearly severed and must be strung together with ferries or bridges or their verbal equivalents.

Like her great-uncle, Miss Bishop is always constructing when she appears to be describing, and the result is a poetry which has the quality of

an engineering exercise. There is a tendency to reduce the most complicated poetic issues to "questions" that are exclusively technical in nature.
Her poem "Large Bad Picture," then, is a highly self-conscious enterprise—
the use of an artificially bad poem to elicit the mood of an artificially
awkward oil painting. Although we marvel at the proficiency of the poem,
there is something curiously absent in such mastery. The emphasis upon
the coalesced perspective tends to be a substitute for any attention to the
personal. Even though we might wish to meet the grizzled amateur painter,
he will always be inaccessible, located somewhere behind his masterpiece.
Behind all the present and past participles of "Large Bad Picture" lurks
only a world that is somehow already *given*, never in the process of being
created. One suspects that this too is part of the map-maker's vision; after
all, a poetic universe that is reducible to a map might well imply that the
person en route is always among the lost. Compared with so much
contemporary poetry that is confessional in its detail of the loss of or
dispersal of selfhood, self-negation is a point of departure in Elizabeth
Bishop's craft. But it is a self-negation that the reader never records and
has no way of measuring, since the loss has occurred *a priori*. For this
reason, the poetry often lacks a distinctive teleology. We see no possibility
of a therapeutic progression in a world so relativized that "North's as near as
West" precisely because hers is at best a two-dimensional craft. There is a
certain surface tension always present in Elizabeth Bishop's art that is at
least partially the result of the loss of *privilege* in every sense in which we
might typically use that word: the narrator's sense of an advantage to
perspective; an access to secrets unknown to other protagonists in her
poems; or even the subtlety of an untrustworthy vision which might
confer aesthetic advantage by granting the reader the right to acknowledge a false subjectivity. She has had far more favorable response from
British critics than from those in this country perhaps because the limits of
her poetry prevent the kind of self-indulgence that G. S. Fraser referred to
as "luxury" in his essay, "Some Younger American Poets" (*Commentary*,
May, 1957). Fraser contrasted Miss Bishop's precise diction with that of
her American contemporaries and came to the conclusion that she had
willingly surrendered a certain polish in order that she might more clearly
say exactly what her poems want to say. He equates that equation,
unfortunately, with what he terms "an immense sense of responsibility
toward a critically cooperative audience." Of course there is a definable
responsibility in such an enterprise only when the word "responsibility" is
made synonymous with a failure to take risks. The etymology of the word
itself involves—as one of its primary meanings—the idea of an "answer"
or a "reply," literally a "speaking again (re-spondere)." And that quality is

seldom characteristic of her poetry because there is never a voice sufficiently distinctive so as to serve as a vehicle for an assumed dialogue.
Responsibility seldom derives from rhetorical questions. In short, it is the
responsibility of the map-maker: a world well-drawn and accurate, given
the nature of current exploration, but exhibiting more and more the
quality of a guidebook:

> The mosquitoes
> go hunting to the tune of their ferocious obbligatos.
> After dark, the fireflies map the heavens in the marsh
> until the moon rises.
> Cold white, not bright, the moonlight is coarse-meshed,
> and the careless, corrupt state is all black specks
> too far apart, and ugly whites; the poorest
> post-card of itself.
>
> ("Florida")

That very ability to turn a traditional landscape into a guidebook, complete with a commentary on the state's gnarled race relations, is a peculiarly unique slant to the contemporary *paysage moralisé*. Travel guides
become post-cards at the end of the journey when the initiate tells the
would-be traveler where to go and what to see.

But the landscape itself is altered in the process so that it always
appears to the reader as if it had been reproduced rather than experienced.
And the moral vision of such a universe is similarly skewed. For, as in so
many twentieth-century sex manuals, occasions that we would expect to
be of great intimacy are charted for us, perhaps too narrowly. If personal
intercourse with the natural world is part of the mythos of the guidebook,
the reader's potentiality is democratized at an enormous price. Not only
does it always look easier than it is, but emotional considerations are
seldom horizontal. For if the poet creates the illusion that technique alone
assures mastery, then we study the craft with an idea of learning it only to
discover that we have become cognizant of a world that is all surface.
From the map, as from the do-it-yourself guide to auto repair, we become
aware only of other surfaces. All of this is to say that Elizabeth Bishop's
poetry is always an *expedition* for which preparation is needed and, though
such is surely part of the Christian metaphor for life itself, her vision is
peculiarly technologized since there is no authentic ground for existence
in her scheme. We have the trappings of direction and guidance without
the emergence, real or promised, of presence. There is no better or
worse, no up or down, but only boundaries that create neutralized
spaces:

At low tide like this how sheer the water is.
White, crumbling ribs of marl protrude and glare
and the boats are dry, the pilings dry as matches.
Absorbing, rather than being absorbed, . . .

("The Bight")

Her images are never organically related nor are they presented in any of Imagism's characteristically durational clusters. Rather her poems appear as if they were strung together, with each metaphoric "set" following the preceding one in some established order of proper priorities. The pattern involves some invisible poetic finger moving across a map and accumulating rather than creating the world: "there is this, and then this, and then this. . . ." The manner is strangely reminiscent of one of Miss Bishop's childhood favorites, Gerard Manley Hopkins, whose verse provides the epigraph to a charming little poem, "Cold Spring." As in Hopkins's progressions, a number of her poems commence *ex nihilo* followed by some highly truncated phrase: "A cold spring:/the violet was flawed on the lawn." Then the universe suddenly proliferates:

Tufts of long grass show
where each cow-flop lies,
The bull-frogs are sounding,
slack strings plucked by heavy thumbs.
Beneath the light, against your white front door,
the smallest moths, like Chinese fans,
flatten themselves, silver and silver-gilt
over pale yellow, orange, or gray.
Now from the thick grass, the fireflies
begin to rise:

("A Cold Spring")

This type of poem usually concludes with some coda that approximates the tone of Hopkins's "Praise him" in its abbreviated reduplication in emotive language of the phenomenal catalogue:

And your shadowy pastures will be able to offer
these particular glowing tributes
every evening now throughout the summer.

("A Cold Spring")

The progression is from nothingness, through an almost incredible enumeration of the discrete, though evanescent particulars of a landscape, and then to a deliberation upon the human significance of the catalogue. We move from the distinctly non-human to the decidedly human by means of an almost imperceptible intrusion of the possessive pronoun "your" which serves to give the reader a kind of power at the very instant that he is being overwhelmed by the fertility of the scene. The use of "and" to link the human coda to the world of nature that precedes it in "Cold Spring" is one of those partial deceptions that deflect Miss Bishop's craft from a certain sincerity. As spring catches slumbering nature by surprise, so the "shadowy pastures" of the concluding lines catch the reader by surprise. Somehow, the location has been shifted, for these pastures are part of an interior landscape, part of the realm of "offer[ings]" and "tribute." At the very instant of rebirth in the book of nature, the reader is also part of the kingdom of sacrifice in the book of grace. But, like the old man's painting in "Large Bad Picture," the reader is never sure how he got there. The poem proceeds within a false *telos* punctuated by "Now, in the evening" to "Now, from the thick grass" to the "And . . ./ now throughout the summer." Yet, the final "now" is not part of the world of presence, but part of the absence of sacrifice and redemption that involves the possibility of return in the future; we have entered a realm of "will be" disguised as "now." Map-making too is an enterprise sufficiently vicarious as to involve a similar confusion between future and present tenses. The cartographer's product is one that continually must be up-dated, which is yet another way of using the word "now" as a refrain.

This constant struggle with the current in Elizabeth Bishop's art is metaphorically represented as a dialectic involving natural landscape and the claims of history. But again, history in her poems appears not as chronological time nor as the presence of the past, but rather as some symbol for every failed connection. For example, the poem "Argu-ment" from the volume *A Cold Spring* seems a lament for some lost love (one of the very few poems in Miss Bishop's canon that involves anything like intimacy), yet the rift is related in terms of a battle between distance and desire on the one hand, and days and voices on the other:

> Days that cannot bring you near
> or will not,
> Distance trying to appear
> something more than obstinate,
> argue argue argue with me
> endlessly
> neither proving you less wanted nor less dear.
> ("Argument")

History never is part of the kingdom of contiguity, but rather serves an opposite function in the dialogue with space:

> Days: And think
> of all those cluttered instruments,
> one to a fact,

> cancelling each other's experience,
> how they were
> like some hideous calendar
> "Compliments of Never & Forever, Inc."
>   ("Argument")

Rather than the accumulation of experience in increments of intensity, the voice of days is merely a record of canceled hopes and fears. It is the absence rather than the presence of connection. The lines themselves are faintly derivative of the kind of emotion that Sylvia Plath wrote about with such poignancy; the female body appears as a calendar torn between the two extremes of human affections: "I *never* want to see you again" and "I shall love you *forever*." The words appear merely as another "compliment," a part of the commercial world affixed to the gift of days as an afterthought. It is something distributed free at holiday time from businesses and corporations we have never encountered in experience. For Elizabeth Bishop, history then is merely another map, a spatialization of relationships that always appears as distance. In the poem "Argument" there is no distinction whatsoever between the language of history and the language of space:

> Distance: Remember all that land
> beneath the plane;
> that coastline
> of dim beaches deep in sand
> stretching indistinguishably
> all the way,
> all the way to where my reasons end?
>   ("Argument")

Actually, the two components of this pseudo-dialogue come to participate in the life of the other. Days are related to the cancellation of experience, and distance is inextricably bound to the processes of memory "stretching indistinguishably" to a point where "reasons end." Again, the poet is almost fixated by boundaries, by the extremity where each participant loses domain. It is the realm of peninsular experience, either brackish water or tidal flats, and is surely a second cousin to the terrain of the Brazilian jungle from which our map-maker continually has drawn translations throughout her poetic career. Perhaps these too are but the poetic equivalent of a Mercator projection. As the solitary speaker of "In Prison" had discovered, the tiniest reduction of space nevertheless provides the occasion for the metaphoric enlargement of boundaries through psychic projection and reprojection. The recognition of imprisonment participates in and leads to the only kind of freedom to which humans have access.

RICHARD HOWARD

"In the Waiting Room"

A decade ago, when she chose "The Man-Moth" for an anthology, Elizabeth Bishop remarked on the misprint (for "mam-moth") by which "an oracle spoke from the page of *The New York Times.* . . . One is offered such oracular statements all the time but often misses them. . .the meaning refuses to stay put." In this recent poem—published since the fortunately mistitled *Complete Poems*—the oracle is, in part, the *National Geographic*, whose "volcano,/black, and full of ashes;/. . .spilling over/in rivulets of fire," just like Herbert's "font, wherein did fall/A stream of blood, which issued from the side/Of a great rock," functions as an instrument of tempering. Pain, war, all the horrors of the flesh, the inadequacies of mere selfhood ("Better than you know me, or (which is one)/Than I myself," Herbert chatters on, as Miss Bishop more laconically discerns: "Without thinking at all/I was my foolish aunt,/I—we—were falling") —these are the means by which we are brought home to ourselves as we must be if we are authentically alive, "new, tender, quick."

Both poems are triumphs of tonality, of patience with material event in its likelihood of revealing what is beyond the material, the image of a speaking voice beguiling us into the deeps until every word (even Bishop's innocuous title, even Herbert's "natural" slip of the tongue: "I found that some had stuff'd the bed with thoughts. I would say *thorns*") turns incandescent in the "spacious furnace" of experience, of experiment, of trial. The result is that the process I have called tempering (the word covers the famous "temperament" of the modern poet as well as the *Temple* in which the metaphysical one lodges his entire utterance) collocates,

From *Preferences*. Copyright © 1974 by Richard Howard. The Viking Press, 1974.

fuses: "held us all together/or made us all just one," for to possess an identity is to acknowledge society ("I felt: you are an I,/ you are an *Elizabeth*,/you are one of *them*."). Such participation is of course explicit in Herbert, for the Sacraments are institutionalized and available, "into my cup for good"; in Bishop, they are momentary and delusive ("the meaning refuses to stay put"), and though at the ultimate source of the word she is a religious poet—religion as a binding together, a unifying of what can never be uniform—there is no redemption for her; there is the waiting room, which like the caldron of affliction is "bright and too hot," and "then I was back in it," just as Herbert goes back to bed. "It" is the world, that "scalding pan" which affords these poets their presumption of membership as well as their "sensation of falling."

JEROME MAZZARO

The Poetics of Impediment

That the seemingly modernist poetry of Elizabeth Bishop should be universally welcomed by postmodern poets illuminates not only a different kind of postmodernism but also the complexity of her own work. Like W.H. Auden's early poetry, which provided the model for the new style, her work abounds in "forthright statement, in which words are in general used denotatively" and images and metaphors bristle "from the exciting exactness with which they apply to experience." Occasionally, as Anne Stevenson proposes in *Elizabeth Bishop* (1966), there is Auden's "erudite colloquialism." The lyric refrain of "Varick Street" offers one instance. Moreover stories like "Then Came the Poor" (1934) contain the same attacks of Auden's Marxist phase on the uselessly idle rich, but she is far more skeptical than he is about the benefit of proletarian revolution. Poems like "The Man-Moth (1936) with its continuity of all life and evolution by chance out of a printer's error convey an implicit Darwinism that may have prompted Randall Jarrell's listing it first among what he cites as "her best poems." This Darwinism continues into such poems as "Night City" (1972) and beyond. But the stress Jarrell and others place on the psychological appears to be the point where most attempts to link Bishop to postmodernism founder. Most critics are willing to go along uneasily with James G. Southworth's statement that, "except for some ten poems," Bishop's poetry "is as objective as poetry can well be."

The consciousness of her control, the conjectural nature of her vision, and her intellectual clarity connect Bishop to Marianne Moore, E.A. Robinson, Wallace Stevens, and "the generation of poets which flourished after World War I." She has praised Moore for her "completely accurate" descriptions and ability to "give herself up entirely to the object under contemplation" and to "feel in all sincerity how it is to be *it*," and she has consistently kept enough details of her life confused or private in order to prevent Freudian interpretation. To offset these resistances to personal imposition and applied psychoanalysis and to allow a determination of her own commitment to what "It All Depends" (1950) calls "the sea" and "the very life" of poetry, a view of denotative syntax like that developed in John Crowe Ransom's two-part essay "Poetry" (1947) is useful. Writing of what he calls "precious objects," Ransom shows how by increasing the density of detail and "impeding" the reader, poets like Shakespeare are able to assert the value of what is being described. Often these objects are, as Ransom points out, familiar yet "always capable of exhibiting fresh aspects." They are comparatively absolute and inviolable, and their very lack of change coupled with familiarity allows the poet to spend more affective time on them than on equally familiar objects which are intended for use. Yet his affection uses no overtly emotive language, and critics of Bishop's writing who find little or no mannerisms and still are unable to accept a view of objectivity are, in effect, responding to the presence of such emotions.

Her tributes for various dead friends and her three Nova Scotia stories convey in contexts that are often more revealing than the poems the basic Imagist attachment of emotion to objects that informs her thinking. In "Gregorio Valdes, 1879–1939" (1939) she states of Valdes's talent: "When he copied, particularly from a photograph, and particularly from a photograph of something he knew and liked, such as palm trees, he managed to make just the right changes in perspective and coloring to give it a peculiar and captivating freshness, flatness, and remoteness." She describes a painting of her rooming house that he did. She had asked him to put more flowers and a Traveller's Palm in the work, and later, showing her a sketch of the palm, he apologized "because the tree really had seven branches on one side and six on the other, but in the painting he had given both sides seven to make it more symmetrical." Coming home one evening, she saw the finished work on the veranda: "In the grey twilight they seemed to blur together and I had the feeling that if I came closer I would be able to see another miniature copy of the house leaning on the porch of the painted house, and so on,—like the Old Dutch Cleanser advertisements." Her piece on Flannery O'Connor (1964) represents as tokens of affection a similar immersion in familiar objects as well as an attentiveness by the ailing fiction writer to the details of a "cross in a bottle" that Bishop sent her. "An Inadequate Tribute" (1967) extends this wedding of emotion and detailed object to Jarrell by connecting him to a part of Cape Cod and a dazzling bright day.

In each of these pieces her ability to recall accurately, vividly, and discretely is connected to affection, repossession, and individuality as much as was Valdes's ability to copy. Each person is identified with a discrete, inviolable world, much as in mnemonics an object to be recalled is associated with a precise token or commonplace. The blurring of these tokens or places leads to lapses and haziness of memory, a crumbling of the "rocklike" and "perfect" appearance of remembered things. In this need of precise recollection, the process of recovery resembles that yearning for fixity described by Robert Lowell in "91 Revere Street" (1955): "Major Mordecai Myers's portrait has been mislaid past finding, but out of my memories I often come on it in the setting of our Revere Street house, a setting now fixed in the mind, where it survives all the distortions of fantasy, all the blank befogging of forgetfulness. There, the vast number of remembered *things* remains rocklike. Each is in its place, each has its function, its history, its drama. There, all is preserved by that motherly care that one either ignored or resented in his youth. The things and their owners come back urgent with life and meaning—because finished, they are endurable and perfect." The process also resembles what Gaston Bachelard designates "reveries of childhood."

In *The Poetics of Reverie* (1960) Bachelard speaks of the "indelible marks" that "the original solitudes"—those of childhood—leave on certain souls. He associates such sensitizing action with "poetic reverie" in which one can relax his aches. In Bishop's case these reveries would have much to do with her early years, spent with her grandparents in Nova Scotia and with her aunt in Boston where, as Stevenson indicates, ill health kept her from attending school regularly. "Instead, she spent long, solitary winters in bed, reading. Her passion for books and for music dates from this period (she was about eight) when, sick and without friends her own age, she began to write poems and to take piano lessons." Bishop's father died eight months after her birth and her mother never recovered from the shock of his death. Stevenson leaves open whether the mother's "nervous collapse and subsequent insanity were entirely the result of her husband's death or whether her disease was an affliction of long standing. . . . The tragedy remains. At the age of eight months Elizabeth Bishop lost, in effect, both parents." Her life in Nova Scotia with her maternal grandparents lasted until she was six; then she spent a year in Worcester, Massachusetts, with the paternal grandparents, until she went to live more or less permanently with her Aunt Maud in Boston. She returned to Nova Scotia summers afterward until she was thirteen.

"The Baptism" (1937) and "Gwendolyn" (1953) show how Bishop's writing connects the transience of this early life to objects. Both stories have identical small-town settings that would seem to resemble the village where the poet spent her early childhood, and except for different narrative points of view, both may derive from the "novel about family life in a Nova Scotia village" that she told the editors of *Magazine* (1934) she was writing. Townsfolk divide into Baptists and Presbyterians, and in the first story the youngest of three sisters decides to join the Baptist congregation in perference to the Presbyterian church that her older sisters belong to. Central to the story which deals with religious despair and the growing insanity of the young girl is the association of death and flowers. The association begins when Mrs. Peppard's conversation moves from the death of "her sister's baby" to a discussion of begonias, and the link recurs in the midst of a vision where lamp smoke rises to the ceiling and smells "very strong and sweet, like rose-geranium." Finally the girl's death shortly after her baptism enlists the gift of "a beautiful plant . . . from the city, a mass of white blooms" along with the townsfolk's cut red, white, and pink geraniums. "Gwendolyn" relates the death of a second young girl from diabetes and, in doing so, associates the frail condition of the dying girl's appearance to that of an unnamed doll that once belonged to the narrator's Aunt Mary.

"In the Village" (1953) recalls the return of the poet's mother to Nova Scotia "in the hope that, in familiar surroundings, she might recover." Instead the visit produced her final breakdown, and she had to be put in a mental hospital in Dartmouth, Nova Scotia. Told as an evocation of that summer with its various noises of the mother's scream, cow flop, the bell at Mealy's candystore, the clanging firebell, and the blacksmith's clang, it recounts what memories the poet may have preserved of that experience. In it, as in Auden's "Musée des Beaux Arts" (1939), suffering "takes place/While someone else is eating or opening a window or just walking dully along." The mother's suffering is incomprehensible to the daughter; the two aunts who try to make things easier cannot. The situation is a variation of that described in "The Baptism," including some of the same townsfolk like Mrs. Peppard, except now the three girls have parents who make their life less isolated. What is established by the story is the relic nature of the poet's most primal needs. The proof of her parents and their love for her is very much tied up with the same objects Bishop describes being unloaded from the crates and boxes that have been shipped from Boston. Things become significant because they are related valuably to the past; but, as "The Sea and Its Shore" (1937) maintains, even this relationship cannot long withstand erosion. In time the flow of life like that of the sea will prove more immediate, and with the eventual dissolution of this immediacy, the value of such relationships will reemerge diminished. Paler they endure to represent in later life the inaccessible place where one would like to live.

"The Sea and Its Shore" speaks directly to these matters of survival and erosion. The story presents art as a temporary extension of life. Edwin Boomer, whose job it is to keep a stretch of beach free from papers, collects the more interesting scraps he uncovers. Eventually he comes to see the beach as an expression of print, but Bishop notes: "The point was that everything had to be burned at last. All, all had to be burned, even bewildering scraps that he had carried with him for weeks or months. Burning paper was his occupation, by which he made his living, but over and above that, he could not allow his pockets to become too full, or his house to become littered." Thus this "most literary" man whose desire was to rescue some print from destruction by nature finds himself aiding nature in its laws. The categories under which he classifies information prove finally irrelevant, and what enjoyment he derives from his bonfires produces no sense of joy at their inevitability. It is easy enough to link the story to both the categories of Bishop's own writing as well as the attitudes that must have resulted from her having lost her parents and maternal grandparents at an early age. That Boomer's name should so closely resemble Bulmer, the name of her maternal grandparents, is perhaps no accident—or that her poetry should convey such seriousness in its recovery of events and objects while at the same time evincing a lack of seriousness about the durability of art. Nowhere does one get the sense that she is writing for more than herself or that she sees the content of life any differently from Boomer—as matter about herself, about people whose lives catch her fancy, and about what seems bewilderingly inexplicable.

In all these prose pieces there is a particular emphasis upon labor—whether the work is the care that Valdes puts into his painting or the affection O'Connor feels at noting that "the rooster has an eyebrow" and the altar cloth is "a little dirty from the fingers of whoever cut it out." Jarrell is seen on the beach "writing in a notebook," and both the dressmaker and blacksmith of "In the Village" are saved by their labor from deep involvement in the sorrows of the house. Even Boomer is rescued from being overwhelmed by the paper he collects by the necessity of burning it as part of his job. In contrast the rich of "Then Came the Poor" are contemptible because they are idle: they cannot be useful. One might connect this work ethic to the poet's New England—Nova Scotia background and her Puritan past or suggest, as she does in her *Shenandoah* interview (1965), that it is related to the socialist temper of the thirties: "Politically I considered myself a socialist, but I disliked 'social conscious' writing. . . . I was all for being a socialist till I heard Norman Thomas speak; but he was *so* dull. Then I tried anarchism, briefly." Nevertheless it represents that same attitude of "going on" which Auden's "Musée des Beaux Arts" will later convey; the ploughman of Pieter Brueghel's *Land- scape with the Fall of Icarus* cannot stop his work to watch the boy's falling out of the sky; a large part of life must go on working as it always has.

Aesthetically what the emphasis on labor does is to promote literary labor as a value, allowing form, as Roland Barthes in *Writing Degree Zero* (1953) suggests, to become "the end product of craftsmanship, like a piece of pottery or a jewel." The purpose of such labor is to contain the tension described by "The Sea and Its Shore" as the erosion of art by life and reinterpreted along Freudian lines in Robert Lowell's "Thomas, Bishop, and Williams" (1946) as a conflict between the death urge (the sea) and civilization (the shore) or, as Sherman Paul in *Hart's Bridge* (1973) is willing to apply it to Hart Crane, the strong tension between the desire to return to childhood and the need to escape that childhood. In Bishop's case the effort may derive from the naturalists' belief in man's evolution from the sea and hence from his struggle to preserve the element he has achieved. Her own depictions have led occasionally to an artificially baroque love poem but more often to an equally conscious stylization of experience or technique of mapping experience that greatly resembles the mapping in the opening poem of *North & South* (1946). At times, as in "Chemin de Fer," the stylization moves into overt formalism but more often it merely tracks. "Maps," as Prince Modupe relates in *I Was a Savage* (1958), "are liars. . . . The things that hurt one do not show on a map." The "airy and easy sweep of map-traced, staggering distances" belittles the journeys that one makes on tired feet. Modupe was to learn from showing his father a map that "the truth of a place is in the joy and the hurt that come from it. . . . With my big map-talk, I had effaced the magnitude of his cargo-laden, heat-oppressed treks." Bishop's journey outward from the emotions of childhood begins with "The Map," and it does so, however obscurely, in terms earned from that childhood.

Among the earliest poems the poet has seen fit to keep is "The Map," which anticipates her own love of travel as well as the predilection for travel books that Lucy in "The Baptism" and the narrator of "In the Village" display. The poem's first observations of Newfoundland and Labrador suggest a starting point in Nova Scotia as the viewer's eye moves eastward toward Norway. The map, as the metaphors of blossom and fishtank convey, represents an outlet for the speaker as exciting and consuming as those hobbies given to children, for the printer, in running the names of seashore towns out to the sea and of cities across neighboring mountains, is said to experience "the same excitement/as when motion too far exceeds its cause." Moreover, just as the narrator can imagine stroking the lovely bays, the "peninsulas take the water between thumb and finger/like women feeling for the smoothness of yard-goods." The feel of both is for the unfinished or what can be worked on. This "unfinished" quality as it applies to land and sea occupies the opening stanza. There the poet wonders if the land lies in the sea or merely draws the sea about it like a cape. Are the shadows growing into the sea or withdrawing from it? She concludes that the land does the "investigating." Mapped waters are quiet and self-contained. In coming to this realization, she wonders whether the colors given to land are assigned or earned since "topography displays no favorites." Echoing the opening of Robert Frost's "West-running Brook" (1928) and its depiction of how that brook got its name, Bishop ends by stating: "More delicate than the historians' are the map-makers' colors."

Frost's poem had dealt as well with contraries as a vehicle to identity, but he treated the problem in historical terms. In Bishop history disappears to be replaced by a denotative flatness. What impresses one immediately about this flatness is the femininity of the speaker. The emotive adjectives are deliberately feminine—"fine tan sandy shelf," "moony Eskimo," "lovely bays"—but equally feminine are the occupational metaphors—flower gardening, caring for fish, dressmaking, and finally map coloring. Norman J.W. Thrower, in *Maps & Men* (1972), notes: "It later became the custom to hand-color the prints of engravings, . . .a practice that prevailed until the end of the nineteenth century. Understandably, map coloring became an important activity in various cartographic centers, and ladies, sometimes those socially prominent, often engaged in this work." Thus the poem iterates the tension between land and sea that "The Sea and Its Shore" codifies into a conflict between the artist and life and, as that work established art as a temporary rather than permanent thing, so too does the poem convey the fragility with the word *delicate*. In the absence of a formal meter or line, its rhymes show a stylization rather than a formalization—something designed to resemble the formal but somehow not itself formal much as maps, by excluding the joys and pains of actual experience, stylize landscapes by bending not to the abstract rules of geometry but to the natural contours of the subject. The very adjectives and metaphors which act to impede the reader establish the value which has been attached to the incidents.

Bishop's oft-noted ability to make her subjects interact with one another as well as speak back to her is conveyed in the images of the peninsula feeling water and Norway's becoming a hare. Like Theodore Roethke, Bishop is a dramatic poet not because she impersonates but because she waits until objects speak to her, which they must do in a mnemonics system. The purpose of mnemonics is to call back with such vividness that whatever is recalled resumes mentally the life it once had. In Christian mnemonics or meditation, memories of God, Christ, or the saints are called up by means of icons, relics, and tokens. In the *Shenandoah* interview the poet states that she became aware of such an approach while she was still at Vassar when reading an eassy on the baroque sermon in preparation for a paper on Gerard Manley Hopkins. One of the scraps of paper Boomer picks up two years later concerns mnemonics. It lists experiences which weaken the memory. This waiting for objects to speak relies, in addition, on a concept of connaturality like that Bishop posits for Moore, a sense that the depth of things and the depth of self are united in some way and can speak to one another. The divisions between man and nature made by traditional religions along lines of man's having a soul and by evolutionists along the necessity for man to distance himself from his origins are, consequently, held in abeyance, although what seems to be evoked in Bishop's poems are less ecstatic states than the observations of a girlhood which, having been lost, seems more edenic than the writer's current state.

"The Imaginary Iceberg," which comes next in the volume, speaks more directly to the matters of the division between man and nature. Its contrast of manmade ship and naturally formed iceberg as vehicles of motion leaves no question of the speaker's preference. Icebergs make both technology and art "artlessly rhetorical"; they move the soul, being, like it, self-made "from elements least visible." One has conveyed by these "obscure" elements a response of what is deepest in man (his soul) to what is deepest in sea life (the iceberg) with a suggestion that is almost naturalistic: that the soul is not God-given but is created by a process similar to that which creates the iceberg. The suggestion is perhaps more a function of the metaphysical style than of theology, although Bishop admits to being "not religious" despite her pleasure at reading various religious poets. Moreover, as the title conveys, the subject is an "imaginary" rather than real iceberg. In this the poem may derive from Stevens. Bishop acknowledges that he was the contemporary poet who most affected her writing while she was in college. Stevenson ventures that the rhetorical questions of "The Map" may well be influenced by "Sea Surface Full of Clouds" (1924) and that the emphasis on the imaginary is in keeping with the "unfinished" stresses of "The Map" as well as what critics have seen as Stevens's view of the imagination. Joseph N. Riddel in "Stevens on Imagination" (1971) notes that for Stevens, "only mind, the unreal, can name and thus conceive beginnings and the order and direction they imply. Only mind can speak of history and form, because mind has created history and form as the space of its being." Like Bishop's iceberg, mind succeeds the world or things as they are in the order of creation, but by its nature becomes essential to the real.

The poems, however, which enlarge upon the notions of history in "The Map" and the travel reading of the poet's youth, are not in *North & South*. They are "At the Fishhouses," "Cape Breton," and "Over 2000 Illustrations and a Complete Concordance" from *A Cold Spring* (1955). Set again in Nova Scotia at a convergence of sea and shore, "At the Fishhouses" describes a chat with an old man who was a friend of the speaker's grandfather. Like Lucy in "The Baptism," this speaker is later revealed to be "a believer in total immersion" and the singer of "A Mighty Fortress Is Our God," listed in the tale as a favorite hymn of Lucy's sister Flora. But most importantly the poem repeats the notions of the world as "flowing and drawn," knowledge as "historical, flowing and flown," and the poem as a mnemonic recollection: "I have seen it over and over, the same sea, the same,/slightly, swinging above the stones,/icily free above the stones,/above the stones and then the world." This late announcement of the poem as recollection gives emotional content to what otherwise might be a belabored silvery description of a cold evening in which an old man sits netting among five fishhouses. His casual talk of "the decline in the population/and of codfish and herring/while he waits for a herring boat to come in" anticipates the diminishing catch of her mental world at the poem's close. The fixed nature of the opening as "cold dark deep and absolutely clear" in its recollection of the sea becomes eventually what "we imagine knowledge to be." Cape Breton, a short distance off from the fishhouses, forms the setting of a second of the poems. The piece is again deceptively descriptive, and again the detail functions as a repossession of the island and betrays the emotional nature of the content. Sea and land are once more in opposition as the silken water "weaving and weaving" to disappear "under the mist" is opposed by the man "carrying a baby" who disappears into a meadow whose poverty is "a snowfall of daisies." The metaphysical statement is that life goes on as ever.

Just as "At the Fishhouses" and "Cape Breton" may be regarded as reflections of Bishop's desire to return to childhood, "Over 2000 Illustrations and a Complete Concordance" reflects the attempt to escape that childhood by realizing its fantasies of escape. The poem has been compared to Charles Baudelaire's "Le Voyage," but it is in light of Bishop's own conflicts that its description and movement can better be seen. The poem depicts a world traveler looking back on the illustrations of her girlhood that inspired her to travel. The book containing the illustrations is like that of "The Baptism." There the isolated sisters are said to have gone "through a lot of old travel books that had belonged to their father. One was called *Wonders of the World*; one was a book about Palestine and Jerusalem. . . . Lucy grew excited over accounts of the Sea of Galilee, and the engraving of the Garden of Gethsemane as it looks to-day brought tears to her eyes. She exclaimed, 'Oh dear!' over pictures of 'An Olive Grove,' with Arabs squatting about it in, and 'Heavens!' at the real, rock-vaulted Stable, the engraved rocks like big black thumb-prints." "In the Village" also speaks of "gilded red or green books, unlovely books, filled with bright new illustrations of the Bible stories" that "drummers sometimes came around selling." In either case the traveler's return to such illustrations is to note a difference from the "serious, engravable" nature of the pictures and the often tawdry realities of the travel. The poem ends with a picture that was not realized—a Nativity's image of domesticity, "a family with pets." The traveler suspects that this picture might have satisfied the child looking at it, rather than have acted, as had the other illustrations, as a lure to disappointing adventure. The poem is undoubtedly indebted to Baudelaire's depiction of the disappointment of travels as compared to imaginary voyages, but how personal and poignant the ending becomes in Bishop's context. The familiar "family with pets" that she never had occurs in the same reveries that produce the desire for travel.

In pursuing the perfect journey, the poem echoes the problems of "In Prison" (1938) and its search for a "true place in the world." The narrator of this story finds that his "proper sphere" is a prison. He desires imprisonment as much as the speaker of "Over 2000 Illustrations and a Complete Concordance" desires travel and with comparably exacting expectations. His prison must contain "a view of a court-yard paved with stone," permit the reading of "one very dull book. . . , the duller the better," and indulge his wish to use the walls of the cell for writing. The prison must also allow him to dress a little differently from the other prisoners and to form a friendship with "an important member of prison society" that will eventuate in the narrator's becoming "an *influence*." But most importantly, like the later poem, there is a final confusion between choice and necessity. The narrator who wishes to believe the Hegelian view that "freedom is knowledge of necessity," must restate the story's premise that "this way is the only logical step for me to take": "I mean, of course, to be acted *upon* in this way is the only logical step for me to take." However much one wishes to claim "necessity" in Bishop's writing, matters of choice intrude: stimulated by childhood books to visit various places, her travelers decide what places to visit. Like Baudelaire's voyagers, however, they cannot choose what they will find. Only in the imagination is the universe ever equal to one's desire: realizations always entail adjustments to the real.

Written as a satire on the narrator's presumption of "necessity," "In Prison" anticipates responses to travel that recur in much of Bishop's poetry. Either the traveler accepts the excitement and novelty of new environments just as the "prisoner" refrains from imagining the contents of his "one dull book," because to do so would "spoil the sensation of wave-like freshness" that he hopes will accompany the book's being handed him, or the traveler willfully represses other environments so that he may accept wholly one place, again much as the "prisoner" discovers that he "could 'succeed' in one place, but not in all places" and protests against ambiguous positions. Critics are right to ally such a prison to the house of "The Sea and Its Shore," the fairy palace of "Jerónimo's House," and finally to the jar which in "Anecdote of the Jar" (1919) Stevens places in Tennessee to "make the slovenly wilderness/Surround that hill." All are shelters "not for living in, for thinking in." The function of each is to provide a temporary stay against confusion—a stay often requiring mental journeying if not the physical journeying that critics like Stevenson are willing to pronounce is the poet's major preoccupation. These places consequently provide the perfect models for the arrangements of detail that in turn the formal arrangements of art emulate, but none becomes so overwhelmingly central that critics may speak of obsession either in what she seeks to recover or in her attitude toward its eventual diminution. The loss of value in one object will merely allow the investment of value in a second.

Nowhere is this change of value more evident than in the recent "Crusoe in England" (1971). The speaker of the poem has lost his attachment for England by having been castaway on an island and, by being returned to England, the "living soul" that his island flute, knife, shrivelled shoes, goatskin trousers, and parasol possessed. These objects still have some value as his own reverie and as a request from the local museum-keeper attest. In this new telling of Daniel Defoe's novel, creativity becomes the means of reinvestment. Crusoe mentions Greek drama, beds of irises, and philosophy in language that is sometimes openly sentimental. He misses his "poor old island" and "miserable, small volcanoes," and he admits to giving way often to self-pity, arguing that " 'pity should begin at home.' So the more/pity I felt, the more I felt at home." He is, at the same time, interested in accepting some kind of duty, and he achieves in his friendship with Friday the equivalent of a friendship with "an important member of prison society" that "In Prison" mentions. His becoming "an *influence*," however, is ended by Friday's death from measles. Friday's being male, moreover, limits the urge toward futurity that the poem identifies with duty to rude artifacts, since the urge cannot be served in biological propagation. Art thus becomes some kind of adjustment to Necessity. The speaker's inability to accept either the judgment of the museum keeper or the death of Friday counters a self-definition comparable to the affirmation that self-pity allowed on his island home. Self-definition now comes from reverie and drawing "vast generalizations, abstractions of the grandest, most illuminating sort, like allegories or poems."

Bishop's greatest achievements in her early collections have been in poems that willfully repress the past in order to focus on one time and place and hence that avoid nostalgia. "The Man-Moth," "Roosters," "The Weed," and "The Fish" from her first volume all present situations that are so vividly and meticulously drawn that they present one's withdrawal into the past. The first concerns a fantasy creature who, like man, inhabits the city and who "must investigate as high as he can climb." His home is the subway tunnels. On rare occasions he visits the surface, thinking the moon "a small hole at the top of the sky/proving the sky quite useless for protection." Everywhere he seems to be challenging death or an *in extremis* condition from which he "falls back scared but quite unhurt." On the basis of this challenging Lowell sees the poem as concerning a "death desire" and other critics think it is about evolutionary progress. If caught, the man-moth will try to palm his sole possession—a tear—which he will relinquish to his captor if that captor is watchful. The tear is "cool as from underground springs and pure enough to drink." In this, the tear complements and opposes that of "The Reprimand" (1935) in which teardrops are seen as the eye's equivalent to the tongue's sighs, eye's "deepest sorrow." In "The Man-Moth" this sorrow becomes a moral for man's ambition and its consequences. Again set up in what appears to be six eight-line stanzas, the poem realizes no formal shape, merely the semblance of form. The very density of ordinary detail lends the work a sense of reality that phrases like "a temperature impossible to record in thermometers" heighten into dream.

"Roosters," in contrast, represents an awakening from sleep. It moves from a predawn "first crow of the first cock" to the emergence of the sun which renders the crows "almost inaudible." The cries which announce an end of night affect first hens, then sleeping wives, and then the history of man, coming to symbolize fall and redemption before they give way to sunlight. Written in triple rhymes to suggest either the number of cock crows accompanying Peter's betrayals of Christ or the number of those betrayals, the pattern of each triplet is a sequence of lines whose length increases and where rhymes may occur between stressed and unstressed syllables. Here the ranging sweep of the sentences catches one in detail much as if one were surveying a vast area before the vision begins its equally vast sweep through time. The bird's combativeness, leading to its death, is balanced by Peter's sin, which typifies the ability of man to earn redemption. In effecting this parallel, live roosters transform into "a new weathervane/on basilica and barn," as art which like Peter may be equally untrue to life but may, all the same, prolong life's message. Tears are again part of the transformation as Peter's tears become glaze on a rooster's sides and spurs. Returning to the present in the final five stanzas, the poem pits rooster against sun, with the sun assuming aspects of the earlier triumphant rooster, God, and Peter. The poem ends with the sun climbing into the barnyard, "following 'to see the end,'/faithful as enemy, or friend." Thus "the gun-metal blue dark" echoed in "the gun-metal blue window" which begins the poem initiates a series of correspondences between the boundless and the bounded that in time cluster about images of war, conflagration, and commemoration.

"The Weed," which Bishop acknowledges "is modelled somewhat on [George Herbert's] 'Love Unknown,' " offers another dream-vision. A weed is seen growing through the heart of the dreamer who suspects that she is dead. The weed splits the heart much as weeds create cracks in stone, releasing in the act a flood of water. Each drop of water contains "a light,/a small, illuminated scene," and the river that the drops comprise is said to "carry all/the scenes that it had once reflected," much as a memory house contains in its separate compartments devices for minute and vivid recollection. Queried by the dreamer about what it was doing there, the weed responds that it grows "but to divide your heart again." In the Herbert poem the ordeals of the heart are turned into benefits: the cleansing in the font, the softening in the furnace, and the sensitizing by means of thorns are attempts to mend what the possessor of the heart had marred. Here the heart has obvious links to the process of memorization, "of learning by heart," as well as to loving: both activities tend to preserve the inviolability of their subjects. The splitting into two and possibly into four suggests the beginning of a concept of love similar to that proposed by Aristophanes in Plato's *Symposium*. There primal man was seen as twice the person man is now, and God's halving him was the reason for love and man's currently seeking his other half. This split has left within him an image of completion as fixed and indelible as that which seems to motivate Bishop's poetic reveries. The heart's being halved and quartered would presumably lead it to seek out its other half or its parts in an action comparable to that described by the Greek playwright.

As if to affirm this action, poems of complementarity abound in Bishop's *Complete Poems* (1969). They range from "The Gentleman of Shallot," a man who sees his bilateral anatomy narcissistically as reason to believe a mirror inhabits his spine and who, should the mirror slip and break, is willing to be quoted as saying "Half is enough," to the hermit of "Chemin de Fer," who wants his actions echoed. At one time Bishop announced that she was working on a verse translation of Aristophanes' *The Birds*, and her interest in Aristophanes may account for the particular myth of love that she selects as well as for her sense of the bizarre, though this second may derive more rightly from the writings of Franz Kafka. What is most striking about "The Weed" is not the bizarre but the poem's possible debt to Emily Dickinson—the decision to realize its message by means of the most humble of messengers, a weed. The minuteness with which the probing growth of this weed is described lends the poem its vividness and mystery despite a feeling that the whole is labored, emblematic, and baroque. One simply forgets Herbert or Dickinson when Bishop relates of the weed that "It grew an inch like a blade of grass;/next one leaf shot out of its side/a twisting, waving flag, and then/two leaves moved like a semaphore./The stem grew thick." Similarly one thinks of the techniques of a naturalist when she describes "the nervous roots" reaching to each side; "the graceful head/changed its position mysteriously,/since there was neither sun nor moon/to catch its young attention."

The theme of pain, once more suggested by tears, preserves the centrality of feeling in Bishop's work. Tears also occur in "Chemin de Fer" and the fourth song in "Songs for a Colored Singer." In the first poem the pond across which the hermit fires his rifle is seen as "an old tear/holding onto its injuries/lucidly year after year," and one suspects that "injuries" may account for the lack of echo in the poem. The falling leaves of the Negro song are compared to "tears when somebody grieves" and become seeds from which "faces" like memories grow, again conveying the recollective nature of Bishop's technique. To see the world as tears or as prompting or resulting from tears seems to promote the world as necessary betrayal, irritation, loss, and pain against which, as "The Weed" suggests, one ought not to become hardened and yet for which betrayals, as "Roosters" indicates, one must atone. Thus, like most of the other postmodernists, her primary approach to experience is psychological rather than philosophical—although one might see her decision to endure despite inevitable losses as a kind of stoical acceptance. Her "*elend*" or wretchedness is no different from that described by Jarrell's "Seele im Raum" (1950), just as the conclusions of her journeys "in/No destination we meant" are no different from that of his "On the Railway Platform" (1939). Even her understanding "that the wickedness and confusion of the age can explain and extenuate other people's wickedness and confusion, but not, for you, your own" is postmodern: it is not only what Jarrell makes true for Auden and Rudyard Kipling but what he makes typical of his generation.

Yet, much as these poems exist by a kind of suffering, "The Fish," whose "fine rosettes of lime" owe to Hopkins's "rose-moles all in stipple upon trout" and whose climax may derive from Mallarmé's "l'azur, l'azur, l'azur, l'azur," offers ostensibly a "fish story": it is a yarn about the proverbial catch "that got away." The poem which delineates the time between the supposed catching of a "tremendous fish" and the narrator's letting it go displays what is perhaps Bishop's most calculated use of detail. The only basis for one's believing that the fish was caught is her ability to describe it minutely. How can one doubt the existence of a fish whose brown skin hangs here and there "in stripes/like ancient wallpaper" and whose pattern of darker brown is also "like wallpaper:/shapes like full-blown roses/stained and lost through age"? Or for that matter why should one question a creature "infested/with tiny white sea-lice" and trailing in glory "rags and green weed"? Yet the detail of such externals is no more reliably expressed or is no more credible than the confessed imagined "coarse white flesh/packed in like feathers" or "the dramatic reds and blacks/of his shiny entrails/and the pink swim-bladder/like a big peony." One simply presumes, as with any good teller of fish stories, that she caught the tremendous fish without having engaged in a fight and looked into its eyes and that the consequence of this look made her throw the fish back.

The obliviousness of the Hopkinsish eyes, "the irises backed and packed/with tarnished tinfoil/seen through the lenses/of old scratched isinglass" offers some clue to the speaker's action. It resonates against the lack of struggle accompanying her landing the fish and suggests that the experience may have disappointed her, much as the traveler of "Over 2000 Illustrations and a Complete Concordance" had been disappointed with travel. The disappointment seems to explain why the "five old pieces of fish-line" which hang from its lips are "like medals with their ribbons/frayed and wavering." No such heroic counterstruggle has occurred here, and the victory which begins to fill up "the little rented boat" has, at least on her part, been made empty. Yet, by virtue of an engine's oil spill, a rainbow parodying God's restoration of dominion to Noah occurs; and the illumi-nation of this rainbow, brought about by accident and technology, becomes the immediate cause of her letting the creature go. This final act may be as perverse as the fish's wanting to be caught, or it may suggest, as evolutionists like Alfred Russel Wallace propose, a transference to machine and tools of what in animals takes place through evolution of body parts. Man's dominion is again (as it was in "The Man-Moth" and "The Imaginary Iceberg") wryly evolutionist. But the effect of her letting the fish go may not merely function to explain to others "how it got away"; it may also work to emphasize the importance of detail as a basis for understanding.

The stylization of content, the suppression of pity, and the attention to detail in all these poems led Jarrell to say of her first collection: "Miss Bishop's poems are almost never forced; in her best work restraint, calm, and proportion are implicit in every detail of organization and workmanship. . . . Her work is unusually personal and honest in its wit, perception, and sensitivity—and in its restrictions too; all her poems have written underneath, *I have seen it.*" He was to add in a review of her second volume (1955): "They have a sound, a feel, a whole moral and physical atmoshere, different from anything else I know. . . . They are honest, modest, minutely observant, masterly; even their most complicated or troubled or imaginative effects seem, always, personal and natural, and as unmistakable as the first few notes of a Mahler song, the first few patches of Vuillard interior." Bishop seems to have reacted favorably enough to the earlier criticism that, in 1957, when she published her translation of *The Diary of "Helena Morley,"* she used a variation of the statement to praise the author. Citing Hopkins's comment in regard to Richard Dana's *Two Years Before the Mast,* she says of the diary: "That, I think, is 'the charm and the main point' of *Minha Vida de Menina. . . . It really happened*; everything did take place, day by day, minute by minute, once and only once, just the way Helena says it did."

If some of these poems succeed by willfully excluding the past and necessity, other poems in the same volume show the presence of necessary behavior. "Florida," for instance, despite its being "the state with the prettiest name," cannot prosper without the intense struggle for survival that necessity demands. The alligator has five distinct calls: "friendliness, love, mating, war, and a warning." Hence the exuberance which critics like Stephen Stepanchev see in certain poems as "irrelevant" becomes irrelevant only because of the lack of choice. Stepanchev can see the effect accurately enough but cannot perceive the cause: "It is as though Miss Bishop stopped along the road home to examine every buttercup and asphodel she saw. The images are dazzling; they call attention to themselves like ambitious actors in minor roles; but they contribute very little to the total effect." To make these examinations contribute to a poem's total effect is to deny precisely their necessity in life. "Seascapes" similarly presents a "heavenly" scene as a moving narrator might see it and contrasts the vision to the hell that a stationary "skeletal lighthouse" has. Here, though mutually exclusive, both points of view seem equally fixed by necessity. Necessity also figures in as a minor theme in "Roosters," where it is represented as a struggle for survival, and in "The Fish," where it is seen in the evolutionary progress.

Equally interesting as these travel poems, which can be divided like Boomer's scraps into matter about one's self and about what seems bewilderingly inexplicable, are poems about people whose lives catch the poet's fancy. Early poems like "Cootchie," "The Prodigal," and "Faustina, or Rock Roses" lead into later works like "The Riverman" and "The Burglar of Babylon" to form a body of poems which is based on attention not to detail but to a corresponding uniqueness of human personality that often repeats in human terms what is going on in the natural world. "Cootchie," for example, speaks to the same problem of art that "The Map" had. It describes Miss Lula's black servant, going "black into white . . .below the surface of the coral-reef." The same lighthouse that earlier appeared in "Seascape" will search "land and sea" for someone else and will dismiss Cootchie's grave as trivial. The dismissal contrasts with the efforts of Miss Lula to commemorate her servant with "melting" pink wax roses. "Cootchie" may be based on a Baudelaire poem—"La Servante" in which an old servant is recollected. The poem leads directly into "Faustina, or Rock Roses," a second poem concerning service, which moves beyond the sentiments of Baudelaire to ally the matter of service with that of necessity.

This second poem about a dying woman, her servant, and a visitor prompts the visitor to question whether death is "freedom at last" or "the very worst,/the unimaginable nightmare." The visitor concludes by wondering of the origin of things: "whence come/all the petals" of the world she inhabits. The bed containing the sick woman is described earlier in rose imagery; and roses have, in the course of the poem, become confused with the servant: hence the word *or* of the title. The visitor's roses are only part of the work's elaborate pattern which may be inspired by the rose imagery of Dante's *Paradiso*. Faustina seems saved from the craziness of the house and bed by an unquestioning devotion to work, by the kind of Sisyphean effort that Albert Camus calls the absurd and which runs through much of Bishop's writing. The intriguing voice of the poem is that of the voyeur-speaker. She seems both separated from the visitor, who is described in third person and yet involved: "The eighty-watt bulb" is said to "betray *us* all,/discovering the concern/within *our* stupefaction."

Later the "acuteness of the question" of man's origin re-creates an image of Satan and Judeo-Christian evil with "a snake-tongue flickering," blunting, proliferating "*our* problems" (italics mine); but one is at a loss as to precisely when and how the third-person visitor becomes a first-person narrator. The poem seems to suggest that not even spectators can divorce themselves from the necessity of nature's laws.

Yet, if "Faustina" speaks of necessity with its parodic Dantean roses, "The Prodigal" speaks with equal power of filth and matters of choice. Realized in two sonnets, it depicts the personal hell of an alcoholic who finds himself often recovering from drunkenness in a pig pen and who finally does "make up his mind to go home." Occasionally the sun "glazing" the barnyard mud with red seems to reassure him, and occasionally "the lantern" casts a religious glow, but "shuddering insights, beyond his control" force him beyond these suggestions of art and religion. He decides to leave, and his decision lies clearly within the realm of choice. In this instance "home" seems to mean by the poem's title the alcoholic's origins, though one is never certain if they are a state of nonbeing or a place. One is almost certain, on the other hand, that the pig pen is meant to suggest worldly existence and that, like "Cootchie" and "Faustina," "The Prodigal" is intended to reflect actual observation more than literary antecedents. "The Riverman" and "The Burglar of Babylon," in contrast, are derivative and form, thereby, equivalents of the "found statements" that Boomer occasionally comes upon. Bishop relates that details of "The Riverman" come "from 'Amazon Town,' by Charles Wagley" and that "The Burglar of Babylon" is "a true story, taken from the newspaper accounts." She "made only two minor changes in the facts." Thus the origin of these character poems, like the subjects of the nature pieces, raises problems of choice.

Written in free verse, "The Riverman" seems to derive from the same mixture of folktale and face that typified "The Man-Moth." Its speaker wishes to become a witch doctor, and he believes that he has been spoken to by the river dolphin and has been given presents by the water spirits. By his initiation it is clear that he has not selected the vocation but rather that the dolphin has selected him. The night setting and the man's nakedness are both suggestive of the libidinous impulses that motivate his actions. In addition his going down into the river is a reversal of the action of most of Bishop's progressive protagonists who, if anything, move inland and away from water. The parallel between the man's house on shore and the mansion beneath the water is clear, as is the mirror imagery which, by its insistence on pristine reflection, comments on the pattern of complementarity that has been evolving in her work. Yet the imitation of prescientific thinking seems less her own than had been the thinking of "The Man-Moth." Nothing here suggests a parable for man's will, as had the earlier poem. Instead what the poem and its version of "total immersion" imply is the power of the irrational over civilization, and in that regard the work perpetuates her view that all the products of man will erode. Perhaps, as with other writers of her generation, the source for such a view is Freud's *Civilization and Its Discontents* (1929), but it need not have been. The view is implicit in Elizabeth Bishop's notion of art as temporary, and it explains why she is able to reject the evolutionist's optimism about the future of man based on his ability to construct tools and systems.

"The Burglar of Babylon" repeats this struggle for existence between the lawless (libido) and the law (superego). Like the poor, its criminal cannot go home again once he has been to Rio. This "home," like the Prodigal's, is never specified, for presumably the criminal is from Rio. His removal earlier to a penitentiary has temporarily separated him but in no way has changed that fact. The separation has, on the other hand, made it imperative that he risk death to see again "his auntie,/who raised him like a son." The reader is thus faced with an existential dilemma: the "home" of the burglar becomes, as with the poet and the alcoholic of "The Prodigal," an origin either worldly or otherworldly that is unrecoverable; and his return and pursuit by the police, who shoot their leader by mistake before killing him, end unexpectedly. His aunt cannot understand why he turned criminal, and others do not know why he was so inept that he "got caught six times—or more." The poem ends darkly: the police are "after another two" criminals who are supposedly not "as dangerous/As the poor Micuçu," but one wonders about the self-destructiveness and self-hate that must underscore Micuçu's actions and beliefs. Why else would he have failed so consistently at his crimes? The ending in a failure to secure all the criminals and, hence, to conquer the irrational drive recalls the failure earlier by art in "The Sea and Its Shore" to achieve the same control. The poem by this failure reinforces the themes of loss and pain that comprise much of Bishop's vision. To heighten this failure of containment, the poet chooses a formal genre, the ballad, a form historically allied with tales of outlawry.

Among the most winning of the character poems is "Invitation to Miss Marianne Moore." Based loosely on Pablo Neruda's "Alberto Rojas Jiménez viene volando," it forms an invitation to the older poet to spend a day with the speaker, talking, shopping, and visiting. In the Neruda poem the dead Jiménez comes flying on one of the paper birds that it was the hobby of the dead writer to construct. Jiménez is first located among the decaying dead. From here he begins his journey over living scenes until he reaches Neruda "sin sombra y sin nombre,/sin azúcar, sin boca, sin rosales." For Bishop, Brooklyn becomes the place where the poet is "buried" and whose smells and hellish "clouds of fiery chemicals" must be overcome. She too must traverse the "live world" of the East River and its "whistles, pennants, and smoke" to join the speaker. But, as ever in Bishop, the poetry that Moore writes and that critics like Wallace Fowlie say bestows immortality on writers is here seen as transient: "dynasties of negative constructions/darkening and dying" despite a "grammar that suddenly turns and shines/like flocks of sandpipers flying." The effect of this brilliance among the dying is compared to a brief "light in the white mackerel sky, . . .a daytime comet."

The poem's basic stoic position—a struggle toward life in the face of inevitable destruction—is depicted in "The Sea and Its Shore" and is repeated in Bishop's remarks about the dying Flannery O'Connor: "Something about her intimidated me a bit: perhaps natural awe before her toughness and courage; perhaps, although death is certain for all, hers seemed a little more certain than usual. She made no show of not living in a metropolis, or of being a believer, she lived with Christian stoicism and wonderful wit and humor that put most of us to shame." In "Invitation" the wit of both Moore and Bishop in the face of inevitable, although not imminent, death converges in the description of the older poet as a fairy godmother:

> Come with the pointed toe of each black shoe
> trailing a sapphire highlight,
> with a black capeful of butterfly wings and bon-mots,
> with heaven knows how many angels all riding
> on the broad black brim of your hat. . . .

With such wit, it seems almost inevitable that a few critics should find the poem "whimsical bravura" and "priceless" and that they should pay less attention to the battle against self-pity which is also part of the vision.

The same preoccupation with the transience of art recurs in "Santarém" (1978), except here inevitable destruction gives way to taste. The speaker's admiration for a wasps' nest contrasts with a fellow traveler's pronouncement that it is an "ugly thing." Naturalists have described how natives with machetes "obtain the whitish, tough-cartoned nests of *Chartergus* for sale to Europeans as curios." In the poem the harvested nest opposes the human community and its various divisions of labor, recalling Darwin's earlier worry over specialization among insects and his defenses against critics who argued that only God could be so ingenious as to grant insects the power to construct such efficient and perfectly shaped cells. Traffic divides into dories, stern-wheeler, side-wheelers, dugouts, and river schooner. Thus technology is again made part of man's natural instincts, and art is only one more kind of technology or, rather, a relic of what once was functional. As in other Bishop poems, art is achieved by going backward to "that conflux of two great rivers"—childhood wish or "the Garden of Eden"; and in almost dialectic fashion, the poem's cathedral like the poem itself arises out of an effort to transcend that mental journey and its discovered oppositions of "life/death, right/wrong, male/female." Like the experienced cathedral and the priest's home, art is not immune to natural disaster, though like the priest, one may be away when destruction comes. The very nature of the residue and recovery of the poem's vision, moreover, links it to "Crusoe in England" and the concerns of technology and travel that mark "Imaginary Iceberg," "The Map," "Over 2000 Illustrations and a Complete Concordance," and the Brazil section of *Questions of Travel*.

Bishop's decision in 1951 to live in Brazil leads to a lessening in *Questions of Travel* (1965) of the struggles for existence that underscore most of the early poems. As both "The Riverman" and "The Burglar of Babylon" imply, the major effort here is against time, as if temporary survival has already been assured and must now be protected. Thus the travelers of "Arrival at Santos" and "Questions of Travel" have a sense of their own being at the onset, and the poems relate their defenses against the "answers" which life will offer to "immodest demands for a different world." One must be careful of the boy with the boat hook, the customs officials who may seize the "bourbon and cigarettes," and the frailty of postage stamps which threaten to come off letters and make them undeliverable. Therefore one heads away from the coast where earlier Bishop's major conflicts had been situated. He moves toward the interior where, as he is asked in the title poem: "Is it lack of imagination that makes us come/to imagined places, not just stay at home?" There the journey proves disturbing with its many waterfalls and crowded streams rushing rapidly to oblivion in the sea. Is the purpose of the interiors (civilization) to return one to barbarism (the sea)? Are writers like Giambattista Vico and Norman O. Brown right in their views of history? Is the enormous effort of such travel into the interior ultimately to be wasted? If so, her speaker asks, what drive in man compels him to see these sights for, despite the effort, he would surely regret having missed them? She concludes that knowledge of necessity is never clear: "The choice is never wide and never free."

Like the man-moth's struggle to "investigate as high as he can climb," man's thirst to realize what he imagines becomes in these late poems a mystery, a part of man's nature that is made more visible for readers by a change in the poet's intent to keep one from withdrawing to the past. Stevens in "Peter Quince at the Clavier" (1915) had seen that mystery. He proposed that unrealized concepts give way to new concepts, but those given body are preserved by memory: "Beauty is momentary in the mind. . ./But in the flesh it is immortal." Experience becomes important in itself because of its memory value and, by the durability of recollection, replaces the importance of conceptualization. This is Bishop's position in "The Sea and Its Shore," and in his discussion of "precious objects," Ransom touches on the psychological nature of this replacement as it might affect poetry. He sees poets who use a quantity of such objects as appealing to sentiment rather than to sensibility and as ignoring that special public which is conditioned to react immediately to the significances of what the poet celebrates for the larger public that needs to experience what is being described before it can react. In the case of Bishop's work, life's final uncertainty and the sometimes self-pitying acceptance of annihilation demand an emphasis on experience as the only reality and a special willingness by readers to accept the often cross-grained nature of that experience. When her vision was couched, as in the early poems, in a complex texture that counteracted the sentimentality, acceptances were easier. M.L. Rosenthal rejected her occlusions early, and in *The Modern Poets* (1960) he dismisses a large part of her work as sentimental, and critics like Nancy McNally have stressed the pain and ugliness of what is being depicted.

Something other than mere sentimentalism is again working in these late poems. Certainly Bishop's response to the false prettiness of Fowlie's *Pantomime, A Journal of Rehearsals* (1951), confirms that the ugliness of many of her recollections is, as Jarrell points out, part of the original experience. "My own first ride on a swan boat occurred at the age of three and is chiefly memorable for the fact that one of the live swans paddling around us bit my mother's finger when she offered it a peanut. I remember the hole in the black kid glove and a drop of blood." Yet the continuing emphasis on labor in her writing keeps her from indulging excessively in feeling for its own sake. "The Armadillo" with its final echo of E.A. Robinson offers the clearest argument in these late pieces against her using "precious objects" merely for sentimental emphasis, though something might be said, independent of the poems, for an imagination that recurs consistently to the unpleasant events of her life. All the tears of her poetry may be meant to evoke an awe from the reader similar to that awe which she expresses for O'Connor. If not sympathy for her sensibility, then some kind of admiration for her having withstood the disappointments is being sought and sought on terms not of accomplishment so much as service. But the poems seem to be echoing more importantly Juvenal's advice in Satire x that, if one would be happy, one must want less. Man has been conditioned to think self-indulgently, and his self-indulgence must be curbed.

The situation of "The Armadillo" is not appreciably different from situations that one meets in the poetry of Robinson or Frost. Existence is seen lying between an origin that has been abandoned and perhaps cannot be known and a purpose which is equally unknowable. Yet Robinson would argue by example that the ensuing destructiveness of an Eben Flood or Miniver Cheevey or Richard Cory, being suicidal, does not destroy others; and Frost would make the situation an occasion for his speaker's taking stock. In contrast the celebration of the Bishop poem is widely ecological. The illegal cometlike balloons which are loosed into the landscape manage to threaten and harm the animals, just as man wherever he has settled has threatened the balance of nature and the existence of wildlife. The point of the poem is opposed, as a consequence, to Robinson's utilitarian posture and Frost's quiet contemplation. No man does injury merely to himself or acts entirely toward his own ends. Man's accomplishments may rise toward sainthood and seem, once up in the sky, like stars or planets; but the consequences still descend to do damage to owl nest, armadillo, rabbit, and, hence, other men. Thus the question raised early by "Large Bad Picture" as to whether the ends of man are determined by "Commerce or contemplation" is turned into a nonquestion. The vital question becomes one of interrelation and a determination of how best the present may preserve for the future what already exists. In such a world shut off from certitude and salvation, one's options become Micuçu's or Flood's; one either tries to recover childhood or its primitive equivalent—a world before man began to impose his egotistical will—or one resorts to isolation, self-pity, drink, and eventually suicide. Bishop makes clear that, for all the exceptional experiences that she has had and dwells upon in her work, she desires the return.

"Manners," "Sestina," "The First Death in Nova Scotia," and "Sunday, 4 A.M." from *Questions of Travel* as well as the late stories, "Gwendolyn" and "In the Village" exemplify this return. They complement the move to a more primitive Brazil with a return by the poet mentally to her origins; the move is equated not with any theological or evolutionary system but with her early life. In bringing her work back to a world determined by others and to childhood as the completion of self, Bishop is least protected against a charge of sentimentalism. "Manners"

simply and nostalgically describes her grandfather's lesson in "good manners." "Sestina" recounts in equally sentimental terms a rainy day spent
with her grandmother drawing while the grandmother busied herself with
chores. "The First Death in Nova Scotia" relates the death of her cousin
Arthur, who is made to resemble a "frosted cake" and supposedly borne off
"to be/the smallest page at court." "Sunday, 4 A.M." shows how much
later the poet's dreams confuse the memories of people who had deeply
impressed her as a child with more recent acquaintances. Only daylight
and its bird song restore order. Yet, however minor these poems may
seem, the logic of the returns is no different from that of the philosopher
who equates man's nature with his orgins, and in proposing the returns,
Bishop accepts a pattern similar to that which a number of postmodern
poets have used. Roethke recurs to such a pattern in *The Lost Son* (1948)
and *Praise to the End!* (1951), Lowell in *Life Studies* (1959), Jarrell in *The
Lost World* (1965), and Berryman in his own late reconstructions of youth.

Returns continue in *Geography III* (1977) in such poems as "In the
Waiting Room," "The Moose," and "Poem." The first pictures the poet on
the verge of her seventh birthday in the waiting room of a dentist's office
in Worcester, Massachusetts. World War I is in progress, and the poem
describes the awareness that she achieves by a growing empathy first with
an aunt, then with others in the dentist's waiting room, and finally with
everyone on earth. In this move to adult awareness, Bishop chooses an
age traditionally linked to the start of moral responsibility, and she
tampers with the actual contents of the *National Geographic*, but rather
than move the subject toward the often personal and, hence, sentimental
lessons of *Questions of Travel*, the tampering broadens the work's appeal.
"The Moose" describes what begins as a bus trip from Nova Scotia to
Boston—first in terms of the coast, then in terms of farms and the past
lives of the passengers. Suddenly the trip out of raw nature is interrupted
by the appearance of a moose, and one discovers that man's technical
progress in no way defeats his fascination with the primitive. "Poem"
details another painting of Nova Scotia. Like that of "Large Bad Picture"
it is painted by the poet's great uncle George Hutchinson. The poet
identifies the painting's subject by the location's general characteristics
and, as the poem gains subjective power, by her own recollection of the
precise place and a history of how she came into possession of the work.
The poem ends with a coincidence of visions, indicating that places
which are personally and deeply felt can be matched by different but
equally deeply and personally felt experience.

In this new corollary of personal and collective experience, Bishop's speakers achieve something akin to what Angus Fletcher in *Allegory*

(1964) describes as the allegorical protagonist. This protagonist acts "as if possessed," implying "cosmic notions of fate and personal fortune." His actions touch on both "human and divine spheres" and make "an appeal to an almost scientific curiosity about the order of things." He is "a conquistador," arbitrating "order over chaos by confronting a random collection of people and events" and "imposing his own fate upon that random collection." As in medieval allegory, the literal sense of a Bishop poem comes first, "it being the meaning in which the others are contained and without which it would be impossible and irrational to come to an understanding of the others, particularly the allegorical." The literal sense permits the factive sense to border at times on rationalism and at times on surrealism. One may see this allegory, moreover, as a necessary solution to what she describes in her interview as a love of religious poetry and a dislike of didacticism. She told Ashley Brown: "Auden's late poetry is sometimes spoiled for me by his didacticism. I don't like modern religiosity in general: it always seems to lead to a tone of moral superiority. . . . Times have changed since Herbert's day." By means of a corresponding and accessible ideal world at one remove from experience, she can assert a "moral" meaning at the same time that she keeps her narrative from overt moralizing.

Out of this ideal world and the manipulation of "precious objects," Bishop has created a significant poetry; and just as one may say that she in her returns is not so individualistic as Robinson, Frost, or Stevens, and hence different from that generation, one may add that she is never so mystical as Roethke or so involved with gaining reader sympathy as are the "confessional poets." Regardless of their conclusions, her poems are still active; and despite their searches for self and their emphases on dream, her reconstructions are not inspired by Freudian analysis and its wish to have one's direction altered by the conscious. Although Bishop returns mentally to her origins, her returns do not reflect any of the pathological compulsion that Sherman Paul detects in Crane's reveries of childhood nor do they reflect the therapeutic aims that seem to lie behind the returns of Roethke, Jarrell, Plath, and Berryman. One has the sense, particularly in these late poems, that, unlike some of her contemporaries, she has lived the life she imagined—with all its necessary disappointments—and that, despite the narrow range of choice and the pain of disappointment, she is willing to see her past as the only kind of life she could have lived. She is not, as are Ignatow, Plath, and Berryman, trying to fix blame; nor is she necessarily, as are Roethke and Jarrell, trying to be sympathetic. Like Baudelaire's voyagers she seems instead to be accepting the conditions of voyaging as the process of a life which itself will arrive meaninglessly at death with perhaps a few poems as a dividend.

In their consistent pessimism about ultimate purpose, the ranges of Bishop's vision relate her to the views of modernist poets like Robinson, Frost, and Stevens as well as to the major questions asked by their successors. Her work is perhaps more profoundly existential than the poetry of any of her contemporaries, and like Ignatow she questions even the evolutionary thrust on which occasionally a poet like Jarrell relies. She can and does believe in "tradition" and a sense of linear history, but not in a tradition or history that concedes the immortality of art. Her "tradition" with its accumulation and reinforcements of feeling is no different from the cumulative effects of experience. Her use of works which have preceded her functions more to reinforce than, as in Jarrell, to effect a death struggle with a father figure and to supplant his image. Her "precious objects" give the reader the only durability that she has discovered, and in presenting this durability, she never fights for an idiosyncratic idiom. Such an idiom would distort the reality she values and would finally prove immaterial, an exercise in will without regard to environment. She thus opposes the "rarity" that poets of her generation have assumed to promote their own egos and work and which, by its occasionally strident assertions of importance, can be as self-pitying as her denial of will. Nonetheless one may wonder what her poetry would have been like if she, like her man-moth, had relinquished her "one tear." A more militant stoicism like that she admires in O'Connor might have resulted and produced an equally interesting body of work, but one with far less emphasis on detail and inclined even more to allegory.

If Bishop's approach to life by its inclusion of impediments seems less "intellectual" than that of other poets, it is that she is finally given more to necessity than they are. She is more willing to see life as a dialectical process involving man and his environment rather than a process of man's will being imposed upon his surroundings. Although man may not be improving in her view, he will survive, much as other animal life has survived; and he will need whatever beauty may be preservable. To accept this vision she must abandon the superstructures that most critics rely on to cope with poets—those structures of thought which by their very separation from experience seem to define the ego. By minimizing the organizational nature of such separations and by placing her definition of being on specific interactions with objects, she embraces a relativism like that of other postmodernist poets but based on situation rather than on voice. Her diverse "characters," as Southworth points out, lie not in personae but in her manner of selecting subjects, in a tonality, and in her varied ways of massing detail into significant form. She emerges, therefore, as a balance to the tendency of other poets of her generation to overstress will and rarity. She reminds one how narrow the choices of life are and how unimportant rarity is. Erosion takes its toll of that, too. When *The Complete Poems* appeared in 1969, readers were thankful mainly for the convenience of having all her poems under one cover. Her tendency there to keep her subjects isolated, small, and circumscribed, worked toward establishing her as a master of the self-contained anthology piece. The poems she published afterward, however, have brought her as close as any contemporary writer to the scope and to the "one significant, consistent, and developing personality" that Eliot makes requisite to great poets. It is a greatness, moreover, linked intimately to postmodernist methods.

DAVID KALSTONE

Questions of Memory,
Questions of Travel

Elizabeth Bishop, to her credit, has always been hard to "place." In the surveys of American poetry she is not linked to any particular school. She has had, from the very start, her share of prizes and praise; her work is admired by many poets who do not admire one another. Though on occasion she has had the grants and university positions which keep poets alive in America, she only rarely gives the public readings which keep poets visible. She has lived abroad for long stretches of her life, most recently in Brazil. Her books of poems, eagerly awaited, appear infrequently: *North & South* (1946); *A Cold Spring* (1955); *Questions of Travel* (1965); *The Complete Poems* (1969); *Geography III* (1976).

Bishop is probably the most honored yet most elusive of contemporary poets. Who else, with some of her best poems still to be written, would have entitled a volume *The Complete Poems?* She was, until very recently, "read unreasonably little and praised reasonably much," as Randall Jarrell said of Marianne Moore. There are many reasons for this, but the ones which interest me here have to do with the accidents of critical attention. Bishop's first book was so individual and striking that certain pieces from *North & South*—poems like "The Fish" and "The Man-Moth"— have been reprinted over and over in anthologies. She has become known as the author of single stunning poems, fewer from the later volumes than from the earlier. Wonderful as the anthologized poems may be, they give, even for anthologies, an unusually stunted version of

From *Five Temperaments*. Copyright © 1977 by David Kalstone. Oxford University Press, 1977.

Bishop's variety, of the way her writing has emerged, of her developing concerns.

There is a second problem: the deceptively simple surface of Bishop's work. Critics have praised her descriptive powers and treated her as something of a miniaturist. As mistakenly as with the work of Marianne Moore, they have sometimes asked if Bishop's is poetry at all. Bishop's early poems show a deep affinity with Marianne Moore's exact observant style: "An appropriately selected foundation for Miss Bishop's work," said Randall Jarrell. But he was also quick to see Bishop as "less driven into desperate straits or dens of innocence, and taking this Century of Polycarp more for granted." Jarrell is one of those critics who urges us to look for the inner landscape and not to treat a poet's descriptive powers as if they were ends in themselves, or a weaker form of expression. He was able to show Moore's accuracy and understatement to be an instrument of ironic self-protectiveness. ("Her Shield" is the title of his essay). By implication, he teaches us to ask similar questions about Bishop. Unlike the relatively armored approach of Marianne Moore, Bishop's precise explorations become a way of countering and encountering a lost world. Merely to praise her "famous eye" would be a way of avoiding larger issues. We need to know what is seen, and how the eye, with what Kenneth Burke calls its "disguised rituals," initiates us into human fears and wishes.

II

Robert Lowell, thinking back to the time before he wrote *Life Studies*, felt that Bishop's work "seemed to belong to a later century." It wasn't so much a matter of experimental forms. In *North & South* (1946) there were a number of emblematic poems—"The Map," "The Monument," "The Gentleman of Shalott" among them—some in formal stanzas, some strictly rhymed. Still, from the very start, there was something about her work for which elegantly standard literary analysis was not prepared. Readers have been puzzled, as when one critic writes about "Florida": "the poet's exuberance provides a scattering of images whose relevance to the total structure is open to question. It is as though Miss Bishop stopped along the road home to examine every buttercup and asphodel she saw." First of all, Bishop writes about alligators, mangrove swamps, skeletons and shells—things exotic and wild, not prettified. More important, there is some notion of neat and total structure which the critic expects and imposes, but which the poem subverts. What makes the quoted critic nervous is a quality which becomes more and more prominent in Bishop's work—her apparent lack of insistence on meanings beyond the surface of the poem, the poem's seeming randomness and disintegration. There is something personal, even quirky, about her apparently straightforward descriptive poems which, on early readings, it is hard to identify. This is an offhand way of speaking which Bishop has come to trust and master, especially in her important book of 1965, *Questions of Travel*, and in the extraordinary poems she has published since then.

I am talking about matters of tone, the kind of authority a single voice will claim over the material included in a poem. Anyone who has heard Miss Bishop read will know how flat and modest her voice is, how devoid of flourish, how briefly she holds her final chords and cadences and allows a poem to resonate. Here is the beginning of "In the Waiting Room":

> In Worcester, Massachusetts,
> I went with Aunt Consuelo
> to keep her dentist's appointment
> and sat and waited for her
> in the dentist's waiting room.

Or another opening ("Filling Station"):

> Oh, but it is dirty!
> —this little filling station,
> oil-soaked, oil-permeated
> to a disturbing, over-all
> black translucency.
> Be careful with that match!

And this is the end of "The Bight":

> Click. Click. Goes the dredge,
> and brings up a dripping jawful of marl.
> All the untidy activity continues,
> awful but cheerful.

I have chosen the plainest and most provocative examples of the apparently random in order to raise questions common to much poetry after Wallace Stevens: how is meaning developed from individual and unamplified details? How does the observer's apparent lack of insistence, devoid of rhetorical pressure, rise to significance (if, indeed, that is the word for it)? Howard Nemerov gives us one answer: "Vision begins with a fault in this world's smooth façade." But Bishop finds that fault, that break from observation into the unknown, almost impossible to locate. "There is no split," she remarks in a letter:

> Dreams, works of art (some) glimpses of the always-more-successful
> surrealism of everyday life, unexpected moments of empathy (is it?),
> catch a peripheral vision of whatever it is one can never really see full-face
> but that seems enormously important. I can't believe we are wholly
> irrational—and I do admire Darwin—But reading Darwin one admires
> the beautiful solid case being built up out of his endless, heroic observa-
> tions, almost unconscious or automatic—and then comes a sudden relax-
> ation, a forgetful phrase, and one feels that strangeness of his undertaking,
> sees the lonely young man, his eye fixed on facts and minute details,
> sinking or sliding giddily off into the unknown. What one seems to want
> in art, in experiencing it, is the same thing that is necessary for its
> creation, a self-forgetful, perfectly useless concentration.

Heroic observation; eyes fixed on facts and minute details, sinking, sliding
giddily off into the unknown; a self-forgetful, perfectly useless concentration. What she sees in Darwin, we can see in her own efforts. Take
"Florida" (the poem our critic found disorganized)—a poem of almost
Darwinian concentration.

The opening line is so disarming, almost trivializing, that we are in
danger of taking what follows for granted: the odd changes of scale that
are among this poem's secrets.

> The state with the prettiest name,
> the state that floats in brackish water,
> held together by mangrove roots
> that bear while living oysters in clusters,
> and when dead strew white swamps with skeletons,
> dotted as if bombarded, with green hummocks
> like ancient cannon-balls sprouting grass.

The scale changes as rapidly as Gulliver's: first the whole state,
afloat, intact with its boundaries, the mapmaker's or aerial photographer's
vision; then an organism (held together by mangrove roots), the geolo-
gist's or botanist's fanciful X ray. Her Florida is a barnacled world refined
to residues. Oysters dot the mangrove roots; dead mangroves strew the
swamps with skeletons. Dead turtles leave their skulls and their shells,
which are themselves hosts to other growths, barnacled. The coastline is
looped with seashells painstakingly and exotically named. There is sedi-
ment in the water; solvents in wood-smoke; charring on stumps and dead
trees. Yet the charring is "like black velvet." The residues studding this
landscape are its principal ornaments as well: artistic and historical growths,
like the "tide-looped strings of fading shells" turning the "monotonous
. . .sagging coast-line" to something else.

At first the description occurs in a free-floating eternal present, a series of phrases which don't commit the observer to any main verb at all. They seem if anything to exclude her, re-awakening memories of geological change that stretch far before and beyond her in scale, habitually repeated historical action. The strange shifts of scale—of size and space—in a seemingly timeless, self-renewing present remind us constantly, by implication, of the frailty of our merely human observer. A descriptive poem, which in other hands, say Whitman's, appropriates landscapes and objects, here makes us aware just how, just why we are excluded from such appropriations.

Only when we get to the buzzards, two-thirds of the way through the poem, is there a form of the present tense (they "are drifting down, down, down") restricted to her particular moment of watching, a definite *now*. Here also, two strange mirrors in which we do not find ourselves. First:

> Thirty or more buzzards are drifting down, down, down,
> over something they have spotted in the swamp,
> in circles like stirred-up flakes of sediment
> sinking through water.
> Smoke from woods-fires filters fine blue solvents.

And then:

> After dark, the fireflies map the heavens in the marsh
> until the moon rises.

The four elements form a self-enclosed world. Creatures of the air mirror the earth's discards (are they really there?) floating through water; and fire, as if completing the cycle, exhales fine smoke into the blue. Then again with the fireflies, air and flickering fire are reflected in the marsh, earth and water together. In other words, alternate creations dwarf or frame the poet's own: the long scale of eroding nature with its fossils and predators (buzzards, mosquitoes with "ferocious obbligatos") and then the daily repeating creations and fadings. When the moon comes up, the landscape pales. Its wonderful sounds and colors—the flashy tanagers, the pelicans gold-winged at sunset, the musical screeching—turn skeletal once more.

The world in its processes provides a delicate model for the poet's work, for art—its shells with beautiful names, its finely observed (and alliterative) oysters in clusters. But the poem continually stresses how such contrivance is made for fading and how nature's contrivances survive the artist's own. Building toward a phrase whose effect is worthy of what she admires in Darwin ("a sudden relaxation, a forgetful phrase"), Bishop sums up the impact of the scene, grasped for the fullness of her own understanding:

> Cold white, not bright, the moonlight is coarse-meshed,
> and the careless, corrupt state is all black specks
> too far apart, and ugly whites; the poorest
> post-card of itself.

At the end Florida contracts to the alligator's five primitive calls ("friendliness, love, mating, war, and a warning"), and with its whimper is restored to darkness and its mysterious identity as "the Indian Princess."

Bishop exposes us to a more ambitious version of her almost toneless observer in a poem which reaches back to her Nova Scotia childhood, "At the Fishhouses." Here is the opening:

> Although it is a cold evening,
> down by one of the fishhouses
> an old man sits netting,
> his net, in the gloaming almost invisible
> a dark purple-brown,
> and his shuttle worn and polished.
> The air smells so strong of codfish
> it makes one's nose run and one's eyes water.
> The five fishhouses have steeply peaked roofs
> and narrow, cleated gangplanks slant up
> to storerooms in the gables
> for the wheelbarrows to be pushed up and down on.
> All is silver: the heavy surface of the sea,
> swelling slowly as if considering spilling over,
> is opaque, but the silver of the benches,
> the lobster pots, and masts, scattered
> among the wild jagged rocks,
> is of an apparent translucence
> like the small old buildings with an emerald moss
> growing on their shoreward walls.
> The big fish tubs are completely lined
> with layers of beautiful herring scales
> and the wheelbarrows are similarly plastered
> with creamy iridescent coats of mail,
> with small iridescent flies crawling on them.

At first, as in "Florida," a landscape seems almost without a spectator, the speaker comically unwelcome in an air which smacks of another element and which makes her eyes water and her nose run. She slowly exposes the scene, present tense, with a tempered willingness to let it speak for itself in declarative simplicity. Things *are*; things *have*. The lone fisherman, a Wordsworthian solitary, is worn into the scene, his net "almost invisible," his shuttle "worn and polished," his "black old knife" with a blade "almost worn away." The dense opening description—deliberately slow, close to fifty lines of the poem—is in all details of sight, sense and sound intended to subject us to the landscape, to draw us deeply into it. "The five fishhouses have steeply peaked roofs/and narrow, cleated gangplanks slant up": even the clotted consonants and doubling of adjectives force these words apart and force us to dwell on them, as if to carve out some certainty of vision. The reader is meant to become what the speaker jokingly claims herself to be later in this poem: "a believer in total immersion."

From this immersion a pattern gathers, unhurried but persistent: present, for example, in the odd half-rhyme of *codfish* and *polished*, or in the unassuming repetition of *iridescent*. The wheelbarrows are "plastered/with creamy iridescent coats of mail,/with small iridescent flies crawling on them." The crudeness and the delicacy of these details are made to appear strokes of the same master, of the landscape's age-old subjection to the sea, to the caking, the plastering, the lining, the silvering-over which turns everything to iridescence or sequins, as at the same time it rusts them and wears them away.

In its fidelity to setting—to what is both jagged and strangely jewelled—the poem accumulates the sense of an artistry beyond the human, one that stretches over time, chiselling and decorating with its strange erosions. The human enterprise depends upon and is dwarfed by the sea, just as the fishhouse ramps lead out of, but back into the water: "Down at the water's edge, at the place/where they haul up the boats, up the long ramp/descending into the water." Precisely by imagining these encircling powers, the speaker wins some authority over them. This is her largest gesture, reflected in some smaller moments of propitiation: offering a cigarette to the fisherman, and with odd simplicity singing Baptist hymns to a moderately curious seal, true creature of that "element bearable to no mortal." Behind them—or more to the point "behind us"—as if left behind in merely human history "a million Christmas trees stand/waiting for Christmas."

This "believer in total immersion," through her patient wooing or conjuring, finally wins a certain elevation of tone, a vision, in a twice-repeated phrase, of the sea "Cold dark deep and absolutely clear."

> . . . The water seems suspended
> above the rounded gray and blue-gray stones.
> I have seen it over and over, the same sea, the same,
> slightly, indifferently swinging above the stones,

icily free above the stones,
above the stones and then the world.
If you should dip your hand in,
your wrist would ache immediately,
your bones would begin to ache and your hand would burn
as if the water were a transmutation of fire
that feeds on stones and burns with a dark gray flame.
If you tasted it, it would first taste bitter,
then briny, then surely burn your tongue.
It is like what we imagine knowledge to be:
dark, salt, clear, moving, utterly free,
drawn from the cold hard mouth
of the world, derived from the rocky breasts
forever, flowing and drawn, and since
our knowledge is historical, flowing, and flown.

The poet returns knowledge to concreteness, as if breaking it down into its elements (dark, salt, clear). The speaker herself seems drawn into the elements: at first jokingly in the fishy air which makes the nose run, the eyes water; then in the burning if one dips one's hands, as if water were a "transmutation of fire that feeds on stones." The absorbing and magical transformations of earth, air, fire and water into one another (as in "Florida") make it impossible—and unnecessary—to distinguish *knowledge* from the *sea*, to determine what, grammatically, is "derived from the rocky breasts/forever." With a final fluency she leaves her declarative descriptions behind and captures a rhythm at once mysterious and acknowledging limitations ("flowing and drawn. . .flowing and flown").

"At the Fishhouses" makes explicit what is usually implicit, invisible and vital in Miss Bishop's poems, like a pulse: a sense of the encircling and eroding powers in whose presence all minute observations are valuably made. She is, in fact, rather like a sandpiper she describes in another poem: the bird pictured as subject to the water's roar, the earth's shaking—imagined in "a state of controlled panic, a student of Blake." He watches the sand, no detail too small ("Sandpiper"):

The world is a mist. And then the world is
minute and vast and clear. The tide
is higher or lower. He couldn't tell you which.
His beak is focussed; he is preoccupied,

looking for something, something, something.
Poor bird, he is obsessed!
The millions of grains are black, white, tan, and gray,
mixed with quartz grains, rose and amethyst.

Here again are those shifts of scale which, instead of unsettling, actually strengthen our perspective. The poem is a critique of Blake's auguries of innocence: his seeing the world in a grain of sand. "The world is a mist. And then the world is/minute and vast and clear." The adjectives appear to make a quiet claim. Yet what an odd collocation— minute and vast and clear. The scales are not really commensurable; one sees the world, one sees the grain of sand, and the clarity comes in making a primitive and definite distinction about what is and is not within our grasp. The bird, on the one hand, is battered and baffled by the waves, the misty "sheets of interrupting water"; on the other hand it attends and stares, is preoccupied, obsessed with the grains of sand, a litany of whose colors, minutely and beautifully distinguished, ends the poem. That is all it knows of the world.

These poems both describe and set themselves at the limits of description. Bishop lets us know that every detail is a boundary, not a Blakean microcosm. Because of the limits they suggest, details vibrate with a meaning beyond mere physical presence. Landscapes meant to sound detached are really inner landscapes. They show an effort at recon-stituting the world as if it were in danger of being continually lost. It is only this sense of *precarious* possession that accounts for the way Bishop looks at the city waking up ("Love Lies Sleeping"):

> From the window I see
>
> an immense city, carefully revealed,
> made delicate by over-workmanship,
>   detail upon detail,
>   cornice upon façade,
>
> reaching so languidly up into
> a weak white sky, it seems to waver there.
>   (where it has slowly grown
>   in skies of water-glass
>
> from fused beads of iron and copper crystals,
> the little chemical "garden" in a jar
>   trembles and stands again,
>   pale blue, blue-green, and brick.)

That human contrivance is frail and provisional is clear not only from the "wavering" but also from the odd, habitual changes of scale: an immense city, carefully revealed, is also a little chemical garden in a jar. That it should be seen as workmanship at all is a miracle of freshness, a confusion of proportions, part aerial vision, part closeup as of some miraculous insect civilization. Bishop triumphs in the surprising coincidence of mechanics and natural growth, fused beads of crystal, a little chemical garden—a balancing act to portray our fragile ingenuity.

The ability to see such accomplishments as provisional explains the power of one of Bishop's apparently random poems, "The Bight." It is subtitled "on my birthday," the only suggestion of much resonance beyond the impression of a tide-battered inlet—muddy at low tide, with dredges, pelicans, marl, sponge boats, sharktails hung up to dry, boats beached, some wrecked. What animates the scene this time is the observer's deliberate activity, celebrating her birthday in an off-key way with an unrelenting and occasionally mischievous series of comparisons: pilings dry as matches; water turning to gas (and which Baudelaire might hear turning to marimba music); pelicans crashing like pickaxes; man-of-war birds opening tails like scissors; sharktails hanging like plowshares. The whole rundown world is domesticated by comparisons to our mechanical contrivances, our instruments of workaday survival, enabling, in turn, an outrageous simile (stove-boats "like torn-open, unanswered letters") and an equally outrageous pun ("The bight is littered with old correspondences"). The letters wickedly enough bring Baudelaire back into the poem, merge with his "correspondences." They are unanswered letters to boot, in a poem where the author has shot off one comparison after another, like firecrackers. No wonder then that a dredge at the end perfectly accompanies this poet's activities:

> Click. Click. Goes the dredge,
> and brings up a dripping jawful of marl.
> All the untidy activity continues,
> awful but cheerful.

This is what she allows for her birthday: the pointed celebration of small-craft victories in a storm-ridden inlet.

It is no accident that much of Bishop's work is carried on at the mercy of or in the wake of the tides. There are divided and distinguished stages in her encounters: moments of civilized, provisional triumph; and then again, times when landscapes leave us behind—the northern seas of "At the Fishhouses," the abundant decay of "Florida" and later, of her adopted Brazil, magnetic poles sensed even in the title of her first volume, *North & South*. Our mortal temperate zones seem in some ways the excluded middle where we possess a language of precarious, even doomed distinctions.

III

The fact that Bishop sought worlds which dwarf us, landscapes from which we are excluded, is best glossed by a wonderful and very important story, "In the Village." The tale reaches back to a Nova Scotia childhood, a version of her own. Her mother was taken to a sanitarium when Bishop was five; she never saw her again. The story is told through the child's eyes. In one scene the young girl watches her mother, who is just back from a sanitarium and coming out of two years of mourning, being fitted for a new dress. "The dressmaker was crawling around and around on her knees eating pins as Nebuchadnezzar had crawled eating grass." The child stands in the doorway.

> Clang.
> *Clang.*
> Oh, beautiful sounds, from the blacksmith's shop at the end of the garden! Its gray roof, with patches of moss, could be seen above the lilac bushes. Nate was there—Nate, wearing a long black leather apron over his trousers and bare chest, sweating hard, a black leather cap on top of dry, thick, black-and-gray curls, a black sooty face; iron filings, whiskers, and gold teeth, all together, and a smell of red-hot metal and horses' hoofs.
> *Clang.*
> The pure note: pure and angelic.
> The dress was all wrong. She screamed.
> The child vanishes.

The child vanishes literally, and metaphorically as well, in that moment of awakening and awareness of inexplicable adult pain. From this point on the story is told in the first person and in the present tense, as if she had been jolted into reclaiming something first seen as a distant tableau and dream. Memories of the mother's scream echo through scenes which are also, as in the pungent energy of the blacksmith shop, rich strong recollections of life in a Nova Scotia village. At the end, the mother gone for good, the threats and village harmonies come together for the last time.

> Every Monday afternoon I go past the blacksmith's shop with the package under my arm, hiding the address of the sanitarium with my arm and my other hand.
> Going over the bridge, I stop and stare down into the river. All the little trout that have been too smart to get caught—for how long now?—are there, rushing in flank movements, foolish assaults and retreats, against and away from the old sunken fender of Malcolm McNeil's Ford. It has lain there for ages and is supposed to be a disgrace to us all. So are the tin cans that glint there, brown and gold.
> From above, the trout look as transparent as the water, but if one did catch one, it would be opaque enough, with a little slick moon-white belly with a pair of tiny, pleated, rose-pink fins on it. The leaning willows soak their narrow yellowed leaves.

Clang.
Clang.
Nate is shaping a horseshoe.
Oh, beautiful pure sound!
It turns everything else to silence.
But still, once in a while, the river gives an unexpected gurgle.
"*Slp*," it says, out of glassy-ridged brown knots sliding along the surface.
Clang.
And everything except the river holds its breath.
Now there is no scream. Once there was one and it settled slowly
down to earth one hot summer afternoon; or did it float up, into that
dark, too dark, blue sky? But surely it has gone away, forever.
Clang.
It sounds like a bell buoy out at sea.
It is the elements speaking: earth, air, fire, water.
All those other things—clothes, crumbling postcards, broken
china; things damaged and lost, sickened or destroyed; even the frail
almost-lost scream—are they too frail for us to hear their voices long, too
mortal?
Nate!
Oh, beautiful sound, strike again!

What sounds like a bell buoy out at sea? The scream? The blacksmith's anvil? The two finally merging? "In the Village" is the vital center
from which many of Bishop's poems radiate, the darker side of their serene
need to reclaim "the elements speaking: earth, air, fire, water." She
printed it among the poems of her 1965 volume, *Questions of Travel*, as if
to make that point.

For a moment "In the Village" offers a radiant primal world,
available to human energies. It is almost unique in Bishop's work for the
way it resolves tensions between the remembered, inaccessible, inhuman
call of the four elements and her affectionate grasp of the more precarious
details of human life. In the glow of memory she is for once licensed to
glide from the scream ("But surely it has gone away, forever") to the noise
of the anvil, the two distantly merged like the bell buoy at sea, the
elements speaking. For once, in the suffused light of childhood, she is
allowed to hear those perfectly inhuman elements as if they were the
voices of paradise, a fulfilled retreat from the intense inescapable world of
change and loss. For once, losing hold of details is not an engulfment or a
drowning, but a situation quietly accepted with a muted question:

All those other things—clothes, crumbling postcards, broken china;
things damaged and lost, sickened or destroyed; even the frail almost-lost
scream—are they too frail for us to hear their voices long, too mortal?

No wonder then that Bishop was drawn again and again to her Northern and tropical landscapes whose scale and temperature are so different from our own. Exile and travel are at the heart of her poems from the very start—and sometimes as if they could reconstitute the vision of "In the Village," as if they led somewhere, a true counter to loss. Bishop is spellbound by the polar world in an early poem, "The Imaginary Iceberg." "Self-made from elements least visible," the iceberg "saves itself perpetually and adorns/only itself." Of that tempting self-enclosed world, a frosty palace of art, she writes, "We'd rather have the iceberg than the ship,/although it meant the end of travel." This is, in an idiom fraught with danger, "a scene a sailor'd give his eyes for."

Again, in the wonderful "Over 2000 Illustrations and a Complete Concordance," a traveller is tantalized by the promise of vision beyond the random encounter. Childhood memories of etchings of the Holy Land in an old Bible make her yearn for something beyond the *and* and *and* of pointlessly accumulated travel. This is the end of the poem:

> Everything only connected by "and" and "and."
> Open the book. (The gilt rubs off the edges
> of the pages and pollinates the fingertips.)
> Open the heavy book. Why couldn't we have seen
> this old Nativity while we were at it?
> —the dark ajar, the rocks breaking with light,
> an undisturbed, unbreathing flame,
> colorless, sparkless, freely fed on straw,
> and, lulled within, a family with pets,
> —and looked and looked our infant sight away.

Like the "scene a sailor'd give his eyes for," that last phrase ("looked and looked our infant sight away") carries a mysterious yearning to stop observing, which it also guards against. Bishop never entirely gives in. She glimpses the terrifying folk truth behind the apparent satisfactions of a sight "we'd give our eyes for." And if we are to see the old Nativity in "Over 2000 Illustrations," if the memory of engravings in a beloved childhood book allows us once more to trust experience as sacramental, if such travel will reconstitute the blasted family of "In the Village" (the poem envisions rocks breaking with light "and lulled within, a family with pets"), then what will it mean to "look and look our infant sight away"? Where or when is *away*? Is it a measureless absorption in the scene? Or, on the contrary, a loss of powers, as in "to waste away"? Or a welcome relinquishment, to be gathered back into the world of childhood, to return to "infant" sight—it keeps its Latin root, "speechless."

Bishop, sensing dangers, only hints at satisfaction. "Over 2000

Illustrations and a Complete Concordance" is almost a farewell to such temptations. There are in her poems no final visions. She moves away from "We'd rather have the iceberg than the ship,/although it meant the end of travel" to the "Questions of Travel" entertained in her third book. There, in tones more relaxed than ever before, she learns to trust the saving, continuous, precise pursuits of the exile's eye.

IV

The volume *Questions of Travel* in effect constitutes a sequence of poems, its Brazilian landscapes not so much providing answers as initiating us into the mysteries of how questions are asked. It is important that the book also includes poems about her Nova Scotia childhood and the central story of that period, "In the Village." In the light of those memories, the Brazilian poems become a model of how, with difficulty and pleasure, pain and precision, we re-introduce ourselves into a world.

There are three important initiating poems: in order, "Arrival at Santos," "Brazil, January 1, 1502" and "Questions of Travel." The first is deliberately superficial, comic, sociable. We watch her straining from tourist into traveller, after the disappointments of Santos, which like all ports is like soap or postage stamps—necessary but, "wasting away like the former, slipping the way the latter/do when we mail the letters we wrote on the boat." The familiar and merely instrumental melt away and we know something more than geographical is meant by the last line: "We are driving to the interior."

We go there by means of one of Bishop's characteristic changes of scale. "Arrival at Santos"—it's not Bishop's usual practice—had been dated at the end, *January, 1952.* The next poem is "Brazil, January 1, 1502," and its first word is the generalizing *Januaries.* No longer in the "here" and "now" of the uninstructed tourist, the poem fans out into the repeating present of the botanist and the anthropologist. Our drive to the interior is through the looking glass of natural history. There is a comforting epigraph from Lord Clark's *Landscape into Art,* "embroidered nature . . . tapestried landscape," that seems to familiarize the scene, appropriate it for European sensibilities. Yet this is a wild burgeoning tapestry, not "filled in" with foliage but "every square inch *filling in* with foliage," tirelessly self-renewing. Its distinctions of shade and color force her into relentless unflagging specificity: "big leaves, little leaves, and giant leaves,/blue, blue-green, and olive." A parade of shades: silver-gray, rust red, greenish white, blue-white. The powers of description are deliberately and delightfully taxed; it's hard for mere humans to keep up.

Then, with a bow to our desire for a familiar tapestry, Bishop draws our attention to something in the foreground. It is first identified as "Sin:/five sooty dragons near some massy rocks." The rocks are "worked with lichens" and "threatened from underneath by moss/in lovely hell-green flames." Then, in a deliberate change of scale, the little morality play turns to something wilder, more riveting, making fun of our tame exaggerations. Those dragons are, in fact, lizards in heat.

> The lizards scarcely breathe; all eyes
> are on the smaller, female one, back-to,
> her wicked tail straight up and over,
> red as red-hot wire.

Then the most daring change of all:

> Just so the Christians, hard as nails,
> tiny as nails, and glinting,
> in creaking armor, came and found it all,
> not unfamiliar.

For a moment, until we unravel the syntax, "just so" identifies the invaders with the lizards in heat. Tiny in scale, dwarfed by the scene, the settlers, after Mass, are out hunting Indian women:

> they ripped away into the hanging fabric,
> each out to catch an Indian for himself—
> those maddening little women who kept calling,
> calling to each other (or had the birds waked up?)
> and retreating, always retreating behind it.

The tapestry—initially it seemed like a device to domesticate the landscape—instead excludes invaders from it. At the beginning we were identified with those settlers of 1502: "Nature greets our eyes/exactly as she must have greeted theirs." At the end that proves to be a dubious privilege. Nature's tapestry endures, renews itself. After our initial glimpse of order, we shrink like Alice or Gulliver—toy intruders, marvelling.

Bishop's book, then, imagines first the mere tourist, then the invader, and finally, in the title poem, faces what is actually available to the traveller. "Questions of Travel" anticipates a new submissive understanding, taking what comes on its own terms, as she does with the magical powers of "The Riverman" or the mysterious quirks of the humble squatter-tenant, "Manuelzinho." The key to this new openness and affection is in the movement of the title poem. It proceeds through a cautious syntax of questions, with tentative answers in negative clauses. The glutted, excluded observer of the two opening poems ("There are too many waterfalls here") hallucinates mountains into capsized hulls, her own sense that travel might turn into shipwreck. Her first questions are asked with a guilty air: "Should we have stayed at home and thought of here? . . . Is it right to be watching strangers in a play . . . ?"

> What childishness is it that while there's a breath of life
> in our bodies, we are determined to rush
> to see the sun the other way around?
> The tiniest green hummingbird in the world?
> To stare at some inexplicable old stonework,
> inexplicable and impenetrable,
> at any view,
> instantly seen and always, always delightful?

You can hear Bishop's spirits rise to the bait of detail, the word "childishness" losing its air of self-accusation and turning before our eyes into something receptive, *childlike*, open to wonder. This is finally a less ambiguous approach than that of the traveller yearning to "look and look our infant sight away." "Questions of Travel" does not expect, as "Over 2000 Illustrations" did, that vision will add up, restore our ancient home. The yearning remains ("Oh, must we dream our dreams/and have them, too?"). But the observer is drawn very cautiously by accumulating detail, and questions themselves begin to satisfy the imagining mind. The following passage, all questions, proceeds by the method Bishop admired in Darwin ("a self-forgetful, perfectly useless concentration"):

> But surely it would have been a pity
> not to have seen the trees along this road,
> really exaggerated in their beauty,
> not to have seen them gesturing
> like noble pantomimists, robed in pink.
> —Not to have had to stop for gas and heard
> the sad, two-noted, wooden tune
> of disparate wooden clogs
> carelessly clacking over
> a grease-stained filling-station floor.
> (In another country the clogs would all be tested.
> Each pair there would have identical pitch.)
> —A pity not to have heard
> the other, less primitive music of the fat brown bird
> who sings above the broken gasoline pump
> in a bamboo church of Jesuit baroque:
> three towers, five silver crosses.
> —Yes, a pity not to have pondered,
> blurr'dly and inconclusively,
> on what connection can exist for centuries
> between the crudest wooden footwear

and, careful and finicky,
the whittled fantasies of wooden cages.
—Never to have studied history in
the weak calligraphy of songbirds' cages.

Bishop has the structuralist's curiosity. She probably enjoys Levi-Strauss, who also studies "history in /the weak calligraphy of songbirds' cages" in the Brazil of *Tristes Tropiques*. Bishop rests in doubts, proceeds by a tantalizing chain of negative questions (surely it would have been a pity. . .not to have seen. . .not to have heard. . .not to have pondered. . .etc.). The closing lines revisit the world of "Over 2000 Illustrations and a Complete Concordance" but with more abandon, more trust to the apparent randomness of travel and the state of homelessness:

> *"Is it lack of imagination that makes us come*
> *to imagined places, not just stay at home?*
> *Or could Pascal have been not entirely right*
> *about just sitting quietly in one's room?*
>
> *Continent, city, country, society:*
> *the choice is never wide and never free.*
> *And here, or there . . . No. Should we have stayed at home,*
> *wherever that may be?"*

I said earlier that details are also boundaries for Elizabeth Bishop, that whatever radiant glimpses they afford, they are also set at the vibrant limits of her descriptive powers. "In the Village" and "Questions of Travel" show us what generates this precarious state. "From this the poem springs," Wallace Stevens remarks. "That we live in a place/That is not our own and, much more, not ourselves/And hard it is in spite of blazoned days." Bishop writes under that star, aware of the smallness and dignity of human observation and contrivance. She sees with such a rooted, piercing vision, so realistically, because she has never taken our presence in the world as totally real.

V

"How had I come to be here?" Bishop asks in a recent poem, "In the Waiting Room." Even more than "In the Village," "In the Waiting Room" invites us to understand Bishop's efforts in an autobiographical light. Revisiting childhood experience, less open to ecstasy than the earlier short story, "In the Waiting Room" recalls the sense of personal loss so often implied behind Bishop's observations. The poem is a melancholy

visitation to a childhood world Bishop has earlier ("In the Village")
described more joyfully. This time she is accompanying her aunt to the
dentist's office.

> . . .while I waited I read
> the National Geographic
> (I could read) and carefully
> studied the photographs:
> the inside of a volcano,
> black, and full of ashes;
> then it was spilling over
> in rivulets of fire.
> Osa and Martin Johnson
> dressed in riding breeches,
> laced boots, and pith helmets.
> A dead man slung on a pole
> —"Long Pig," the caption said.
> Babies with pointed heads.
> wound round and round with string;
> black, naked women with necks
> wound round and round with wire
> like the necks of light bulbs.
> Their breasts were horrifying.

The scream of "In the Village" is heard once again in a return to
youthful memories of women in pain. But the scream, this time, is not
banished.

> Suddenly, from inside,
> came an oh! of pain
> —Aunt Consuelo's voice—
> not very loud or long.
> I wasn't at all surprised;
> even then I knew she was
> a foolish, timid woman.
> I might have been embarrassed,
> but wasn't. What took me
> completely by surprise
> was that it was me:
> my voice, in my mouth.
> Without thinking at all
> I was my foolish aunt,
> I—we—were falling, falling,
> our eyes glued to the cover
> of the National Geographic,
> February, 1918.

The memory is astonishing, especially in the telling: the way in which "inside" allows us the little girl's own moment of confusion, as the cry seems to be her own. The child, entirely a spectator to others' pain "In the Village," finds unexpectedly that she is prey to it herself at the moment which sentences her to adulthood "In the Waiting Room."

Observation, the spectator's clear and lonely power, is a kind of life-jacket here. The poem is detailed and circumstantial: the child clings to details so as to keep from "sliding/beneath a big black wave,/another, and another."

> But I felt: you are an *I*
> you are an *Elizabeth*,
> you are one of *them*.
> Why should you be one, too?

The "I" that enters this poem, bearing her very name (the first time Bishop uses it in a poem) has the same staying power, no more, no less than the furniture of the waiting room, the arctics, the overcoats, the shadowy gray knees of the adults in the waiting room—all the sad imprisoning litany of human identity, like the numbers she takes pains to mention: three days until she is seven years old; the fifth of February, 1918. These read like incantations to "stop/the sensation of falling off/the round, turning world/into cold, blue-black space." The very plainness of the poem is what saves her; she is a realist *faute de mieux*, she observes because she has to.

"In the Waiting Room," like other poems Bishop has published since her *Complete Poems* appeared in 1969, rounds a remarkable corner in her career. My impression is that these pieces, collected in *Geography III* (1976), revisit her earlier poems as Bishop herself once visited tropical and polar zones, and that they refigure her work in wonderful ways. "Poem" looks to a small landscape by what must be the same great-uncle, an R.A., who painted the "Large Bad Picture" in her first book, *North & South*. "In the Waiting Room" revisits an awakening to adulthood as seen by a child, the world of "In the Village." "The Moose" recalls the pristine wonder of her Nova Scotia poems, and "Crusoe in England" looks back at a Southern hemisphere even more exotic than her tropical Brazil. In these and other poems, returning to earlier scenes, Bishop has asked more openly what energies fed, pressured, endangered and rewarded her chosen life of travel and clear vision.

Her "questions of travel" modulate now, almost imperceptibly, into questions of memory and loss. Attentive still to landscapes where one can feel the sweep and violence of encircling and eroding geological powers, poems such as "Crusoe in England" and "The Moose" pose their problems retrospectively. Crusoe lives an exile's life in civilized England, lord in imagination only of his "un-rediscovered, un-renamable island." In "The Moose" we are city-bound, on a bus trip away from Nova Scotia, and the long lean poem reads like a thread the narrator is laying through a maze—to find her way back?

"Crusoe in England" re-creates the pleasures and the pains of surviving in a universe of one. News that a new volcano has erupted trips Crusoe's memories of his own island. His way of thinking about it is that an island has been *born*:

> at first a breath of steam, ten miles away;
> and then a black fleck—basalt, probably—
> rose in the mate's binoculars
> and caught on the horizon like a fly.
> They named it. But my poor old island's still
> un-rediscovered, un-renamable.
> None of the books has ever got it right.

The shock of birth, the secret joy of naming, of knowing a place "un-renamable"—these emotions shadow the surface, as they do for the child of "In the Waiting Room." Crusoe's whole poem is pervaded by the play of curiosity. He asks questions, concentrates and then, as Bishop says elsewhere of Darwin, one sees him, "his eye fixed on facts and minute details, sinking or sliding giddily off into the unknown." The drifts of snail shells on Crusoe's island look from a distance like beds of irises. The next thing we know, they *are* iris beds:

> The books
> I'd read were full of blanks;
> the poems—well, I tried
> reciting to my iris-beds,
> "They flash upon that inward eye,
> which is the bliss. . . ." The bliss of what?
> One of the first things that I did
> when I got back was look it up.

No point in finishing Wordsworth's quote: *imagination* would fill the blank better than *solitude* in this case, but neither is necessary in the presence of Crusoe's joy in the homemade and under the pressure of having to re-invent the world: "the parasol that took me such a time/remembering the way the ribs should go"; the baby goat dyed red with the island's one kind of berry "just to see/something a little different"; a flute, "Home-made, home-made! But aren't we all?" The poem is crowded with fresh experience: hissing turtles, small volcanoes. Crusoe has his longings—one fulfilled when Friday appears. He also has his nightmares. When he is on the island, he dreams about being trapped on infinite numbers of islands, each of which he must in painful detail explore. Back in England the nightmare is just the opposite: that such stimulation, imaginative curiosity and energy will peter out. His old knife ("it reeked of meaning, like a crucifix") seems to have lost its numinous power. The whole poem poses a question about imagination when it is no longer felt to be intimately related to survival. Bishop seems involved with the figure of Crusoe because of the questions *after* travel, a kind of "Dejection Ode" countered by the force and energy that memory has mustered for the rest of the poem. It acts out ways of overcoming and then re-experiencing loss.

Elizabeth Bishop has always written poetry to locate herself—most obviously when she is challenged by the exotic landscapes of North and South. She now performs her acts of location in new ways—sometimes showing the pains and joys of domestication, in poems like "Five Flights Up" and "12 O'Clock News" (the imaginative transformation of the writer's desk into a war-torn landscape). More important is the relocation in time, no longer seeing herself and her characters in long geological—Northern or tropical—perspectives, but in a landscape scaled down to memory and the inner bounds of a human life. What she finds are the pleasures and the fears of something like Crusoe's experience: the live memories of naming, the sudden lapse of formerly numinous figures. Early morning "Five Flights Up," listening to an exuberant dog in a yard next door, to a bird making questioning noises, she feels alive enough to imagine

> gray light streaking each bare branch,
> each single twig, along one side,
> making another tree, of glassy veins. . .

apart enough to conclude

> —Yesterday brought to today so lightly!
> (A yesterday I find almost impossible to lift.)

In another sense the past has its sustaining surprises. "Poem" is about the feelings awakened by a small painting passed down in her family, a landscape apparently by the great-uncle responsible for the "Large Bad Picture" which Bishop approached with diffidence and only submerged affection in North & South. In the new poem, the painter's work is welcomed as it brings alive, slowly, a scene from her childhood.

I never knew him. We both knew this place,
apparently, this literal small backwater,
looked at it long enough to memorize it,
our years apart. How strange. And it's still loved,
or its memory is (it must have changed a lot).
Our visions coincided—"visions" is
too serious a word—our looks, two looks:
art "copying from life" and life itself,
life and the memory of it so compressed
they've turned into each other. Which is which?
Life and the memory of it cramped,
dim, on a piece of Bristol board,
dim, but how live, how touching in detail
—the little that we get for free,
the little of our earthly trust. Not much.
About the size of our abidance
along with theirs: the munching cows,
the iris, crisp and shivering, the water
still standing from spring freshets,
the yet-to-be-dismantled elms, the geese.

I hear in these guarded, modest, still radiant lines a new note in Bishop's work: a shared pleasure in imaginative intensity, almost as if this remarkable writer were being surprised (you *hear* the surprise in her voice) at the power over loss and change which memory has given her writing. What else is it that we hear in "The Moose," as the bus gets going though a lovingly remembered trip from salt Nova Scotia and New Brunswick, world of her childhood, toward Boston where she now lives? The fog closes in, "its cold, round crystals/form and slide and settle/ in the white hens' feathers." They seem to enter an enchanted forest, and she is lulled to sleep by voices from the back of the bus, "talking the way they talked/in the old featherbed,/peacefully, on and on." A long chain of human speech reassures her: " 'Yes. . .' that peculiar/affirmative. 'Yes . . .'/A sharp indrawn breath,/half groan, half acceptance." It is almost as if this discourse and its kinship to her own powers, the storyteller's powers handed down, summon up the strange vision which stops the bus: a moose "towering, antlerless. . .grand, otherworldly"—primitive, but giving everyone a "sweet/sensation of joy." It is "homely as a house/(or, safe as houses)" like the very houses the quieting talk on the bus recalls. The moose seems both to crystallize the silence, security and awe of the world being left behind and to guarantee a nourishing and haunting place for it in memory.

In "The End of March" Bishop follows a looped cord along a deserted beach to a snarl of string the size of a man, rising and falling on the waves, "sodden, giving up the ghost. . . ./A kite string?—But no kite." It might be an emblem for these recent poems which touch on lost or slender connections. Bishop seems more explicit about that than she used to be. Where loss was previously the unnamed object against which the poems ventured forth, it is now one of the named subjects. Her poems say out very naturally: "the little that we get for free,/the little of our earthly trust. Not much." Memory is her way of bringing to the surface and acknowledging as general the experience of losing which has always lain behind her work and which the work attempts to counter. "One Art" is the title Bishop gives to a late villanelle which encourages these very connections.

> The art of losing isn't hard to master;
> so many things seem filled with the intent
> to be lost that their loss is no disaster.
>
> Lose something every day. Accept the fluster
> of lost door keys, the hour badly spent.
> The art of losing isn't hard to master.

The effort to control strong feeling is everywhere in this poem. What falls away—love, homes, dreams—is hopelessly intertwined with the repeating rhymes which challenge each other at every turn: *master, disaster*.

> I lost my mother's watch. And look! my last, or
> next-to-last, of three loved houses went.
> The art of losing isn't hard to master.
>
> I lost two cities, lovely ones. And, vaster,
> some realms I owned, two rivers, a continent.
>
> I miss them, but it wasn't a disaster.
> —Even losing you (the joking voice, a gesture
> I love) I shan't have lied. It's evident
> the art of losing's not too hard to master
> though it may look like (*Write* it!) like disaster.

The last stubborn heartbreaking hesitation—"though it may look like (*Write* it!) like disaster"—carries the full burden, and finally confidence, of her work, the resolve which just barely masters emptiness and succeeds in filling out, tight-lipped, the form.

If Bishop's writing since *Complete Poems* still displays her tough idiosyncratic powers of observation, it also makes a place for those observations in very natural surroundings of the mind. The title *Geography III* (and its epigraph from "First Lessons in Geography") is at once a bow to her real-life relocation and a deep acknowledgment of the roots of these poems in childhood memory and loss. The time and the space these poems lay claim to are more peculiarly Elizabeth Bishop's own—less geological, less historical, less vastly natural; her poems are more openly inner landscapes than ever before.

JOHN HOLLANDER

Elizabeth Bishop's Mappings of Life

G eography III is a magnificent book
of ten poems whose power and beauty would make it seem gross to ask for
more of them. Its epigraph is a catechistic geography lesson quoted from a
nineteenth-century textbook, claimed for parable in that seamless way of
allowing picture to run into image that the poet has made her own, in this
instance, by her own added italicized questions about mapped bodies—of
land, of water—and about direction, following the epigraph in its own
language but now become fully figurative. The opening poem of Miss
Bishop's first volume, *North & South*, is called "The Map"; in all the work
that has followed it, the poet has been concerned with mappings of the
possible world. More generally, she had pursued the ways in which
pictures, models, representations of all sorts, begin to take on lives of their
own under the generative force of that analogue of loves between persons
which moves between nature and consciousness. We might, somewhat
lamely, call it passionate attention. Its caresses, extended by awareness
that pulses with imagination, are not only those of the eye and ear at
moments of privileged experience, but rather at the times of composition,
of representing anew. The map-makers' colors, "more delicate than the
historians'," are as much part of a larger, general Nature as are the raw
particulars of unrepresented sea and sky, tree and hill, street and store-
front, roof and watertank. Much of the praise given Miss Bishop's work
had directed itself to her command of observation, the focus of her vision,
the unmannered quality of her rhetoric—almost as if she were a novelist,

From *Parnassus* (Fall 1977). Copyright © 1977 by Poetry in Review Foundation.

and almost as if love of life could only be manifested in the accuracy and interestingness of one's accounts of the shapes which human activity casts on nature.

But the passionate attention does not reveal itself in reportage. Love remains one of its principal tropes, just as the reading, interpreting and reconstituting of nature in one's poems remains a model of what love may be and do. The representations—the charts, pictures, structures, dreams and fables of memory—that one makes are themselves the Geographies which, in our later sense of the word, they map and annotate. The radical invention of a figurative geography in *North & South*, the mapping of personal history implicit there, are perhaps Miss Bishop's *Geography I*; after the Nova Scotian scenes and urban landscapes to the south of them in *A Cold Spring*, lit and shaded by love and loss, the grouped Brazilian poems and memories, rediscoveries even, of childhood yet further to the north, asked questions of travel. A literal geographic distinction, a north and south of then and now, gained new mythopoetic force; all that intensely and chastely observed material could only have become more than very, very good writing when it got poetically compounded with the figurative geography books of her earlier poems. *Questions of Travel* is thus, perhaps, her *Geography II*.

This new book is a third, by title, by design and, by its mode of recapitulation, a review of the previous two courses as well as an advanced text. Like all major poetry, it both demands prerequisites and invites the new student, and each of these to far greater degrees than most of the casual verse we still call poetry can ever do. The important poems here seem to me to derive their immense power both from the energies of the poet's creative present and from the richness and steadfastness of her created past ("A yesterday I find almost impossible to lift," she allows in the last line of the last poem in the book). Yes, if yesterdays are to be carried as burdens, one would agree; but even yesteryears can themselves, if one is imaginatively fortunate, become monuments to be climbed, to be looked about and even ahead from, to be questioned and pondered themselves.

And so here with the monuments of the earlier Bishop poetry: the reader keeps seeing them in these later poems—in the background or in pictures hung as it were on their walls. Rhetorically, a villanelle echoes the formal concerns of the earlier sestinas and, at a smaller level, the characteristic use of repeated terminal words in adjacent lines, whether in a rhymed or unrhymed poem, continues to be almost synecdochic, in these poems, of the imperceptible slip from letter into spirit of meaning. The magnificent earlier "The Monument," echoed in this volume in part of "The End of March" (of which more later) resounds even through Miss Bishop's wonderful translation of an Octavio Paz homage to Joseph Cornell—a string of boxed tercets. "12 O'Clock News" recapitulates a whole cycle of emblematic poems in her previous work, this strange prose poem being a kind of Lilliputian itinerary of the poet's own desk, a microcosmography of the world of work. The piece called briefly—but hardly simply—"Poem" is something of a meditation upon the earlier poem "Large Bad Picture" as well as, manifestly, upon the small good one which presents a view, a spot of time, in Nova Scotia, a moment in the past which is recollected from its fragments in the attempt to puzzle out an ambiguous sign, a representation of a *something* that may or may not be part of one's own life. (. . . *Well, of somebody's*, we are tempted to go on in one of Miss Bishop's characteristic tones—there is no lack of human significance in the pictures of life in the world about which she broods, and the problem with them is rather one of mapping the directions in which they urge the viewer to turn.) The scene in this little painting has assembled itself out of contemplation, rather than commerce; the artist turns out to have been a great-uncle "quite famous, an R.A." The poet goes on:

> I never knew him. We both knew this place,
> apparently, this literal small backwater,
> looked at it long enough to memorize it,
> our years apart. How strange. And it's still loved,
> or its memory is (it must have changed a lot).
> Our visions coincided—"visions" is
> too serious a word—our looks, two looks:
> art "copying from life" and life itself,
> life and the memory of it so compressed
> they've turned into each other. Which is which?

But "vision" is, of course, not too serious a word (as, I suppose, "serious" is too unvisionary a one). A major rhetorical device in American poetry of the past century and more has been a mode of evasion of the consequences of visionary seriousness; it can take the form of a pretending, for example, whether in Hawthorne or Frost, that anecdote is merely that and not myth showing a momentary face, a defense of whimsy or skepticism. Stevens' way was to pretend to a theory of just that sort of pretending, to discuss the ground-rules by which experiences and names for them play with each other. Elizabeth Bishop is not obviously Stevensian, even when she makes figures of figures (as in that wrenching early epigram, "Casabianca"); and in her celebrated and profoundly original diction there are few echoes of the whole of harmonium (save perhaps for the trace of

"Disillusionment of Ten O'Clock" in her "Anaphora" from *North &
South*, where day "sinks through the drift of classes/to evening, to the
beggar in the park/who, weary, without lamp or book/prepares stupendous
studies"). Her personal mode of rhetorical questioning, of demands for
truth directed toward the mute objects she has herself invented, is certainly an analogue of Stevensian turnings in the wind of the leaves of
imagery itself. These questionings ("Are they assigned, or can the countries pick their colors?") occur in her earliest poems, and continue to
quicken all her fictions, giving the breath of life—as do Stevens'
"qualifications"—to her molded figures and scenes. Miss Bishop's characteristic mythopoetic mode is one in which description, casually and
apparently only heuristically figurative, bends around into the parabolic.
What happens in the latter part of "At the Fishhouses" is possibly the *locus
classicus* of this movement in her work: the almost painted scene offers up
its wisdom not with the abrupt label of a moralization, but gradually, as
images of place begin to be understood—almost to understand themselves—as
images of the condition of consciousness itself.

It is that poem which seems to lie in the background of the
powerful "The Moose" in the new book. Although its anecdotal frame
might suggest "The Fish" as a prototype, the nonviolent encounter with
the animal presence here is very different and far more profound: a bus
ride southward from maritime provinces of the past is halted at the end of
the poem as a she-moose emerges "out of/the impenetrable wood/and
stands there, looms, rather,/in the middle of the road." Underscored by a
deceptively disarming cadence of lightly-rhymed stanzas of six trimeter
lines, the account of the bus-ride becomes parabolic with its ability to
contain the past rather than merely to observe traces of it through the
windows; a sort of Sarah Orne Jewett dialogue between two ancestral
voices emerges from the back seats of the bus and the poet's mind as they
move toward Boston, and the great creature appearing out of the woods,
at a kind of border between the possibility of one sort of life and that of
another, comes into the poem as a great living trope of the structures
which get wrecked in crossing such borders—"high as a church,/homely as
a house/(or, safe as houses)." The appearance of the creature is a phenomenon at once unique and paradigmatic, an "embodiment" in momentary
dramaturgy of something in nature analogous (the antlerless form?) which
came of the poet's crying out to life for "original response" ("As a great
buck it powerfully appeared"). The moose's powerful appearance is too
important a manifestation, as always in Bishop's poetic world, to occasion
the squandering of poetic diction. Even the gently ironic homeliness of
the chorus of other travellers (" 'Sure as big creatures.'/'It's awful

plain.'/'Look! It's a she!' ") echoes point by point the narrator's admittedly guarded mythologizing ("high," "homely," "safe"), and with the effect of domesticating even more the awe and the pressure of significance. We are tempted to think of her language at the most sublime moments of her travel talks as "cold" or "casual," but it is neither of these. Her great originality has always washed other kinds of voice away, and notwithstanding her "Invitation to Miss Marianne Moore," in A Cold Spring, to descend as a tutelary muse upon her, Miss Elizabeth Bishop's work seems as self-begotten as any in our time. What seems cold in her language is warmed by the breath of its own life.

Of the two major masterpieces in Geography III, the astonishing longish poem called "Crusoe in England" engages some of the larger meditative consequences of this self-sufficiency. It is a great dramatic monologue of the famous Solitary returned to a world of memory and discourse, the larger isle of England, "another island,/that doesn't seem like one, but who decides?" It is as if the narrator had come from an island of myth (the fable of what one was? what one made, and made of one's life?) to our overhearing and growing suspicion that he had been as responsible for the lay of the land upon which he had been cast up as for his own survival in it. As usual, a tone of detached gazetteering (again, suggesting the distanced detailings of "The Monument" and, even more, the narrative cadences of "The Riverman") colors a stanza of frighteningly powerful vision:

> The sun set in the sea; the same odd sun
> rose from the sea,
> and there was one of it and one of me.
> The island had one kind of everything:
> one tree snail, a bright violet-blue
> with a thin shell, crept over everything,
> over the one variety of tree,
> a sooty, scrub affair.
> Snail shells lay under these in drifts
> and, at a distance,
> you'd swear that they were beds of irises.
> There was one kind of berry, a dark red.
> I tried it, one by one, and hours apart.
> Sub-acid, and not bad, no ill effects;
> and so I made home-brew. I'd drink
> the awful, fizzy, stinging stuff
> that went straight to my head
> and play my home-made flute
> (I think it had the weirdest scale on earth)
> and, dizzy, whoop and dance among the goats.

> Home-made, home-made! But aren't we all?
> I felt a deep affection for
> the smallest of my island industries.
> No, not exactly, since the smallest was
> a miserable philosophy.

The very island is an exemplar, a representation; it is a place which stands for the life lived on it as much as it supports that life. Its unique species are emblems of the selfhood that the whole region distills and enforces, and on it, life and work and art are one, and the home-made Dionysus *is* (rather than blesses from without or within) his votary. "Solitude" itself is a forgotten word in this place of isolation. Terrors of madness assaulted, even as they necessitated, the retreat into poetry of the Crusoes and Castaways of William Cowper, solitaries to whom the very tameness of the animals was frightening as a mark of wildness that had never known the human, nor ever learned to fear and be fearsome, solitaries who would "start at the sound" of their own voices. But for Bishop's Crusoe, madness is not the problem, particularly the eighteenth-century madness kept at bay by faith. The one mount of speculation on his island is named "*Mont d'Espoir* or *Mount Despair*" indifferently (for Defoe's Crusoe, "Despair" only), and he is rescued from one insulation to another in a different, colder sea enisled, "surrounded by uninteresting lumber."

But one cannot begin to do this splendid piece justice in a brief essay: it is the centerpiece of the book's geographies, and a poem of the first importance. So, too, is "The End of March," a beach-poem in which, again, "vision" is not too serious a word, a strange, late domestication of the poet's earlier Nova Scotia sea-scapes. But this time it is not a meditation on a scene so much as a movement against a scene, a classic journey out and back, toward a treasured image of imagined fulfillment, along a stretch of beach that yields up none of the comforts of place ("Everything was withdrawn as far as possible,/indrawn: the tide far out, the ocean shrunken"), past objects from which meaning itself has withdrawn. The goal is never reached, and the walk back presents glimpses of an almost infernal particularity:

> On the way back our faces froze on the other side.
> The sun came out for just a minute.
> For just a minute, set in their bezels of sand,
> the drab, damp, scattered stones
> were multi-colored,
> and all those high enough threw out long shadows,
> individual shadows, then pulled them in again.
> They could have been teasing the lion sun,
> except that now he was behind them . . .

This moment is itself, in its replacement of a wrecked hope, a splendid monument to a poetry that has always remained measured, powerful in imagination and utterly clear—radiantly and distinctly—in its language. If it seems to manifest rhetorical or eschatological withdrawals, these are never movements away from truth, or even from the struggle for it. Miss Bishop's poems draw themselves in when they do, like wise and politic snails, from the rhetorics of self-expression, the figures of jealousy and pity, the boring industry of innovation. Withdrawn or not, so many of her poems have moved themselves into the few unoccupied corners of perfection that seem to remain, that we can only end as readers where philosophy is said to begin, in wonder.

HELEN VENDLER

Domestication, Domesticity
and the Otherworldly

Elizabeth Bishop's poems in *Geography III* put into relief the continuing vibration of her work between two frequencies—the domestic and the strange. In another poet the alternation might seem a debate, but Bishop drifts rather than divides, gazes rather than chooses. Though the exotic is frequent in her poems of travel, it is not only the exotic that is strange and not only the local that is domestic. (It is more exact to speak, with regard to Bishop, of the domestic rather than the familiar, because what is familiar is always named, in her poetry, in terms of a house, a family, someone beloved, home. And it is truer to speak of the strange rather than of the exotic, because the strange can occur even in the bosom of the familiar, even, most unnervingly, at the domestic hearth.)

To show the interpenetration of the domestic and the strange at their most inseparable, it is necessary to glance back at some poems printed in *Questions of Travel*. In one, "Sestina," the components are almost entirely innocent—a house, a grandmother, a child, a Little Marvel Stove, and an almanac. The strange component, which finally renders the whole house unnatural, is tears. Although the grandmother hides her tears and says only "It's time for tea now," the child senses the tears unshed and displaces them everywhere—into the dancing waterdrops from the teakettle, into the rain on the roof, into the tea in the grandmother's cup.

> . . . the child
> is watching the teakettle's small hard tears

From *Part of Nature, Part of Us: Modern American Poets*. Copyright © 1980 by The President and Fellows of Harvard College. Harvard University Press, 1980.

> dance like mad on the hot black stove
> the way the rain must dance on the house . . .
> . . . the almanac
> hovers half open above the child,
> hovers above the old grandmother
> and her teacup full of dark brown tears.

The child's sense of the world is expressed only in the rigid house she draws (I say "she," but the child, in the folk-order of the poem, is of indeterminate sex). The child must translate the tears she has felt, and so she "puts. . .a man with buttons like tears" into her drawing, while "the little moons fall down like tears/from between the pages of the almanac/into the flower bed the child/has carefully placed in the front of the house."

The tercet ending the sestina draws together all the elements of the collage:

> *Time to plant tears*, says the almanac.
> The grandmother sings to the marvellous stove
> and the child draws another inscrutable house.

The absence of the child's parents is the unspoken cause of those tears, so unconcealable though so concealed. For all the efforts of the grand-mother, for all the silence of the child, for all the brave cheer of the Little Marvel Stove, the house remains frozen, and the blank center stands for the definitive presence of the unnatural in the child's domestic experience— *especially* in the child's domestic experience. Of all the things that should not be inscrutable, one's house comes first. The fact that one's house always *is* inscrutable, that nothing is more enigmatic than the heart of the domestic scene, offers Bishop one of her recurrent subjects.

The centrality of the domestic provokes as well one of Bishop's most characteristic forms of expression. When she is not actually representing herself as a child, she is, often, sounding like one. The sestina, which borrows from the eternally childlike diction of the folktale, is a case in point. Not only the diction of the folktale, but also its fixity of relation appears in the poem, especially in its processional close, which places the almanac, the grandmother, and the child in an arrangement as unmoving as those found in medieval painting, with the almanac representing the overarching Divine Necessity, the grandmother as the elder principle, and the child as the principle of youth. The voice speaking the last three lines dispassionately records the coincident presence of grief, song, necessity, and the marvelous; but in spite of the "equal" placing of the last three lines, the ultimate weight on inscrutability, even in the heart of the domestic, draws this poem into the orbit of the strange.

A poem close by in *Questions of Travel* tips the balance in the other direction, toward the domestic. The filling station which gives its name to the poem seems at first the antithesis of beauty, at least in the eye of the beholder who speaks the poem. The station is dirty, oil-soaked, oil-permeated; the father's suit is dirty; his sons are greasy; all is "quite thoroughly dirty"; there is even "a dirty dog." The speaker, though filled with "a horror so refined," is unable to look away from the proliferating detail which, though this is a filling station, becomes ever more relentlessly domestic. "Do they live in the station?" wonders the speaker, and notes incredulously a porch, "a set of crushed and grease-/impregnated wickerwork," the dog "quite comfy" on the wicker sofa, comics, a taboret covered by a doily, and "a big hirsute begonia." The domestic, we perceive, becomes a compulsion that we take with us even to the most unpromising locations, where we busy ourselves establishing domestic tranquillity as a demonstration of meaningfulness, as a proof of "love." Is our theology only a reflection of our nesting habits?

> Why the extraneous plant?
> Why the taboret?
> Why, oh why, the doily? . . .
>
> Somebody embroidered the doily.
> Somebody waters the plant,
> or oils it, maybe. Somebody
> arranges the rows of cans
> so that they softly say:
> ESSO-SO-SO-SO
> to high-strung automobiles.
> Somebody loves us all.

In this parody of metaphysical questioning and the theological argument from design, the "awful but cheerful" activities of the world include the acts by which man domesticates his surroundings, even if those surroundings are purely mechanical, like the filling station or the truck in Brazil painted with "throbbing rosebuds."

The existence of the domestic is most imperiled by death. By definition, the domestic is the conjoined intimate: in American literature the quintessential poem of domesticity is "Snowbound." When death intrudes on the domestic circle, the laying-out of the corpse at home, in the old fashion, forces domesticity to its ultimate powers of accommodation. Stevens' "Emperor of Ice-Cream" places the cold and dumb corpse at the home wake in grotesque conjunction with the funeral baked meats, so to speak, which are being confected in the kitchen, as the primitive impulse to feast over the dead is seen surviving, instinctive and barbaric, even in our "civilized" society. Bishop's "First Death in Nova Scotia" places the poet as a child in a familiar parlor transfixed in perception by the presence of a coffin containing "little cousin Arthur":

> In the cold, cold parlor
> my mother laid out Arthur
> beneath the chromographs:
> Edward, Prince of Wales,
> with Princess Alexandra,
> and King George with Queen Mary.
> Below them on the table
> stood a stuffed loon
> shot and stuffed by Uncle
> Arthur, Arthur's father.

All of these details are immemorially known to the child. But focused by the coffin, the familiar becomes unreal: the stuffed loon becomes alive, his taciturnity seems voluntary, his red glass eyes can see.

> Since Uncle Arthur fired
> a bullet into him,
> he hadn't said a word.
> He kept his own counsel . . .
>
> Arthur's coffin was
> a little frosted cake,
> and the red-eyed loon eyed it
> from his white, frozen lake.

The adults conspire in a fantasy of communication still possible, as the child is told, "say good-bye/to your little cousin Arthur" and given a lily of the valley to put in the hand of the corpse. The child joins in the fantasy, first by imagining that the chill in the parlor makes it the domain of Jack Frost, who has painted Arthur's red hair as he paints the Maple Leaf of Canada, and next by imagining that "the gracious royal couples" in the chromographs have "invited Arthur to be/the smallest page at court." The constrained effort by all in the parlor to encompass Arthur's death in the domestic scene culminates in the child's effort to make a gestalt of parlor, coffin, corpse, chromographs, loon, Jack Frost, the Maple Leaf Forever, and the lily. But the strain is too great for the child, who allows doubt and dismay to creep in—not as to ultimate destiny, oh no, for Arthur is sure to become "the smallest page" at court, that confusing place of grander domesticity, half-palace, half-heaven; but rather displaced onto means.

> But how could Arthur go,
> clutching his tiny lily,
> with his eyes shut up so tight
> and the roads deep in snow?

Domesticity is frail, and it is shaken by the final strangeness of death. Until death, and even after it, the work of domestication of the unfamiliar goes on, all of it a substitute for some assurance of transcendent domesticity, some belief that we are truly, in this world, in our mother's house, that "somebody loves us all." After a loss that destroys one form of domesticity, the effort to reconstitute it in another form begins. The definition of death in certain of Bishop's poems is to have given up on domesticating the world and reestablishing yet once more some form of intimacy. Conversely, the definition of life in the conversion of the strange to the familial, of the unexplored to the knowable, of the alien to the beloved.

No domesticity is entirely safe. As in the midst of life we are in death, so, in Bishop's poetry, in the midst of the familiar, and most especially there, we feel the familiar as the unknowable. This guerrilla attack of the alien, springing from the very bulwarks of the familiar, is the subject of "In the Waiting Room." It is 1918, and a child, almost seven, waits, reading the *National Geographic*, while her aunt is being treated in the dentist's office. The scene is unremarkable: "grown-up people,/arctics and overcoats,/lamps and magazines," but two things unnerve the child. The first is a picture in the magazine: "black, naked women with necks/wound round and round with wire/like the necks of light bulbs./Their breasts were horrifying"; and the second is "an *oh!* of pain/—Aunt Consuelo's voice" from inside. The child is attacked by vertigo, feels the cry to be her own uttered in "the family voice" and knows at once her separateness and her identity as one of the human group.

> But I felt: you are an *I*,
> you are an *Elizabeth*,
> you are one of *them*.
> Why should you be one too?
>
> What similarities—
> boots, hands, the family voice
> I felt in my throat, or even
> the *National Geographic*
> and those awful hanging breasts—
> held us all together
> or made us all just one?

In "There Was a Child Went Forth" Whitman speaks of a comparable first moment of metaphysical doubt:

> . . .the sense of what is real, the thought if after all it should
> prove unreal,
> The doubts of day-time and the doubts of night-time, the curious
> whether and how,
> Whether that which appears so is so, or is it all flashes and specks?
> Men and women crowding fast in the streets, if they are not flashes
> and specks what are they?

It is typical of Whitman that after his momentary vertigo he should
tether himself to the natural world of sea and sky. It is equally typical of
Bishop, after the waiting room slides "beneath a big black wave,/another,
and another," to return to the sober certainty of waking fact, though with
a selection of fact dictated by feeling.

> The War was on. Outside,
> in Worcester, Massachusetts,
> were night and slush and cold,
> and it was still the fifth
> of February, 1918.

The child's compulsion to include in her world even the most unfamiliar
data, to couple the exotica of the *National Geographic* with the knees and
trousers and skirts of her neighbors in the waiting room, brings together
the strange at its most horrifying with the quintessence of the familiar—
oneself, one's aunt, the "family voice." In the end, will the savage be
domesticated or oneself rendered unknowable? The child cannot bear the
conjunction and faints. Language fails the six-year-old. "How—I didn't
know any/word for it—how 'unlikely.' "

That understatement, so common in Bishop, gives words their full
weight. As the fact of her own contingency strikes the child, "familiar"
and "strange" become concepts which have lost all meaning. "Mrs. An-
derson's Swedish baby," says Stevens, "might well have been German or
Spanish." Carlos Drummond de Andrade (whose rhythms perhaps suggested the trimeters of "In the Waiting Room") says in a poem translated
by Bishop:

> Mundo mundo vasto mundo,
> se eu me chamasse Raimundo
> seria uma rima, não seria uma solução.

If one's name rhymed with the name of the cosmos, as "Raimundo"
rhymes with "mundo," there would appear to be a congruence between

self and world, and domestication of the world to man's dimensions would seem possible. But, says Drummond, that would be a rhyme, not a solution. The child of "In the Waiting Room" discovers that she is in no intelligible relation to her world, and, too young yet to conceive of domination of the world by will or domestication of the world by love, she slides into an abyss of darkness.

In "Poem" ("About the size of an old-style dollar bill") the poet gazes idly at a small painting done by her great-uncle and begins yet another meditation on the domestication of the world. She gazes idly—that is, until she realizes that the painting is of a place she has lived in: "Heavens, I recognize the place, I know it!" In a beautiful tour de force "the place" is described three times. The first time it is rendered visually, exactly, interestedly, appreciatively, and so on: such, we realize, is pure visual pleasure touched with relatively impersonal recognition ("It must be Nova Scotia; only there/does one see gabled wooden houses/painted that awful shade of brown"). Here is the painting as first seen:

> Elm trees, low hills, a thin church steeple
> —that gray-blue wisp—or is it? In the foreground
> a water meadow with some tiny cows,
> two brushstrokes each, but confidently cows;
> two minuscule white geese in the blue water,
> back-to-back, feeding, and a slanting stick.
> Up closer, a wild iris, white and yellow,
> fresh-squiggled from the tube.
> The air is fresh and cold; cold early spring
> clear as gray glass; a half inch of blue sky
> below the steel-gray storm clouds.

Then the recognition—"Heavens, I know it!"—intervenes, and with it a double transfiguration occurs: the mind enlarges the picture beyond the limits of the frame, placing the painted scene in a larger, remembered landscape, and the items in the picture are given a local habitation and a name.

> Heavens, I recognize the place, I know it!
> It's behind—I can almost remember the farmer's name.
> His barn backed on that meadow. There it is,
> titanium white, one dab. The hint of steeple,
> filaments of brush-hairs, barely there,
> must be the Presbyterian church.
> Would that be Miss Gillespie's house?
> Those particular geese and cows
> are naturally before my time.

In spite of the connection between self and picture, the painting remains a painting, described by someone recognizing its means—a dab of titanium white here, some fine brushwork there. And the scene is set back in time—those geese and cows belong to another era. But by the end of the poem the poet has united herself with the artist. They have both loved this unimportant corner of the earth; it has existed in their lives, in their memories and in their art.

> art "copying from life" and life itself,
> life and the memory of it so compressed
> they're turned into each other. Which is which?
> Life and the memory of it cramped,
> dim, on a piece of Bristol board,
> dim, but how live, how touching in detail
> —the little that we get for free,
> the little of our earthly trust. Not much.

Out of the world a small piece is lived in, domesticated, remembered, memorialized, even immortalized. Immortalized because the third time that the painting is described, it is seen not by the eye—whether the eye of the connoisseur or the eye of the local inhabitant contemplating a past era—but by the heart, touched into participation. There is no longer any mention of tube or brushstrokes or paint colors or Bristol board; we are in the scene itself.

> . . . Not much.
> About the size of our abidance
> along with theirs: the munching cows,
> the iris, crisp and shivering, the water
> still standing from spring freshets,
> the yet-to-be-dismantled elms, the geese.

Though the effect of being in the landscape arises in part from the present participles (the munching cows, the shivering iris, the standing water), it comes as well from the repetition of nouns from earlier passages (cows, iris), now denuded of their "paint" modifiers ("two brushstrokes each," "squiggled from the tube"), from the replication of the twice-repeated early "fresh" in "freshets" and most of all from the prophecy of the "yet-to-be-dismantled" elms. As lightly as possible, the word "dismantled" then refutes the whole illusion of entire absorption in the memorial scene; the world of the child who was once the poet now seems the scenery arranged for a drama with only too brief a tenure on the stage— the play once over, the set is dismantled, the illusion gone. The poem, having taken the reader through the process that we name domestication and by which a strange terrain becomes first recognizable, then familiar, and then beloved, releases the reader at last from the intimacy it has induced. Domestication is followed, almost inevitably, by that dismantling which is, in its acute form, disaster, the "One Art" of another poem:

> I lost my mother's watch. And look! my last, or
> next-to-last of three loved houses went . . .
>
> I lost two cities, lovely ones. And, vaster,
> some realms I owned, two rivers, a continent . . .
>
> the art of losing's not too hard to master
> though it may look like (*Write* it!) like disaster.

That is the tone of disaster confronted, with whatever irony.

A more straightforward account of the whole cycle of domestication and loss can be seen in the long monologue, "Crusoe in England." Crusoe is safely back in England, and his long autobiographical retrospect exposes in full clarity the imperfection of the domestication of nature so long as love is missing, the exhaustion of solitary colonization.

> . . . I'd have
> nightmares of other islands
> stretching away from mine, infinities
> of islands, islands spawning islands,
> like frogs' eggs turning into polliwogs
> of islands, knowing that I had to live
> on each and every one, eventually
> for ages, registering their flora,
> their fauna, their geography.

Crusoe's efforts at the domestication of nature (making a flute, distilling home brew, even devising a dye out of red berries) create a certain degree of pleasure ("I felt a deep affection for/the smallest of my island industries"), and yet the lack of any society except that of turtles and goats and waterspouts ("sacerdotal beings of glass. . ./Beautiful, yes, but not much company") causes both self-pity and a barely admitted hope. Crusoe, in a metaphysical moment, christens one volcano "*Mont d'Espoir* or *Mount Despair*," mirroring both his desolation and his expectancy. The island landscape has been domesticated, "home-made," and yet domestication can turn to domesticity only with the arrival of Friday: "Just when I thought I couldn't stand it/another minute longer, Friday came." Speechless with joy, Crusoe can speak only in the most vacant and consequently the most comprehensive of words.

> Friday was nice.
> Friday was nice, and we were friends.
> . . . he had a pretty body.

Love escapes language. Crusoe could describe with the precision of a geographer the exact appearances of volcanoes, turtles, clouds, lava, goats, and waterspouts and waves, but he is reduced to gesture and sketch before the reality of domesticity.

In the final, recapitulatory movement of the poem Bishop first reiterates the conferral of meaning implicit in the domestication of the universe and then contemplates the loss of meaning once the arena of domestication is abandoned.

> The knife there on the shelf—
> it reeked of meaning, like a crucifix.
> It lived . . .
> I knew each nick and scratch by heart . . .
> Now it won't look at me at all.
> The living soul has dribbled away.
> My eyes rest on it and pass on.

Unlike the meanings of domestication, which repose in presence and use, the meaning of domesticity is mysterious and permanent. The monologue ends:

> The local museum's asked me to
> leave everything to them:
> the flute, the knife, the shrivelled shoes . . .
> How can anyone want such things?
> —And Friday, my dear Friday, died of measles
> seventeen years ago come March.

The ultimate locus of domestication is the heart, which, once cultivated, retains its "living soul" forever.

This dream of eternal and undismantled fidelity in domesticity, unaffected even by death, is one extreme reached by Bishop's imagination as it turns round its theme. But more profound, I think, is the version of life's experience recounted in "The Moose," a poem in which no lasting exclusive companionship between human beings is envisaged, but in which a series of deep and inexplicable satisfactions unroll in sequence, each of them precious. Domestication of the land is one, domesticity of the affections is another, and the contemplation of the sublimity of the nonhuman world is the third.

In the first half of the poem one of the geographies of the world is given an ineffable beauty, both plain and luxurious. Nova Scotia's tides, sunsets, villages, fog, flora, fauna, and people are all summoned quietly into the verse, as if for a last farewell, as the speaker journeys away to Boston. The verse, like the landscape, is "old-fashioned."

> The bus starts. The light
> is deepening; the fog
> shifting, salty, thin,
> comes closing in.
>
> Its cold, round crystals
> form and slide and settle
> in the white hens' feathers,
> in gray glazed cabbages,
> on the cabbage roses
> and lupins like apostles;
>
> the sweet peas cling
> to wet white string
> on the whitewashed fences;
> bumblebees creep
> inside the foxgloves,
> and evening commences.

The exquisitely noticed modulations of whiteness, the evening harmony of settling and clinging and closing and creeping, the delicate touch of each clause, the valedictory air of the whole, the momentary identification with hens, sweet peas, and bumblebees all speak of the attentive and yielding soul through which the landscape is being articulated.

As darkness settles, the awakened soul is slowly lulled into "a dreamy divagation/. . ./a gentle, auditory, slow hallucination." This central passage embodies a regression into childhood, as the speaker imagines that the muffled noises in the bus are the tones of "an old conversation":

> Grandparents' voices
>
> uninterruptedly
> talking, in Eternity:
> names being mentioned,
> things cleared up finally . . .
>
> Talking the way they talked
> in the old featherbed,
> peacefully, on and on . . .
>
> Now, it's all right now
> even to fall asleep
> just as on all those nights.

Life, in the world of this poem, has so far only two components: a beloved landscape and beloved people, that which can be domesticated and those who have joined in domesticity. The grandparents' voices have mulled over all the human concerns of the village:

> what he said, what she said,
> who got pensioned;
>
> deaths, deaths and sicknesses;
> the year he re-married;
> the year (something) happened.
> She died in childbirth.
> That was the son lost
> when the schooner foundered.
>
> He took to drink. Yes.
> She went to the bad.
> When Amos began to pray
> even in the store and
> finally the family had
> to put him away.
>
> "Yes. . ." that peculiar
> affirmative. "Yes. . ."
> A sharp, indrawn breath,
> half-groan, half-acceptance.

In this passage, so plainly different in its rural talk and sorrow from the ravishing aestheticism of the earlier descriptive passage, Bishop joins herself to the Wordsworth of the *Lyrical Ballads*. The domestic affections become, for a moment, all there is. Amos who went mad, the son lost at sea, the mother who died, the girl gone to the bad—these could all have figured in poems like "Michael" or "The Thorn." The litany of names evoking the bonds of domestic sympathy becomes one form of poetry, and the views of the "meadows, hills, and groves" of Nova Scotia is another. What this surrounding world looks like, we know; that "Life's like that" (as the sighed "Yes" implies), we also know. The poem might seem complete. But just as the speaker is about to drowse almost beyond consciousness, there is a jolt, and the bus stops in the moonlight, because "A moose has come out of/the impenetrable wood." This moose, looming "high as a church/homely as a house," strikes wonder in the passengers, who "exclaim in whispers,/childishly, softly." The moose remains.

> Taking her time,
> she looks the bus over,
> grand, otherworldly.

Why, why do we feel
(we all feel) this sweet
sensation of joy?

What is this joy?

In "The Most of It" Frost uses a variant of this fable. There, as in
Bishop's poem, a creature emerges from "the impenetrable wood" and is
beheld. But Frost's beast disappoints expectation. The poet had wanted
"counter-love, original response," but the "embodiment that crashed"
proves to be not "human," not "someone else additional to him," but
rather a large buck, which disappears as it came. Frost's beast is male,
Bishop's female; Frost's a symbol of brute force, Bishop's a creature "safe as
houses"; Frost's a challenge, Bishop's a reassurance. The presence approaching from the wood plays, in both these poems, the role that a god
would play in a pre-Wordsworthian poem and the role that a human
being—a leech-gatherer, an ancient soldier, a beggar—would play in
Wordsworth. These human beings, when they appear in Wordsworth's
poetry, are partly iconic, partly subhuman, as the Leech-Gatherer is part
statue, part sea-beast, and as the old man in "Animal Tranquillity and
Decay" is "insensibly subdued" to a state of peace more animal than
human. "I think I could turn and live with animals," says Whitman,
foreshadowing a modernity that finds the alternative to the human not in
the divine but in the animal. Animal life is pure presence, with its own
grandeur. It assures the poet of the inexhaustibility of being. Bishop's
moose is at once maternal, inscrutable, and mild. If the occupants of the
bus are bound, in their human vehicle, to the world of village catastrophe
and pained acknowledgment, they feel a releasing joy in glimpsing some
large, grand solidity, even a vaguely grotesque one, which exists outside
their tales and sighs, which is entirely "otherworldly." "The darkness
drops again," as the bus moves on; the "dim smell of moose" fades in
comparison to "the acrid smell of gasoline."

"The Moose" is such a purely linear poem, following as it does the
journey of the bus, that an effort of will is required to gaze at it whole.
The immediacy of each separate section—as we see the landscape, then
the people, then the moose—blots out what has gone before. But the
temptation—felt when the poem is contemplated entire—to say something
global, something almost allegorical, suggests that something in the sequence is more than purely arbitrary. The poem passes from adult observation of a familiar landscape to the unending ritual, first glimpsed in
childhood, of human sorrow and narration, to a final joy in the otherworldly, in whatever lies within the impenetrable wood and from time to

time allows itself to be beheld. Beyond or behind the familiar, whether the visual or the human familiar, lies the perpetually strange and mysterious. It is that mystery which causes those whispered exclamations alternating with the pained "Yes" provoked by human vicissitude. It guarantees the poet more to do. On it depends all the impulse to domestication. Though the human effort is bent to the elimination of the wild, nothing is more restorative than to know that earth's being is larger than our human enclosures. Elizabeth Bishop's poetry of domestication and domesticity depends, in the last analysis, on her equal apprehension of the reserves of mystery which give, in their own way, a joy more strange than the familiar blessings of the world made human.

WILLARD SPIEGELMAN

Elizabeth Bishop's "Natural Heroism"

In her genial invitation to Marianne
Moore to come flying over the Brooklyn Bridge one fine morning for a *fête
urbaine*, Elizabeth Bishop conjures up an image of Miss Moore borne aloft
like the good witch of Oz, shoes trailing sapphires, cape full of butterflies,
hat decked with angels. Defined by fey and glittering objects, and not
quite a part of this world, Moore rises "above the accidents, above the
malignant movies" of profane life, while listening to "a soft uninvented
music," like Keats's spiritual toneless ditties. She floats up, "mounting the
sky with natural heroism." This is a curious phrase, since we are likely to
think of the hero as one set apart in his superiority or struggle, and of his
status as one not easily achieved. If anything, herosim and nature are
antithetical. In Bishop's work, however, the "natural hero" occupies a
privileged position which is unattainable by the super- or unnatural exploits of masculine achievement which the poetry constantly debunks. For
Bishop, as for Stevens, "the man-hero is not the exceptional monster."
This, in itself, is nothing new: ever since Wordsworth attempted to
democratize the language and the subjects of poetry, his Romantic heirs
have focused on ordinariness and on the self-conscious meditative habits
which turn heroism inward. But Bishop goes even beyond Wordsworth's
radical break with the past. Her hero replaces traditional ideas of bravery
with a blend of domestic and imaginative strengths. The highest value in
Bishop's work is a politely skeptical courage which neither makes outrageous demands on the world nor demurely submits to the world's own.

From *Centennial Review* 22 (Winter 1978). Copyright © 1978 by *Centennial Review*.

To understand Bishop's natural heroism, and her kinship with, yet movement beyond, Wordsworth, I wish to look at three types of poems, all tinged with her qualifying skepticism. First, there are those which trace the outline of heroic situations or devices and then negate or undercut them; second, those which internalize an encounter or conflict and, in the manner of a Romantic crisis lyric, make the act of learning itself a heroic process, but which also dramatize the avoidance of apocalypse that Geoffrey Hartman has located at the heart of Wordsworth's genius; and finally those in which the *via negativa* of denial or avoidance implies Bishop's positive values, poems where a dialectical struggle between two contestants is resolved by an assertion of heroic worth.

At her most playful, Bishop insinuates heroic, mythological allusions, often with a tentative, amused tone, so that their full impact is softened. In "House Guest," she wonders, "Can it be that we nourish/one of the Fates in our bosoms?" but Clotho is only an inept seamstress. Eros (in "Casabianca") is reduced to the obstinate boy standing on the burning deck, trying to recite Mrs. Hemans' "The boy stood on the burning deck." Hyperion-Apollo, the Romantics' fair-haired youth of morn, becomes some "ineffable creature" whose daily appearance and fall (in "Anaphora") are purposely rendered by a series of effects on his beholders, as if Bishop is too modest to describe or even name the god himself.

More important in Bishop's habitual tactic of diminution or undercutting is the way certain ideas of masculine greatness are filed down or eroded to their essential littleness. "The Burglar of Babylon" deprives its eponymous hero of his glory by recounting, in childlike ballad quatrains, his life as a petty criminal sought by a whole army of police who finally, and unceremoniously, kill him. As Ezra Pound is revealed through the expanding stanzas (modeled on "This is the house that Jack built") of "Visits to St. Elizabeth's," his simple nobility is smothered by the weakness, fragility, and insipidity of the other inmates. The stanzas enlarge, and as Pound is seen in a setting (the literal one of the hospital, the figurative one of the syntactic, grammatical units of increasing complexity) he moves from "tragic," "honored," and "brave," to "cranky," "tedious," and "wretched."

The clichés of masculine conquest are also explored in "Brazil, January 1, 1502," and in the first half of "Roosters." In the first poem, the Portuguese invaders are no better than aroused, predatory jungle lizards. Their "old dream of wealth and luxury" provokes them to the attempted rapacious destruction of landscape and native women. In "Roosters," virility and combativeness, "the uncontrolled, traditional" virtues that create "a senseless order," are mocked by the image of the roosters as pompous, puffed-up military dictators ("Deep from protruding chests/in green-gold medals dressed") and as colorful metallic map-marking pins (the lizards and Christians in the previous poem were also hard, glinting, metallic): "glass-headed pins,/oil-golds and copper greens,/anthracite blues, alizarins,/each one an active/displacement in perspective;/each screaming, 'This is where I live.'" Like Stevens' Chief Iffucan, Bishop's roosters virtually squawk "Fat! Fat! Fat! Fat! I am the personal," and she witnesses the "vulgar beauty" of their iridescence as well as their lunatic, pseudo-heroic fighting swagger. Even the unmilitary Gentleman of Shalott, who has been domesticated (as if Sir Lancelot, originally seen in the mirror in Tennyson's poem, has come indoors to replace the lady who died for love of him), and who is reflected in profile by the mirror, is only a shadow of his total self. Resigned and uncertain, "he loves/that sense of constant re-adjustment./He wishes to be quoted as saying at present:/'Half is enough.'" His partner in Bishop's first volume is the Man-Moth, a curious creature from an imaginary bestiary, the inspiration for whose creation (a newspaper misprint for "mammoth") epitomizes Bishop's metamorphosizing and whimsical imagination. As mammoth, he is literally extinct, as man-moth, confected and precarious.

It is tempting to write off these playful inhabitants of Bishop's world as cousins of Moore's fanciful animals and flowers. But even the most fragile bear weightier implications. The bravado, false heroics, and metallic sheen of the cocks, for example, as well as the speaker's scorn and patronizing amusement, are replaced in the second half of "Roosters" by a new perspective and a softer voice. No longer mock-warriors, the roosters become emblems of human sin and the promise of Christian forgiveness. Peter's denial of Christ at the cock's crowing is sculpted in stone as a tangible reminder of his weakness and his master's love. Even the little rooster is "seen/carved on a dim column in the travertine." If you look hard enough, in other words, the fighting cock of the first part of the poem can be seen anew. Peter's tears and the cock's call are bound together, both in action and its symbolic representation: "There is inescapable hope, the pivot;/yes, and there Peter's tears/run down our chanticleer's/side and gem his spurs." As Peter was long ago forgiven, so we still learn that "'Deny deny deny'/is not all the roosters cry." Spurs encrusted with tears mark the transformation of militancy into humility.

In the poem's last section, Bishop returns to her opening picture of daybreak, and the difference in her imagery alerts us to the distance between braggadocio and the roosters' subsequent Christian meekness. The opening was a military fanfare:

> At four o'clock
> in the gun-metal blue dark
> we hear the first crow of the first cock
>
> just below
> the gun-metal blue window
> and immediately there is an echo
>
> off in the distance,
> then one from the backyard fence,
> then one, with horrible insistence,
>
> grates like a wet match
> from the broccoli patch,
> flares, and all over town begins to catch.

The final view moves us to a slightly later stage of the dawn, gentler and tamed, as the roosters have literally ceased to crow, their threat having been figuratively replaced by the promise of forgiveness and natural harmony:

> In the morning
> a low light is floating
> in the backyard, and gilding
>
> from underneath
> the broccoli, leaf by leaf;
> how could the night have come to grief?
>
> gilding the tiny
> floating swallow's belly
> and lines of pink cloud in the sky,
>
> the day's preamble
> like wandering lines in marble.
> The cocks are now almost inaudible.
>
> The sun climbs in,
> following "to see the end,"
> faithful as enemy, or friend.

Moving as it is, "Roosters" is not typical of Bishop's work. For one thing, the vocabulary of Christian belief appears only rarely in her poetry, and her imagination is more secular than religious (in "A Miracle for Breakfast," there are mysterious hints of communion, or of the miracle of the loaves and fishes, but these are never clarified). For another, the studied symmetry, the juxtaposition of opposing views which augment one another seems too easy. More typical is "Wading at Wellfleet," a short, early lyric which encompasses the tensions I've discussed and diminishes or deflects heroic action more subtly than "Roosters":

In one of the Assyrian wars
a chariot first saw the light
that bore sharp blades around its wheels.

That chariot from Assyria
went rolling down mechanically
to take the warriors by the heels.

A thousand warriors in the sea
could not consider such a war
as that the sea itself contrives

but hasn't put in action yet.
This morning's glitterings reveal
the sea is "all a case of knives."

Lying so close, they catch the sun,
the spokes directed at the shin.
The chariot front is blue and great.

The war rests wholly with the waves:
they try revolving, but the wheels
give way; they will not bear the weight.

The poem is deceptively simple; even its playfulness shows Bishop's ability to take a natural event (named in the title), establish it within a larger metaphoric context, and then surprise us by defusing the bomb she herself has lit. As in "Roosters," glittering danger—here in the opening military details—is evoked like a "false surmise" and then reduced, but unlike "Roosters," "Wading at Wellfleet" avoids simple dualisms. It is, instead, both neatly divided into three parts and, at the same time, seamless in its verbal repetitions and unity. The three pairs of stanzas are isolated by rhyme and subject matter. In the first, we have a backward historical glance at biblical battles (with, I suspect, a whispered reminder of Byron's "The Destruction of Sennacherib"); in the second, the central image of the beach on Cape Cod; and in the third, a dialectical synthesis which paradoxically unites and separates the terms of the first two. The first section introduces the poem's major concept (danger) in the guise of military activity, and its first important image (sharp light) in the off-handed pun of line 2. The same wit is present in lines 5 and 6, where "rolling" sets us up for the last stanza ("revolving") and "heels" reminds us of the title ("Wading"). The second section explicitly combines the light and dazzle of the first with this day's water, and brings the Assyrian warriors into an imaginary relationship with the speaker (they become *any* warriors). The pivotal image is conditional and deliberately vague: we want to know whether any sea has ever put into action its threat, or whether the Atlantic, this particular ocean on this particular day, has been withholding its power. As it surprisingly turns out, the sea is a paper tiger, like the roosters, because it is constitutionally incapable of making real the threat which the human observer has imagined (like the paranoid speaker in Frost's "Once by the Pacific," who supposes that the waves "thought of doing something to the shore/That water never did to land before"). The dialectical synthesis of the last stanzaic pair, then, is imagistic only (the sea-chariot-light configuration). The waves reflect, but can never duplicate, the knifelike sharpness of the sun, itself an image of the chariot wheel (the pun in Herbert's "case of knives" suggests the same weakening of the military motifs); their revolution is their destruction as they roll over and past the feet of the wader.

The frequency with which Bishop attacks and transforms military formulas, forays, and glory shows her grappling with received values and ideas, and struggling towards new ones. In "Roosters," the replacement is clear and easy, while in "Wading at Wellfleet" it is cunningly avoided by disarming the military apparatus, which is the poem's unifying force, without filling the void it leaves. In their dealings with large themes, these poems are relatively minor when compared with others which bring us to the very edge of imaginative revelation and then hold back. Skepticism, an unwillingness to approve either major conflicts or major revelations, is common to both groups. If heroism is undercut in the first poems, we should not be surprised to learn in the next group, that even meditative, epistemological problems (i.e., encounters between a speaker and a natural scene or object) can be subjected to the same deflating treatment. The dangers and traumas of knowledge are posed and then removed. This is, as Geoffrey Hartman has shown, the standard strategy of Wordsworth, who first plunges into some shadowy terrain within the heart or mind of man and then, when scared by what he might learn there, withdraws and calls it "nature." To raise a threat and then to dissipate it, not so much out of fear or cowardice as out of ontological skepticism (which, in "Wading at Wellfleet" and other poems, is disguised as polished light-heartedness) is Bishop's way as well.

"Cape Breton" and "The Moose," two of her longer poems, sustain the anxieties of the shorter lyrics and build towards larger statements. Masquerading as a description of a natural scene, "Cape Breton" is a glimpse into a heart of darkness. Indeed, Bishop's vision is to Conrad's as Marlow's is to Kurtz's:

> He had made that last stride, he had stepped over the edge, while I had been permitted to draw back my hesitating foot. . . .perhaps. . .all truth, and all sincerity, are just compressed into that inappreciable moment of time in which we step over the threshold of the invisible.

Throughout, descriptive data are balanced by suggestions of absence, disappearance, and vacancy: "Cape Breton" is more about what is not there than what is. The opening images are negated: we see an uneven line of birds, but their backs are toward us; we hear sheep whose fearfulness, we are parenthetically told, causes them occasionally to stampede over the rocks into the sea. Water and mist are the salient features of this world, melting into each other, "weaving. . .and disappearing," and "the pulse,/rapid but unurgent, of a motorboat" is incorporated into the mist, while the boat's invisible body is obliterated.

The delicate beauty enfolded within and by the secret ministry of mist evinces both dissipation ("like rotting snow-ice sucked away/almost to spirit") and erosion ("the ghosts of glaciers drift/among those folds and folds of fir. . .dull, dead, deep peacock-colors"). Having set the scene in a primal, almost Gothic chill, the speaker proceeds to human, domestic details, but with the same plan of taking away with one hand what the other offers. There is a road along the coast with "small yellow bulldozers" but no activity: "without their drivers, because today is Sunday." There are "little white churches" (all the human details are deliberately dwarfed) in the hills, but they too are vestiges of some unknown past, "like lost quartz arrowheads." The central revelation comes now, and as we might expect, it is one of human and epistemological emptiness:

> The road appears to have been abandoned.
> Whatever the landscape had of meaning appears to have been abandoned,
> unless the road is holding it back, in the interior,
> where we cannot see,
> where deep lakes are reputed to be,
> and disused trails and mountains of rock
> and miles of burnt forest standing in gray scratches
> like the admirable scriptures made on stones by stones—

The disappointment is double: the evidence of the eye leads us to nothing (we see no meaning), and the possibility of hidden truth is buried beneath hearsay ("reputed to be") and the geological palimpsests which can be seen and read only by the Kurtzes of the world. All that the speaker is able to hear these regions "say for themselves" is the song of the small sparrows, themselves too fragile to last, sustain meaning, or provide comfort: "floating upward/freely, dispassionately, through the mist, and meshing/in brown-wet, fine, torn fish-nets."

The next verse paragraph looks as if it will announce a major turn in the poem, but we learn that Bishop's singular devotion to painting emptiness here deceives us with apparently human images. A bus, packed

with people, comes into view, but once again a parenthetical afterthought
reduces fullness to relative emptiness:

> (On weekdays with groceries, spare automobile parts, and pump parts,
> but today only two preachers extra, one carrying his frock coat on
>   a hanger.)

Passing a closed roadside stand, a closed schoolhouse ("where today no
flag is flying"), the bus finally emits two passengers, a man with a baby,
who immediately vanish in "a small steep meadow,/which establishes its
poverty in a snowfall of daisies," to return "to his invisible house beside
the water." The human dimension is teasingly put into, and then erased
from, the picture where even natural details are muted, softened, and so
delicately and charmingly miniaturized that we might almost forget the
accumulated horror that they are surely meant to convey. Indeed, as the
bus itself pulls off, the birds keep on singing, normal activity, such as it is,
resumes, and the poem ends like a surrealistic movie (e.g., *Blow-Up*)
where, in a field, a man stands and then quite simply vanishes, as if he
were never there. There remains only the mist which covers and swallows
all:

> The thin mist follows
> the white mutations of its dream;
> an ancient chill is rippling the dark brooks.

Who has been dreaming, really: the mist which encompasses everything,
or the human viewer who thought she saw a man on a bus? Both the
landscape and its meaning have been abandoned in a cinematic sleight-of-
hand that calls into question the very grounds of our knowing.

Though not as chilling in its implications, "The Moose" follows a
similar course of isolating the speaker, and presenting her with the potential dangers of encounter with the unknown; but here, instead of remaining uncertain and tantalizing, the threat is destroyed. A heart of darkness,
in "Cape Breton," is implied but experientially unknowable; in "The
Moose," the midnight danger is tamed and domesticated, its sting removed. The poem begins as a series of farewells, as a bus moves west and
south in late afternoon, from Nova Scotia to Boston. The light darkens,
the fog gathers round, "a lone traveller" says goodbye to family and dog.
Moonlight surrounds the bus as it enters New Brunswick's forests, and the
passengers sink together into their private dreams, divagations, and con-
versations, some overheard by others ("—not concerning us,/but recognizable, somewhere,/back in the bus"). Two-thirds of the way through the
poem, as a sense of comfort enables the travellers to succumb finally to

sleep, the bus stops with a jolt, halted by a creature from the deep, dark interior:

> A moose has come out of
> the impenetrable wood
> and stands there, looms, rather,
> in the middle of the road.

But the moose is no memento of the inner depths, nor a visitor from the heart of the night. The only revelation is of the beast's harmless, almost personable, curiosity as she sniffs the bus. And yet the very plainness of the beast, an emblem of the plainness of the experience of confrónting it, provokes a question which Bishop refrains from answering directly:

> Taking her time,
> she looks the bus over,
> grand, otherworldly.
> Why, why do we feel
> (we all feel) this sweet
> sensation of joy?

Grand but "awful plain," the moose becomes an occasion for a shared experience, a common sense of surmounting a momentary fright (which in this case is hardly heroic) followed by the reunion, in separate contentment, of the passengers with one another.

Habitually, then, we see Bishop constructing situations in which disaster is averted, or at worst insinuated gently enough so as to appear harmless. We can go even further, however, to discover in a third group of poems that active confrontation with physical or intellectual danger may yield lessons of wisdom and strength of purpose to narrators and characters.

Bishop's "natural" (i.e., either automatic, "in the nature of things," or common, "universal") heroism becomes clear in many of these poems, among them the terrifying "In the Waiting Room," the only one in which her own name appears. The seven-year-old Elizabeth, waiting while her aunt is in the dentist's chair, learns two primal lessons: of human pain and mortality, as she hears her aunt scream; and of unity in spite of human differences as she looks at African pictures in a *National Geographic*, and sinks into a confused semiconsciousness. She speaks her name ("you are an *I*,/you are an *Elizabeth*"), asserting her essential individuality, while simultaneously entertaining a nightmare vision of the universal sameness of all people: herself, Aunt Consuelo, the native African women, and the other patients in the office. This crisis lyric describes both a revelation and the joint horror and acceptance it provokes in the girl who has now, irrevocably, entered into her rational maturity. For all its differences in tone and language, it is Bishop's "Immortality" ode, where we see the light of common day begin its irreversible movement in the child's consciousness. For Wordsworth, years bring the philosophic mind to the adult who is, at the same time, borne down by the accumulated baggage of deadly custom and stale imitation. But where Wordsworth's manic willingness to be cheerful in the face of frost ("We in thought will join your throng") is the key to his own heroism, Bishop tentatively accepts continuity and community as bulwarks against separateness. Hence the circular structure of the poem which nakedly returns to the opening details of time and place, relocating the child, after her momentary blackout, in this very world, "which is," in Wordsworth's phrase, "the world of all of us." The "sweet sensation of joy" which unites the riders in "The Moose" is now replaced by an awful wonder at the fact of unity when one feels most alone:

> Why should I be my aunt,
> or me, or anyone?
> What similarities—
>
> . . . held us all together
> or made us all just one?
> How—I didn't know any
> word for it—how "unlikely". . .

The unlikely but perfectly natural realization that we have all of us one human heart is the crucial beginning, in Bishop's view of the self, of a transformation of isolation into community (on the egoism of the child, cf. Wordsworth's remark, "I was often unable to think of external things as having external existence"). In maturity, as opposed to childhood, it is joy that brings the separate travellers together.

It is no surprise that Bishop should instinctively be a poet of *places*, because the conditions of placement—stasis, domesticity, routine, community—compensate for her natural humility in the face of the greater "world" where she often feels estranged. The attractions of travel are its dangers ("Questions of Travel" presents the philosophical dimensions of the debate between movement and rest): hence poems like "Cape Breton" and "The Moose," which depict the avoidance of revelation of which I've written (significantly, the passengers in the bus are united by joy when the bus is stopped; when it starts up again, it leaves behind "a dim/smell of moose, an acrid/smell of gasoline"). Conversely, the domestic coziness of Bishop's Brazilian poems invokes traditional pastoral ideas of rest and also the relief that accompanies a sense of belonging in a harmonious community. In this context, the apparent oxymoron in "natural heroism" is erased: the heroic self does not stand apart from his tribe by virtue of either suffering or action (nor is he isolated like Man-Moth, Portuguese invaders, or Pound); rather, by synecdoche, he exemplifies his community.

Since he does not stand alone, the hero is usually presented as part of a group, or especially a pair. The confrontations between people in Bishop's work are sometimes ambivalent and tricky: high and low, victor and victim, master and servant, are likely to change places. The relationship of patron and tenant-farmer in "Manuelzinho" turns upon the seeming inequality between them and upon their reversal of roles, when "superior" and "inferior" lose all meaning. Manuelzinho, a blessed fool, magical and hexed, can grow nothing, and the frustrations of his employer, affectionately but exasperatingly listed, proclaim the distance between his childlike wonder and her mature sensibleness. But this distance is reduced by love, first the patronizing affection of adult for child, then, gradually, the accumulated sense of dependence on Manuelzinho for more than mere amusement. Figurative exaggerations become statements of fact, just as fancy begins to assume solidity:

> Account books? They are Dream Books.
> In the kitchen we dream together
> how the meek shall inherit the earth—
> or several acres of mine.

Colorful harlequin, aged child, and useless necessity, Manuelzinho, without his knowing it, occasions humility and warmth in his patron, so that at the poem's end, their positions have been reversed. In this quasi-feudal relationship, propriety demands courteous generosity from both, especially from the patron whose plea for understanding and forgiveness is one of those gestures in Bishop's work that reaffirm human community between equals and prove that heroism need be neither grandiose nor excessive. Having mocked Manuelzinho's ridiculous, painted hats, the speaker doffs her own to him in a kind act of homage:

> One was bright green. Unkindly,
> I called you Klorophyll Kid.
> My visitors thought it was funny.
> I apologize here and now.

> You helpless, foolish man,
> I love you all I can,
> I think. Or do I?
> I take off my hat, unpainted
> and figurative, to you.
> Again I promise to try.

"I could have laughed myself to scorn to find/In that decrepit Man so firm a mind," Wordsworth's surprised response to his leech-gatherer, is equivalent to the sustenance which this speaker derives from Maneulzinho. Where Bishop surpasses Wordsworth, however, where her egoism is simply less intense, is in her continual insistence on the need for symbiosis: mutual support, rather than epiphanies wrought by otherworldly visitors, is the key to natural polity, as well as piety. Her other long poem about master and servant ("Faustina, or Rock Roses") also dramatizes "service," but through images that reflect and complement one another, it turns hierarchy into a bizarre democracy. Here it is difficult to know who is master—the white woman, shrivelled and dying, or Faustina, the black servant whose own freedom is imminent but whose current status is ambivalent. The uncertainty of the human relationship is depicted in the opening stanza:

> Tended by Faustina
> yes in a crazy house
> upon a crazy bed,
> frail, of chipped enamel,
> blooming above her head
> into four vaguely roselike
> flower-formations,
>
> the white woman whispers to
> herself.

We must infer an initial ellipsis ("The rock roses are. . .tended by Faustina") to grasp the full, functional ambiguity of the lines: the servant is caretaker of sculpted flowers (which metamorphose into a visitor's gift of real flowers at the end of the poem) and of the white woman, equally "frail" and "chipped," lying in "white disordered sheets/like wilted roses," beside a crooked table littered with chalky powder, cream, and pills, in a room where each rag contributes "its/shade of white, confusing/as undazzling." The poem is a still life, a study in desiccated whiteness, with a human analogue. Faustina's "terms of. . .employment" ("terms" suggesting both time and condition) are complained of, and explained to, the visitor. Her "sinister kind face" poses an unanswerable riddle of her own feelings about the mistress' approaching death and her own survival; the ambiguous antecedent of "it" is both the señora's *and* the servant's conditions:

> Oh, is it
> freedom at last, a lifelong
> dream of time and silence,
> dream of protection and rest?

Or is it the very worst,
the unimaginable nightmare
that never before dared last
more than a second?

"There is no way of telling" is the closest thing to a response as mistress and servant, polar opposites, one dying and one living, converge in the ambivalent haze of this syntax.

We do not normally think of Bishop as a poet of struggle; the tension in her poems is mostly internalized, and confrontations, when they occur, are between the self, traveling, moving, or simply seeing, and the landscape it experiences. But in "Manuelzinho" and "Faustina" we have two pairs of agonists, locked in relationships of affection and struggle from which there is no release in life. In fact, Bishop's most anthologized poem, "The Fish," is more typical of its author than we might suspect. It depicts external and internal conflict, and a heroic action which is perfectly "natural" in its motivation and accomplishment. It follows the pattern I have traced for all of Bishop's poems so far, thus making it a paradigm of her work: an action is intimated and then undercut; next, a mild revelation, hardly heralded, occurs, and then a positive reaction proves the speaker's heroism. The simple experience literally surrounds the reasons for it: "I caught a tremendous fish" (line 1), "and I let the fish go" (line 76). We first see deflation: the tremendous fish is caught with no struggle whatsoever, and, like the moose, turns out to be anything but dangerous: "He hung a grunting weight,/battered and venerable/and homely." It is not for the absence of a good fight, or as a testimony to the grim veteran who has struggled in the past, that the speaker releases her catch. More important to her action are the accumulated details of her revelation. These involve an anthropomorphizing of the adversary (as in "Roosters" and "The Moose") and, as a result of a camaraderie, an aesthetic epiphany which preempts and therefore obliterates the military antagonism hinted at earlier in the poem.

The description of the fish (the bulk of the poem) domesticates him (his skin is like wallpaper; there are rosettes of lime and rags of seaweed on him; the swim-bladder is like a peony), while not omitting reminders of his potential danger ("the frightening gills. . .that can cut so badly," "his sullen face,/the mechanism of his jaw"). Stressing the fish's familiarity *and* otherness, the speaker transforms him into a veteran fighter, a survivor of many contests who wears the remnants of old fish-lines in his lower lip like battle scars or "medals with their ribbons/frayed and wavering,/a five-haired beard of wisdom/trailing from his aching jaw."

The revelation has two parts: first, the new picture which the speaker's imaginative perception has created; and second, the way this new image of the fish colors and alters her environment. For an analogue to the heroic dimension of the poem we have only to look at Wordsworth's encounters with spectral, ghastly figures (leech-gatherer, beggar, discharged soldier) who are shocking, at first, because of their subhumanness, but who subsequently chastise and instruct Wordsworth in the "unlikely" connections among us all. In his famous description, the leech-gatherer is changed from a rock into a giant sea-beast before finally assuming his full human identity. Likewise, Bishop's fish undergoes, a series of revisions which build to create his final symbolic weight.

The aesthetic nature of this experience, by which the fish is literally *seen* and metaphorically tamed, is the final cause of the speaker's release of him. Looking hard at her opponent, Bishop moves beyond military conquest to a "victory" in which both contestants have a part: "I stared and stared/and victory filled up/the little rented boat." The last twelve lines return us to the model of the Wordsworthian nature lyric, first in their insistence on a mesmerizing vision (cf. "I gazed and gazed" in "I Wandered Lonely as a Cloud"), next in the metaphoric "wealth" which this show brings, and last, in a muted reminder of the covenant and the natural piety emblemized by a rainbow, inspiring confidence and joy through a feeling of connection with the world (it is a nice detail that this feeling comes in a "rented boat," where the speaker is a natural outsider):

> I stared and stared
> and victory filled up
> the little rented boat,
> from the pool of bilge
> where oil has spread a rainbow
> around the rusted engine
> to the bailer rusted orange,
> the sun-cracked thwarts,
> the oarlocks on their strings,
> the gunnels—until everything
> was rainbow, rainbow, rainbow!
> And I let the fish go.

Victory, then, comes with neither the catching of the fish (almost accidental) nor its release (virtually automatic) but with the conjunction of two antagonists, heroic by virtue of their endurance (the fish, like the leech-gatherer, is admirable for merely surviving), their embodiment or perception of natural beauty, and the harmony of visual detail which reflects their personal connections. For Bishop, natural heroism becomes not the elimination, or conquest, of the enemy, but the embracing, subsuming, and internalizing of him. In the largest sense, separateness is denied, and victory is earned: another word for her heroism is love.

ANNE R. NEWMAN

Elizabeth Bishop's
"Roosters"

We know more of the actual compo-
sition of "Roosters" than of most of Elizabeth Bishop's poems. It "was
inspired by a newspaper reproduction of one of Picasso's roosters"; and at
one point, she has commented, she was having difficulties until she heard
a Scarlotti sonata. Two of Elizabeth Bishop's strong interests, painting and
music, are thus seen to have had an immediate effect on the poem; which
is not surprising, as "Roosters" is itself an extremely skillful combination
of visual and rhythmical effects. Through her art the raucous barnyard
fowl is transformed into a symbol of hope.

"Roosters" begins rather matter-of-factly, as do many of her poems:

> At four o'clock
> in the gun-metal blue dark
> we hear the first crow of the first cock.

But the realistic subject is gradually transformed; and the symbolic episode
of Peter's denial of Christ, which is used as the basis of this transcendence, is enclosed within a larger natural cycle. Elizabeth Bishop sees the
ideal and the real, permanence and decay, affirmation and denial in both
man and nature. But she sees them as a pattern, and everything in the
poem works toward a realization of balance and synthesis. The duality
which was once integrated naturally and mythically by man must now be
consciously integrated through perception and art. This is a major theme

From *Pebble: A Book of Rereadings in Recent American Poetry*, no. 18–19–20 (1980).
Copyright © 1979 by Greg Kuzma.

in her work as a whole, and in "Roosters" we have one of her finest aesthetic realizations of the theme as all is brought together through the imaginative relationship of the real roosters with the small bronze statue of a cock on a column outside the Papal buildings in Rome:

> Old holy sculpture
> could set it all together
> in one small scene, past and future:

The highly controlled verse form of "Roosters" supports the concept of conscious art as an integrating factor for civilized man. The complex pattern is modeled on Crashaw's poem "Wishes to his supposed Mistress," but it is modified in both rhythm and rhyme. In place of Crashaw's strict dimeter, trimeter, tetrameter lines (in that sequence), Miss Bishop establishes a norm of two, three, and four stresses in the lines; and she uses many partial rhymes instead of consistently perfect ones. This combination gives "Roosters," one of her more formal pieces, that naturalness of tone which is characteristic of her poetry.

The cries gradually increase in number and intensity as the roosters begin answering each other from "off in the distance" to "the backyard fence":

> then one, with horrible insistence,
>
> grates like a wet match
> from the broccoli patch,
> flares, and all over town begins to catch.

Being wakened before dawn is not, as a rule, a pleasant experience; and one begins to feel that this may be even more than an ordinary awakening. The words and images in these early stanzas seem to be the resentful reactions of a reluctant waker commenting on a familiar scene. The "flare" sets off all the roosters and "cries galore" come realistically from "the water-closet door" and "the dropping-plastered henhouse floor." Here a new element of noise and confusion is introduced as "in the blue blur/their rustling wives admire." They are hens, surely, but they are also "wives" in the mind of the waker; and "admire" gives an impression of mindless clucking in the henhouse. The comparison of women and hens creeps in rather insidiously, and the man-fowl comparison continues as "the roosters brace their cruel feet and glare." They are quite literally cruel, considering the dangerous spurs; but the line becomes a comment on human relationships. The mindless admiration for strength, cruelty and stridency is carried further in the next stanza:

> with stupid eyes
> while from their beaks their rise
> the uncontrolled, traditional cries.

The juxtaposition of "stupid," "uncontrolled," and "traditional," follow-ing the human connotations, is powerful. The roosters are beginning to appear as more than unpleasant barnyard fowl; for the tradition seems to be one of admiration for war-like cruelty, for flamboyant and pompous strength:

> Deep from protruding chests
> in green-gold medals dressed,
> planned to command and terrorize the rest.

Their panoply and strutting stance appear to be directed at, or for the benefit of,

> the many wives
> who lead hens' lives
> of being courted and despised;

witty lines, certainly, but they suggest that the uncontrolled tradition has been based on sexual and power urges. The idea is continued: "deep from raw throats / a senseless order floats / all over town," a brutal image. The rooster has succeeded not only in waking man but also in having man identify himself with the baser animal characteristics, or passions; awaken-ing him thus in two senses—to the objective world and to his own limitations. It is at this point that "a rooster gloats." Thus the first ten stanzas have established part of the theme, the scene, and the identification.

In stanza eleven the implication of all mankind is suggested as the cries spread everywhere, "over our beds," and

> over our churches
> where the tin rooster perches
> over our little wooden northern houses,

The weathervane rooster is introduced here as a natural part of the scene, but this first mention of a different kind of rooster and its association with "our churches" give a subtle foreshadowing of the pivotal image of the statue of the cock.

The roosters then spread out,

> making sallies
> from all the muddy alleys
> marking out maps like Rand McNally's:

a humorous and delightful image in which rooster tracks are compared to map markings; but also a comment upon how each, in war-like attire, claims his territorial rights. The shining, metallic images of the cocks which follow suggest that neither human nor natural qualities are in control; unfeeling, mechanical ones have taken over. "Each one an active / displacement in perspective" implies that the traditional perspective is indeed warped—seen through "stupid, cruel eyes."

The action so far has taken place in pre-dawn, a time between waking and sleeping which Miss Bishop often uses, a time when consciousness and unconsciousness merge. That this is not a gentle hour here has been evident from the first few lines. Blue is the predominant color, but it is "gun-metal blue," not the expected soft blue of half-light. The colors which follow support the metallic feeling and focus it on the roosters which are "green gold," "oil golds," "copper greens," "anthracite blues," "alizarins." Throughout this section, images combine colors and metals. The harsh, metallic overtones of the colors are in keeping with the hard, senseless awakening. Frequent suggested color and texture images such as "dropping-plastered henhouse floor," "rusty iron sheds," "fences made from old bedsteads," and "glass-headed pins" also add to the impression of cold, mindless brutality and decay. Visual perceptions are strongly supported by other adjectives which describe the roosters: "stupid eyes," "protruding chests," "raw throats"; and the action words: "grates," "flares," "brace," "command," and "gloats." And underlying all is the sound imagery, increasing in intensity and stridency from "the first crow" and "an echo" to a "cry with horrible insistence," and so on, until it becomes "screaming, screaming." The scene is presented in sensory images, filtered through the resentful consciousness of a person commanded to awaken to a life which she feels as a cruel reality.

This tone is carried through even in the rhyme, mainly masculine end-rhyme, with the final accent of the line falling strongly on the rhymed (or partially rhymed) words; so that although there is much enjambment and the flow seems natural and easy, the effect of harshness is maintained. The cacophonous effect is heightened by frequent consonance of hard k, g, ch, and d sounds and assonance of long vowels. The rhythmic norm takes on the staccato quality of the roosters' cries. Everything in this section develops the impression of an ugly pre-dawn hour.

Stanza seventeen begins a subtle shift in perspective and tone. The poetic voice becomes more personal as the waker, in her mind, addresses the roosters directly. The scene extends from mental images based on the actual scene to broader conceptions and relationships. There is a hint that she is questioning the authority of the roosters in the line, "Roosters, what are you projecting?" after she has felt their command to "Get up! Stop dreaming!" There are touches of humor, as though she is amused by her own extreme reaction. She tries to reduce the serious resentment with which she has taken the cocks' cries and deliberately tries to undercut her horrified perception. The tone is thus not allowed to become heavy; but the humor takes a serious turn as the more she tries to question the authority of the roosters the more totally bleak her vision becomes. Concentrating upon the images of cruelty and war which the roosters evoke, she questions thus:

> You, whom the Greeks elected
> to shoot at on a post, who struggled
> when sacrificed, you whom they labeled
>
> "Very combative . . ."

Through the reference to Greek culture the perspective of the poem is extended, pointing up a dreadful kind of continuity. The earlier image of the weathervane comes to mind, but here there is a live rooster on a post. The struggling cock is offered as a sacrifice to appease warlike gods; later a sacrificial image suggests redemption as a metaphorical post becomes a pivot symbolic of hope. The waker continues to question the rooster's right to give commands and

> cry "Here!" and "Here!"
> and wake us here where are
> unwanted love, conceit and war?

It is indeed a bleak vision, reminiscent of the awakening of the consciousness to the reality of "the darkling plain" in the closing lines of Arnold's "Dover Beach." Conceit and war images are carried on in the next two stanzas:

> The crown of red
> set on your little head
> is charged with all your fighting blood.
>
> Yes, that excrescence
> makes a most virile presence
> plus all that vulgar beauty of iridescence.

References to ancient Greece and increasing emphasis upon the human qualities of the roosters tend to distance the poem from the literal barnyard scene. In the last five stanzas of this part of the poem, there is a surrealistic sense of removal from specific reality as the characteristics of cock and man become more and more fused and universalized. The scene actually returns to the village, but the feeling is more timeless and placeless. The poem continues with a battle—inevitable, really, after the qualities which have been displayed.

> Now in mid-air
> by twos they fight each other.
> Down comes a first flame-feather,

cockfights, and epic single combats;

> and one is flying,
> with raging heroism defying
> even the sensation of dying.

and heroism which is futile and blind, signifying death.

> And one has fallen,
> but still above the town
> his torn-out, bloodied feathers drift down;

all the harsh cries of defiance are gone now; the feathers drift quietly:

> and what he sung
> no matter. He is flung
> on the gray ash heap, lies in dung
> with his dead wives
> with open, bloody eyes,
> while those metallic feathers oxidize.

The touch of beauty and heroism in the stanzas above is bitterly counteracted in the last two stanzas through the sense of waste and hopelessness in the image of the dead cock, now also fallen hero, among the dead wives. In this battle scene colors are integrated with images of blood; and the shrill cries which heralded "unwanted love, conceit and war" are translated into action. Finally, in the stillness of death, the metallic image of the feathers recurs—all their flamboyant colors fading, on the ash heap, in excrement.

The poem seems, so far, to have been presented through a feminine voice. Undertones of loss add a sense of personal drama and imply an explanation for her bleak reactions to "Stop dreaming!". Waking to "unwanted love, conceit and war" can take on personal connotations. There is a hint of disgust combined with sympathy in the attitude toward the gullible "hen-wives"; and bitterness toward the stupid, destructive pride of the cocks. A similar attitude is implied in the second part of the poem with the comparison of Magdalen's sin and Peter's—hers of the "flesh alone," his of the "spirit." The male-female comparisons are interesting and add a personal dimension to the poem, but they do not take precedence over the concern for all mankind. The voice becomes less personal, more universalized, as she moves into the second part, in which pain and despair are transcended.

This part begins with an abrupt shift of scene; from its lowest point it is time to begin turning on the pivot. Lloyd Frankenberg speaks of this turn in

> the long magnificently incantatory "Roosters:" . . . Sustained and accelerating, its three-line form constantly suggesting the rooster's triple blast, the poem moves from a country morning to the morning of Christianity. The symbolic triple rebuke of Peter becomes a sign of his forgiveness.

The section opens with St. Peter; the cock is not mentioned until the fifth stanza.

> St. Peter's sin
> was worse than that of Magdalen
> whose sin was of the flesh alone;
>
> of spirit, Peter's,
> falling, beneath the flares,
> among the "servants and officers."

The image of Peter's spiritual "falling beneath the flares" brings to mind earlier images such as "Down comes a first flame-feather," and "one has fallen"—thus identifying Peter somewhat with the fallen cock. Continuity in the poem is maintained not only through rhythm, verse pattern, and progression of theme but, as here, through resonance of imagery.

Transformation begins at this point:

> Christ stands amazed,
> Peter, two fingers raised
> to surprised lips, both as if dazed.
>
> But in between
> a little cock is seen
> carved on a dim column in the travertine,
>
> explained by *gallus canit*;
> *flet Petrus* underneath it.
> There is inescapable hope, the pivot;

Through the "old holy sculpture" the brutal qualities of man and nature are transcended; and the word "inescapable" suggests that hope is as much a part of the world as despair, just as the once strident cock is now quiet, small, but enduring. Peter, "heartsick," "still cannot guess" that "his dreadful rooster" might "mean forgiveness." But the next image of "a new weathervane / on basilica and barn," shows that Peter has been forgiven. The proof to mankind is portrayed through art: "outside the Lateran"

> there would always be
> a bronze cock on a porphyry
> pillar so the people and the Pope might see
> that even the Prince
> of the Apostles long since
> had been forgiven, and to convince
> all the assembly
> that "Deny, deny, deny"
> is not all the roosters cry.

The cry, silent for many stanzas, is brought back here with a hint of its original tone: but now "affirm, affirm, affirm" is suggested as the other half of the cry. After the pivot, "Peter's tears / run down our chanticleer's / sides and gem his spurs." This is the first time the rooster has been called "chanticleer," a more cheerful herald of dawn. Echoes of earlier images enter, and the "cruel feet" are now spurs gemmed by human tears, precious and enduring.

This second part of the poem is more contemplative, controlled more directly through the poetic consciousness, which transforms the real into the symbol. Abstractions are still presented largely through images, but overall there is less bold sensory imagery than in the first part: colors tend to be muted; and action words are quieter, implying continuity and permanence mixed with a conditional quality. The "inescapable hope" is there; nevertheless, it must be perceived through art. In keeping with the overall softening of reality in this part, there is a higher proportion of feminine rhyme and slant rhyme, a gentler sense of flow through a general lessening of attention focused on the rhyming words, fewer harsh consonants, a softening of vowel sounds, and fewer jammed accented syllables. The effect is cumulative and subtle; the tone gradually changes as the theme develops. Certainly the end of this section is affirmative in comparison with the first; the denial is still present, but subdued. And it is out of the denial itself that the hope comes; affirmation and denial are recognized as the two sides of humanity—and they have been reconciled through art.

The last part, in five stanzas, takes us back to the original scene and extends the theme to the natural world, where duality is also intrinsic. Earlier this scene has been presented in images formed through the consciousness of a person who resents being wakened to harsh reality; following the symbolic transcendence, she becomes aware of natural beauty.

In a toned-down way, Elizabeth Bishop often uses archetypal patterns in
her poetry, as when the human progression from despair to hope is
reflected here in the natural cycle. This integration gives the Christian
parable an archetypal resonance at the same time that it defines the
natural process in human terms as death and rebirth of the spirit.

The world is transformed by the coming of dawn in a natural time
progression from the four o'clock dark. Change comes through the play of
light on the same objects which were revealed in the "blue blur" of the
first section, especially the broccoli patch:

> In the morning
> a low light is floating
> in the backyard, and gilding
>
> from underneath
> the broccoli, leaf by leaf;
> how could the night have come to grief?

The colors have changed and now all is gilding and pink; even the
metallic suggestion of *gilding* is given a progressive form so that the effect is
of a play of golden light rather than any static quality. The sense of release
and lightness comes in the sounds of the words which in turn produce the
more easily flowing movement. Everything is gently moving in stanzas
forty through forty-three; the repetition of "floating, gilding, gilding,
floating," "leaf by leaf," the suggested swallow's flight, the streaks of light
in the sky as "wandering lines." The alliteration of l's is especially
prominent, taking precedence over the earlier harsh consonant sounds;
vowels are somehow lighter and quicker moving; sprung rhythm effect is
toned down as the rhythm becomes more regular. Language itself seems
transfigured by the dawn:

> gilding the tiny
> floating swallow's belly
> and lines of pink cloud in the sky,
>
> the day's preamble
> like wandering lines in marble.
> The cocks are now almost inaudible.

What has taken place naturally in the world and consciously through art
are now united as she sees the beauty and wonder of the scene with a
symbolic richness.

And then Miss Bishop does what she so often does in the final
lines of a poem: she brings us back to an awareness that the epiphany is
neither complete nor permanent. The roosters have been "almost inaudible," not quite, and now

The sun climbs in,
following "to see the end,"
faithful as enemy, or friend.

The ambiguity which is suggested in the sun symbol is actually central to the ideas of the poem. The beautiful vision has been only part of reality; and though one wishes to hold on to it, the last stanza is a reminder that human emotions are as subject to change as natural phenomena are. But there is also the reminder of permanence within the shifting pattern itself. The last stanza is a shattering image; but it is part of Elizabeth Bishop's essential honesty to recognize that, as the pre-dawn bleakness has not lasted, neither will the shining affirmation of the dawn. As the cock can both deny and affirm, the sun impartially brings pain and pleasure; and the perceptive observer is now ready to accept the full reality of day.

PENELOPE LAURANS

"Old Correspondences":
Prosodic Transformations

The bight is littered with old correspondences.

from "The Bight"

When asked, in a 1966 *Shenandoah*
interview, what she especially liked about George Herbert, whose poetry
she said had influenced her own poem, "The Weed," Elizabeth Bishop
explained that she admired "the absolute naturalness of tone." In the few
reviews and critical pieces Bishop has written, she returns several times to
spontaneity as a poetic quality she values. A pleasant but gently critical
review of Wallace Fowlie's autobiographical book *Pantomime* concludes
with the dry remark that Fowlie is "more spontaneous than he gives
himself credit for." And it is for spontaneity, among other principal
virtues, that she praises Marianne Moore in her early review of Moore's
poems.

Bishop's concern with tone is not surprising, since few aspects of
composition have been more troublesome for that generation of poets
following the great moderns. Most of them have tried for just that
"naturalness" and "spontaneity" they learned to value from their Romantic progenitors, but the difficulty has been to define these qualities in

From *Elizabeth Bishop and Her Art*, edited by Lloyd Schwartz and Sybil P. Estess. Copyright
© 1983 by The University of Michigan. University of Michigan Press, 1983.

mid-twentieth century terms. Bishop's own definition is suggested in the *Shenandoah* discussion where she describes her early discovery of an essay on seventeenth century baroque prose which "tried to show that baroque sermons . . . attempted to dramatize the mind in action rather than in repose." The sense of the mind actively encountering reality, giving off the impression of involved, immediate discovery, is one of Bishop's links to the Romantics, as the recurrence of the word "spontaneous" in her critical vocabulary emphasizes.

This high valuation on the natural in Bishop's critical statements is especially interesting in light of the range of metrical variation and complicated versification in her poems. For some contemporary poets the "natural" has implied a certain disrespect for form. Bishop's poetry, on the contrary, has always displayed a wide range of formal inventiveness. Yet, if one asked a competent reader for an extempore comment on formal variation in Bishop's poetry, he might answer that he didn't remember much—it is that subtly done. The appearance of regularity in the face of so much variation is partly evidence of Bishop's technical versatility, but it is also directly connected with the way formal qualities are related to thematic ones in her poetry. It is consistent with Bishop's own preference for the natural that, in her poems, form always yields to the exigency of what she is trying to say. Her patterns are a result of her insistence that formal structures adapt to the developing progression of the poem, rather than predetermine that progression. Of course no good poet allows form to dictate what he is going to say. But many will let it guide them in making choices. Bishop, however, rarely seems to permit this to happen.

While it appears to be true that formal adaptiveness—the subordination of form to meaning—gives Bishop's poetry some of that sense of spontaneity she admires, it also seems true, paradoxically, that this same adaptiveness works to restrict the meaning of spontaneity in her work quite narrowly. Thematically, Bishop's poetry tends toward Romantic subject matter: problems of isolation, of loss, of the quest for union with something beyond the self, press with dramatic force in her work. These highly charged questions, however, are nearly always countered by the way they are presented, which has earned for the tone of her verse such critical characterizations as "matter-of-fact and understated" and "flat and modest." Indeed, it seems to me that Bishop exercises her technical proficiency to cut her poetry off from any of that "spontaneous overflow of powerful feeling" so immediately central to the Romantic imagination. Frequently it is this quality of restraint that keeps the poetry from sentimental excess and gives it its elegantly muted, modernist quality.

A well-modulated lyric like "The Armadillo" demonstrates how the formal qualities of Bishop's poetry help to hold the reader's emotional response in check. "The Armadillo" meditates on the Brazilian custom of floating celebratory fire balloons on saints' day and festival days. It depicts the almost unearthly beauty of these fragile, dangerous objects which rise in the night sky, seeming to imitate stars and planets, but which also sometimes fall flaming to earth, disrupting and destroying natural life. The animals in the poem, driven from their nests by a fallen balloon, emerge frightened and mystified, all, from the ancient owls to the baby rabbits, vulnerable in the face of this disaster. Even the ordinarily well-protected armadillo is defenseless before the incomprehensible and terrifying shower of fire.

The question for the critic of this poem is how Bishop shapes the reader's response to this beautiful and cruel event. One could say that the poem, by its factual presentation alone, asks us to recognize the chaos these illegal balloons generate. Yet, until the final stanza, there is little to indicate that Bishop's involvement in the scene is anything more than an aesthetic one. The dramatic beauty of the fire balloons and the vulnerable beauty of the animals are both described with equal power.

The distancing that goes on through most of "The Armadillo" is a way of keeping the poem free of a sentimentality that the depth of underlying feeling might generate. Although the beauty and delicacy of the finished work make this seem unlikely, less authorial control might well reduce it to moralizing (i.e. when men float fire balloons they may do violence to the natural life around them). Instead, Bishop exercises her command of the formal constituents of verse and her descriptive powers to hold the poem back from any easily paraphrasable "meaning" and to give it moral resonance.

The primary way Bishop manages this control is metrical variation. This form of variation is characteristic of Bishop's sure sense of herself: it shows her commanding tradition by apparently allowing her poems to develop spontaneously. At the same time that this variation gives the reader the impression that the poem is progressing naturally, however, it also carefully limits the intensity of response he can have to it. The habitually shifting rhythms of the poem do not allow the reader to lose himself in its lyric music; instead, they keep jolting him to recognition, thereby keeping him from "taking sides"—from becoming, that is, too caught up either in the beauty of the balloons or the terror of the animals.

The way this works is clear in these first stanzas:

> This is the time of year
> when almost every night
> the frail, illegal fire balloons appear.
> Climbing the mountain height,

rising towards a saint
still honored in these parts,
the paper chambers flush and fill with light
that comes and goes, like hearts.

Once up against the sky it's hard
to tell them from the stars—
planets, that is—the tinted ones;
Venus going down, or Mars,

or the pale green one. With a wind,
they flare and falter, wobble and toss;
but if it's still they steer between
the kite sticks of the Southern Cross

It would certainly not be true to say that these quatrains have no music. They do, but it is a distinctly variable one. The shift from two quatrains of three stress lines, each with a five stress third line that mirrors the appearance of the fire balloons and their flushing and filling with light, to the varying three and four stress lines of the next quatrains, keeps the reader constantly readjusting the meter in his head. Even in the first apparently regular stanzas there are examples of the roughness Bishop prefers: the first full sentence ends in the third, rather than in the fourth line of the opening stanza, countering the regular flow of the meter. And in the second stanza, the abab rhyme scheme shifts, retaining a hint of rhyme from the first stanza in "saint" and then picking up one of its full rhymes in "light," but setting the precedent for more variation in the following stanzas. Throughout the rest of the poem, the lines have either three or four stresses, but these stresses vary so from stanza to stanza that the poem projects a sense of constant shifting in spite of its recognizable lyric pattern.

With such extensive shifting it soon becomes clear that this is not simply the ordinary variation all good poets exercise to keep their poems from becoming too regular. Rather, it is variation that preserves a lyric quality while at the same time strictly delimiting lyric effusiveness. While reading this poem the reader is never allowed to forget himself and to be transported by the momentum of the verse. Instead, the metrical roughness keeps him detached, his attention concentrated on the complexity of the event the poet is describing.

Another characteristic technique Bishop uses to great effect in "The Armadillo" is that of drawing back from emotional intensity at just the point where a Romantic poet would allow such intensity to break through most completely. These stanzas from the center of the poem show something of how this works:

Last night another big one fell.
It splattered like an egg of fire
against the cliff behind the house.
The flame ran down. We saw the pair

of owls who nest there flying up
and up, their whirling black-and-white
stained bright pink underneath, until
they shrieked up out of sight.

The ancient owls' nest must have burned.
Hastily, all alone,
a glistening armadillo left the scene,
rose-flecked, head down, tail down,

and then a baby rabbit jumped out,
short-eared, to our surprise.
So soft!—a handful of intangible ash
with fixed, ignited eyes.

The medial pause of the final line of the first quatrain here, together with the series of enjambed lines following it, lead the reader to feel the fright and confusion of the owls, forced from their nest by the shattered balloon. But, typically, Bishop quickly draws back from this intensity. Just after this metrical excitement there is a change: the lines alter from the tetrameter of the former quatrains to three, four, and five stress lines, and the lines also become more end-stopped and more interrupted in their flow. This change mirrors the difference in the animals' response to their plight: the owls fly up shrieking, while the armadillo scurries away alone, and the baby rabbit jumps out, as if lost and mystified. Part of Bishop's achievement here is to catch the specific response of each animal and to convey it in the lyrical gesture of the verse as well as in the language.

But more important than the way Bishop catches the individual quality of each animal here is the way she controls the reader's response to the main event by choosing, just at this point, to reserve intensities and to begin patiently to *describe* the animals. The exactitude of the description determines the final meaning of the poem: it forces the reader to slow down and to visualize the particular vulnerability of each of these creatures when faced with this incendiary accident. Yet until the very end, Bishop directs the reader to the animals' trauma only obliquely, through the description itself, while the way she breaks and controls her verse holds him back from sympathizing with them too effusively. The italics which emphasize that the baby rabbit is "*short*-eared" physically stop the flow of the verse, obliterating much of the reader's momentary empathy for the animal by compelling him to focus on its physical uniqueness. And the exclamation "So soft!" to describe the rabbit is daring in another way. Its use of cliché is made to seem naive, as if Bishop were too unpracticed to find a more original way to describe the rabbit; but when followed by so subtle and exact a metaphor as "a handful of ash," the old cliché assumes renewed force, as if this direct simplicity were the only possible way to render the quality of the small animal. Again, the very fact of the exclamation keeps the reader from being spellbound by the ongoing impulse of the poetry.

After all this holding off, the final quatrain can be interpretive and dramatic without risking sentimentality:

> *Too pretty, dreamlike mimicry!*
> *O falling fire and piercing cry*
> *and panic, and a weak mailed fist*
> *clenched ignorant against the sky!*

All of the animals' panic and misery is conveyed in Bishop's own summation (italicized to separate it from the rest of the poem). In these final lines, their plight extends subtly to become our own. We, of course, understand the fire balloons. But, mailed as we are, with our own strength and intelligence, we cannot protect ourselves from the equally mystifying and terrible events that shake us. It is surely important to note, at this point, that Bishop dedicated this poem to Robert Lowell, who became a conscientious objector when the Allied command began fire-bombing German cities. Bishop's poem points directly to these fire-bombings, which wreaked the same kind of horrifying destruction on a part of our universe that the fire balloons wreak on the animals. In the last quatrain, the "mailed fist," besides being a familiar figure of speech for threats of war-making, represents the protective "armor" of a soldier which is suggested by the armadillo's carapace. The whole quatrain, with its exclamations and enjambed lines, leads upward in intensity to the expression of helplessness in the face of such terror. But because this intensity has been preceded by so much reticence, the emotion here seems earned. There is no sense of false moralizing about this poem; in fact, no sense of moralizing at all, although the moral dimension of the poem is inescapably present.

II

There are Bishop poems in which the proficiency apparent in "The Armadillo" gives the poetry not just the technical control, but also the special quality of reserve that is Bishop's hallmark. In an early poem like

"Large Bad Picture" it seems as if Bishop uses her technical command to place ironic distance between herself and her subject. But the matter does not settle itself so simply as that. Bishop's poetry often concerns her quest to belong somewhere, to find a home: "Large Bad Picture" expresses both Bishop's desire to establish connection with a member of her family she never knew, and her recognition that she has moved beyond the point where this connection is possible. This complicated attitude is conveyed in a poem which never mentions these matters at all, one where meaning is controlled through description and through the formal composition of the poem itself, not through any direct expression of attitude or opinion.

The entire poem describes a scene painted by Bishop's great-uncle of points somewhat to the north of where Bishop grew up. The picture is primitive art at its most primitive, appealing but unsophisticated: the painted waves running along the bay are "perfect" as real waves never are; the spars of the little ships are "burnt match-sticks," like a child's naive depiction of spars; and the birds "hanging in n's in banks" are "scribbled," not rendered, but only approximated as well as the artist's talent allows.

Bishop's emphasis on the technical aspects of the picture, like the title of the poem itself, shows her distinct awareness of the limitations of her great-uncle's art. On the other hand, her involvement with the picture obviously goes far beyond any objective judgment of it. Whatever artistic sophistication her ancestor lacked, his picture captures the essential mood of the scene well enough to make Bishop recognize her own attraction for such a landscape, and to impel her imagination onward. By the sixth quatrain she begins to live in the scene deeply enough to hear sounds in it. Even though she characteristically uses the impersonal "one" instead of "I," the reader perceives that she is caught up enough to hear the crying of the birds in the awesome, eerie landscape, and to catch the mysterious sighing of some great animal of the deep:

> One can hear their crying, crying,
> the only sound there is
> except for occasional sighing
> as a large aquatic animal breathes.

Yet by the end of the poem there is a paradoxical sense in which Bishop has both joined in the scene of the picture and remained separate from it:

> In the pink light
> the small red sun goes rolling, rolling,
> round and round and round at the same height
> in perpetual sunset, comprehensive, consoling,

> while the ships consider it.
> Apparently they have reached their destination.
> It would be hard to say what brought them there,
> commerce or contemplation.

This landscape is irresistible—anyone might be attracted by it. Those aboard the ships might well have been induced there by the same attractions that made Bishop's great-uncle wish to paint the scene, or that make Bishop herself admire it now. Seafarers, artist, and observer, in that case, are all linked in their shared appreciation. But this kind of Romantic merging, in which distant and separate people are brought spiritually close to one another, is countered by the technical limitations of the picture, which stop Bishop and do not allow her to go past a certain point in her interpretation of it. If the ships were more distinctly rendered by the painter it might indeed be possible to tell "what brought them there." But since they are not, the observer is necessarily kept at a distance from the scene.

What finally separates Bishop from her ancestor, however, and complicates the deep spiritual connection with him that the picture initiates, is Bishop's mastery of her craft. If the "large bad picture" is an example of naive art, the poem that describes it displays the technical command of an artist in such control that she makes her poem appear as simplistic as the picture, until a closer look reveals the difference. If there is condescension in the poem (and it seems to me there is a little), then it is not personal but artistic. It is not at all toward her uncle, with whom she clearly feels a deep kinship in spite of the fact she never met him, but toward the inherent technical limitations of the genre of art for which his talents suit him. The point is that her uncle loved the scene and was able to convey this love in an appealing but unsophisticated medium; but it is clear from the poem that if this is a medium Bishop appreciates, it is nevertheless one she has left far behind.

A closer look at "Large Bad Picture" shows how this is so. The poem looks at first as if it might be in regular ballad meter. In fact, however, the meter varies dramatically, and the poem as a whole cultivates a formal roughness that makes it seem the product of an artistically naive imagination. The poem begins with a quatrain in four stress lines that is made to look as if its pattern of rhyming might settle down to be aabb, if only the poet could manage it:

> Remembering the Strait of Belle Isle or
> some northerly harbor of Labrador,
> before he became a schoolteacher
> a great-uncle painted a big picture.

In the very next quatrain Bishop drops this playfully clumsy scheme, picking up alternating lines of four and three stresses and changing the rhyme to a true abcb:

> Receding for miles on either side
> into a flushed, still sky
> are overhanging pale blue cliffs
> hundreds of feet high

After two more quatrains that follow this pattern, the meter veers rapidly, changing four times in four stanzas and making the reader jolt and jog as he struggles to adapt to its changeable flow. The rhyme also occasionally augments this jolting, with such off rhymes as "ships" and "sticks" and "is" and "breathes."

Unlike the technical roughness of her great-uncle's picture, these jagged outcroppings are merely Bishop's imitations of roughness, which call attention to their creator's poetic refinement. And it is this refinement which finally separates Bishop from the great-uncle to whom the picture tantalizingly seems to offer access. In the uncle's picture, everything is cheerfully and awkwardly approximated, but in spite of the fact that the mood is caught exactly, the picture is limited by the attractive but narrow quality of the art. In Bishop's own poem, on the contrary, everything is unsaid, but in spite (or perhaps because) of its purposeful reticence and formal clumsiness, the reader is made to perceive a world of complicated emotion.

"Made to perceive" is a phrase worth emphasizing here, since the fact is that the formal strategy of the poem keeps the reader at a certain remove from Bishop's feelings. Still, it is this very remove that paradoxically makes the nexus of deep feeling at the poem's center more poignant to us. Bishop's unstated (perhaps not fully recognized) suffering is that she longs to be a part of that from which she has been cut off—not only by time and distance, but also by her gifts. The distance she has come as an artist is the distance she is removed from the uncle she never knew. She likes her uncle's picture, but while her personal feelings generate this affection, her artistic integrity forces her to judge the accomplishment, almost in spite of herself. Like many of us, she is nostalgic for a past she has gone beyond. The strength of the poem is that it allows us to share this longing and pain without either belaboring or sentimentalizing it. The reticence about the human emotion, all contained in what is unstated, makes the reader sense it more, not less, strongly. In the end, "Large Bad Picture" is a poem full of a nostalgic Romantic ardor, charged with Bishop's longing to be united with her past; but it is ardor in an unspoken dimension, countered by the poem's descriptive and technical accomplishment.

III

"The Armadillo" and "Large Bad Picture" are written in forms that Bishop adapted from traditional ones. Many of Bishop's major poems, however, like "The Man-Moth," "The Monument," "Over 2000 Illustrations and a Complete Concordance," "At the Fishhouses," "Brazil, January 1, 1502," and "Questions of Travel" are in free verse, or, as one might expect with Bishop, in her own version of free verse. In these longer poems Bishop often manipulates form in much the same way she does in her smaller lyrics. Her delicate exploitation of iambic pentameter in her free verse poems is an example of how she can use a regular meter to give intensity, and then shift the meter to pull it sharply back from this intensity.

One sees this technique at work in a rich and difficult poem like "The Monument." In the poem an admiring speaker seems to be describing an object to a second speaker, who resists seeing it as a work of art. Indeed, the monument is admittedly queer-looking, mysterious, and changeable in its form. The act of contemplating it occasions for Bishop the creation of a poetics, in which the monument becomes the symbol for that noble artistic presence which cannot be defined or explained, but is a product of knowledge, imagination, and faith.

The poem is constructed as a dialogue, predominantly in free verse. Bishop varies its progression several times, most pointedly in one of its important and difficult lines:

> The monument is one-third set against
> a sea; two-thirds against a sky.
> The view is geared
> (that is, the view's perspective)
> so low there is no "far away,"
>
> aňd wé | aře fár | ăwáy | wĭthín | thĕ view.

In these lines, the speaker attempts to break down the barrier between the monument and the observer, implicating the observer in the structure of the work of art itself. Bishop underlines the importance of this implication by allowing the meter, at just this significant moment, to break into metrical regularity and to carry the poem along:

> A sea of narrow, horizontal boards
> lies out behind our lonely monument,
> its long grains alternating right and left
> like floor-boards—spotted, swarming-still,

> and motionless. A sky runs parallel,
> and it is palings, coarser than the sea's:
> splintery sunlight and long-fibred clouds.

After the pentameter has temporarily prevailed, the second speaker begins his prosaic questioning, and free verse again returns to deflect the flow of the poem and to keep the reader from losing himself in the first speaker's magical description.

This technique—of allowing the poem to break in and out of pentameter—is used in varying degrees and with varying effects in other major poems such as "Over 2000 Illustrations and a Complete Concordance," or "Brazil, January 1, 1502." In the latter, Bishop injects a line of pentameter here and there toward the end of the poem before she allows it to break fully into pentameter just before its intense conclusion. She even carries over this technique to a poem that has some five stress lines, but no pentameter at all, "At the Fishhouses":

> I have seen it over and over, the same sea, the same,
> slightly, indifferently swinging above the stones,
> icily free above the stones,
> above the stones and then the world.
> If you should dip your hand in,
> your wrist would ache immediately,
> your bones would begin to ache and your hand would burn
> as if the water were a transmutation of fire
> that feeds on stones and burns with a dark gray flame.
> If you tasted it, it would first taste bitter,
> then briny, then surely burn your tongue.
> It is like what we imagine knowledge to be:
> dark, salt, clear, moving, utterly free,
> drawn from the cold hard mouth
> of the world, derived from the rocky breasts
> forever, flowing and drawn, and since
> our knowledge is historical, flowing, and flown.

Here at the magnificent end of her poem, Bishop twice deflects lyrical intensity. In the first instance, the anaphora which conveys the power of the sea ("the *same* sea, the *same*, / . . . swinging *above the stones*, / icily free *above the stones*, / *above the stones* and then the world") is countered by the mundane conditional clause ("*If* you should dip your hand in"). After bringing the reader down to earth this way, Bishop builds the verse again, and then once more ("If you tasted it") brings it down before she allows it to swing lyrically into its passionate conclusion. These interruptions do not permanently counteract the Romantic impulse of a poem which mystically identifies the cold northern waters of Nova Scotia as the n inexplicable power. But they do *curb* this impulse by metrically, as well as thematically, recalling the reader to the pragmatic expressions of everyday life, and by firmly keeping him from sentimentalizing the power of the primal source Bishop is conjuring.

IV

Bishop's recent book, *Geography III*, shows her using meter and versification to move even farther in the direction her earlier lyrics suggest. In these newer poems there is an increased tendency not just to pull back from a lyric intensity that might allow sentimentality, but sometimes to hold back from this intensity altogether. One way Bishop manages this is to make use of meters which have only two or three stresses to a line.

In the first poem of this book, "In the Waiting Room," Bishop describes going to the dentist's office as a small child with her aunt and sitting in the waiting room while her aunt's teeth are attended to. The experience of seeing pictures of naked African women, a shocking and frightening experience for a young North American girl, of sensing the unattractive presence of other patients around her, and of hearing her aunt's cry of pain from the inner office as if it were her own, gives Bishop an alarming sensation of the strangeness of her existence and of her uncomfortable connection with the rest of humanity. Since the poem is partly about a child's discovery of her own mortality, the waiting room becomes not merely a place where Bishop awaits her aunt, but, by extension, a place where she begins to await her death.

> I said to myself: three days
> and you'll be seven years old.
> I was saying it to stop
> the sensation of falling off
> the round, turning world
> into cold, blue-black space.
>
> I knew that nothing stranger
> had ever happened, that nothing
> stranger could ever happen.
> Why should I be my aunt,
> or me, or anyone?
> What similarities—
> boots, hands, the family voice
> I felt in my throat, or even

the *National Geographic*
and those awful hanging breasts—
held us all together
or made us all just one?

This moment of sudden awareness is obviously one of great emotional intensity for Bishop, a "spot of time" that causes her momentarily to lose ordinary consciousness and penetrate life more deeply. Yet the verse that describes the experience holds the reader back from immediately sharing it. Bishop's rather awkward three stress lines here vary rhetorically, but they do not otherwise bend or give—three stress lines in English simply do not have that flexibility. The reader, then, is made to follow this dramatic moment in a kind of flattened verse that leaves him reflecting on, rather than immediately engaging in, the experience with the poet. It is not that the poem does not contain deep feeling or that it does not have emotional impact; but the feeling is tightly controlled by the formal configuration of the words, which keep it from being either cheap or easy, and the impact is deflected to give it subtler resonance.

It is a tribute to Bishop's technical excellence that she is able to produce an important poem in such a meter. What stands behind her achievement is the free verse movement, which taught poets how to use what Williams called the "variable foot" to give poems more flexibility of manner than stricter forms allowed. If one scans a few passages of "In the Waiting Room," one finds that, as in any good free verse poem, the feet vary from line to line to keep the poem from monotony and to give it rhetorical scope:

I knéw | that nóthing | stránger
had éver | háppened, | that nóthing
stránger | could éver | háppen.

Hów— | I dídn't | knów any
wórd for it | hów "un | líkely" . . .
Hów had I | cóme to | be hére

Here the line break and meter in the first passage focus attention on the important word "stranger," and the variable feet in the second passage emphasize Bishop's existential puzzlement. But while the variable feet give the lines rhetorical latitude as they do in free verse lines, the actual three stress meter of the poem restricts the poem's direct emotional appeal more than might be true in a free verse poem of irregular line lengths. Once again Bishop has adapted tradition to her own ends: instead of using the variable foot to intensify the emotional appeal of a poem, she uses it to give rhetorical variation to a meter that limits this appeal.

Finally, in a poem like "The End of March," one is able to see how reluctant Bishop is to allow technical intensity and thematic passion to correspond in her work. She parcels out her poem's appeal to the reader's emotions charily, using prose passages to contradict what she expressly states, and lyric passages to imply what she is disinclined to make plain. Prose passages are hardly new in Bishop's poetry; they have been there almost from the beginning in poems like "The Bight," "At the Fishhouses," "Cape Breton," and "Manuelzinho." In *Geography III*, however, these passages grow more frequent, conveying the impression that as Bishop's security as a poet has solidified (Bishop has always shown great self-assurance in her writing) she has felt free to include more of these prose passages in her poems.

In "The End of March," for example, fully one third of the poem is prose arranged in verse lines. The poem concerns a walk along a Duxbury beach on a cold, windy, changeable day at the end of winter, and Bishop's desire to reach a rickety house she has spotted on her walk. The house represents a retreat and a release from a world where, as Bishop confides in "Five Flights Up," the final poem of the book, yesterdays are "almost impossible to lift." Living in such a place, one could occupy oneself merely by existing, enjoying the experience of life in its purest, most self-indulgent form. In fact, however, Bishop soon admits that such a dream is "impossible." The house is boarded up—one could not even get into it. And then the day is too cold to allow Bishop to get that far anyway.

Bishop calls the shack a "proto-dream-house," a "crypto-dream-house," and thematically presents it as an unattainable ideal to be approached but never reached. Yet, while the words say one thing, the metrical impulse of the poem communicates precisely the opposite to the reader. The passage in which Bishop describes the house and her wish to reach it contains far and away the most neutral, prose-like writing of the poem:

> I wanted to get as far as my proto-dream-house,
> my crypto-dream-house, that crooked box
> set up on pilings, shingled green,
> a sort of artichoke of a house, but greener
> (boiled with bicarbonate of soda?),
> protected from spring tides by a palisade
> of—are they railroad ties?
>
> There must be a stove; there *is* a chimney,
> askew, but braced with wires,
> and electricity, possibly

> —at least, at the back another wire
> limply leashes the whole affair
> to something off behind the dunes.

Everything in the diction and movement of the verse here—its ordinariness, its prosy, conversational sound and flow, as if Bishop were simply talking to the reader—works to diminish the excitement of the ideal she is imagining. Here is the "naturalness" Bishop likes, with a vengeance.

There is real verbal and metrical excitement in this poem, however, at its conclusion:

> For just a minute, set in their bezels of sand,
> the drab, damp, scattered stones
> were multi-colored,
> and all those high enough threw out long shadows,
> individual shadows, then pulled them in again.
> They could have been teasing the lion sun,
> except that now he was behind them
> —a sun who'd walked the beach that last low tide,
> making those big, majestic paw-prints,
> who perhaps had batted a kite out of the sky to play with.

Although in the poem Bishop leads the reader to believe she longs for life in the "crooked box" house, the beauty of the language and the movement of the verse show that she finds considerable pleasure in living in a world as vast and unknowable as the house is self-contained and intelligible. The forces she describes in this last passage seem beneficent ones: the great rocks come alive as playful beings, capable of "teasing" a receptive "lion sun," who like a small cub might take enjoyment in batting around a kite. But the energy behind all this playfulness is potentially tremendous and terrifying. The description here is of a universe where immense and dangerous power is contained but smouldering. The sun may act like a cub, but it is actually the "lion sun," a force of nature as capable of destroying men's kites (and men themselves) as it is of playing with them.

The quality of the sun as it is presented here is the quality of the end of March itself, a time when elemental forces first begin to seem friendly and contained, but are lurking dangerously in the atmosphere nonetheless. The dynamic way in which Bishop allows these lines to swing into a kind of lyric movement that is often rationed in her poetry shows that this is an energy Bishop values too much to make the other, more passive state her permanent ideal, no matter what she says directly. In fact, the final five lines of the poem make their own small, passionately lyrical stanza—two lines of pentameter, interspersed with two four stress lines, and completed by a long six stress line. Their climactic movement works to persuade the reader that, while Bishop says she longs for a rickety house on a hill, what she actually values is the large, dangerous universe where "all the untidy activity continues, / awful but cheerful."

The point here is that Bishop's daydream—the thing she says, however whimsically and momentarily, she desires—is described in the most flat, dead-pan verse, while a deeper, unspoken ideal is conveyed by the later momentum of the poetry. Significantly, Bishop releases her poem lyrically only at a moment which is not explicitly its thematic high point. Of course this moment becomes its high point, but that is another matter. The important fact is that Bishop seems reluctant to allow metrical intensity and plain-spokenness to correspond, as if she were afraid that the one might spoil or cheapen the other. In this case she uses this reluctance, craftily, to give the poem a more intricate resonance than it otherwise might have had.

V

What this essay has meant partly to address is the way that the reticence of Bishop's poetry is related to the intensity of feeling at its core. It is sometimes assumed that the cool surfaces of Bishop's poems reveal their lack of emotional depth; in fact, Bishop often uses such reticence as a strategy to make a deeper, more complex emotional appeal to the reader. Meter is one means by which she achieves this reticence, one technique she uses to circumscribe feelings so strong that their expression in unremittingly lyrical terms might make her poems seem easy or cloying to contemporary tastes. Such refined use of a technical aspect of poetry adds subtlety to utterance, and seems to me one of the less-recognized reasons that Bishop's poetry has retained its freshness and interest.

DAVID LEHMAN

"In Prison":
A Paradox Regained

Traditionally, poets have dwelled in paradoxical prisons. To enter bonds of queen and country is to affirm one's freedom, Donne seductively argued; Lovelace, equally extravagant if less playful, insisted on liberty as a function of spiritual innocence. He denied not the actuality of stone walls and iron bars, just their right to cohere into prisons and cages, in a passage that schoolchildren were presumed once upon a time to know by heart:

> If I have freedom in my love,
>   And in my soul am free,
> Angels alone, that soar above
>   Enjoy such liberty.
> ("To Althea, from Prison")

If Lovelace could look upon imprisonment as "an hermitage," a time to rededicate himself to a courtly ideal, Hamlet's princely mobility could scarcely preclude a bout of claustrophobia. "Denmark's a prison," he announces, and follows with a characteristic verbal gesture, robust hyperbole collapsing into poignantly prosaic understatement:

> O God, I could be bounded in a nutshell and
> count myself a king of infinite space, were it not
> that I have bad dreams.
>   (act 2, scene 2)

From *Elizabeth Bishop and Her Art*, edited by Lloyd Schwartz and Sybil P. Estess. Copyright © 1983 by The University of Michigan. University of Michigan Press, 1983.

It is, as Hamlet acknowledges, a classic opposition of mind and matter. Whatever his present difficulties, he does not doubt the mind's supremacy over the world it beholds: "There is nothing either good or bad but thinking makes it so." As far as Hamlet is concerned, man's potential to breathe the infinite space of angels is, despite the narrow dimensions of his cell, still available, though not right here, not just now.

It would be interesting to determine when *despite* in that last clause turned into *because of*, when the emphasis shifted and poets actively sought a species of imprisonment because only there would the soul learn true freedom, or goodness, or the peace that passeth understanding. The argument, a recurrent one in medieval Christian theology, has in effect been rewritten, its paradox completed, by agents of the Romantic imagination. In the same spirit in which he commends duty as the "Stern Daughter of the Voice of God," Wordsworth solemnly wills a curtailment of his freedom, identifying form as a necessary jail in his sonnet on the sonnet:

> In truth the prison, unto which we doom
> Ourselves, no prison is: and hence for me,
> In sundry moods, 'twas pastime to be bound
> Within the Sonnet's scanty plot of ground;
> Pleased if some Souls (for such there needs must be)
> Who have felt the weight of too much liberty,
> Should find brief solace there, as I have found.
> ("Nuns Fret Not At Their Convent's Narrow Room")

To Paul Pennyfeather, the beleaguered hero of Evelyn Waugh's *Decline and Fall*, prison ironically allows for the autonomy of the self, its independence from social pressures, its release from "the weight of too much liberty":

> The next four weeks of solitary confinement were among the happiest of Paul's life. . . . It was so exhilarating, he found, never to have to make any decision on any subject, to be wholly relieved from the smallest consideration of time, meals, or clothes, to have no anxiety ever about what kind of impression he was making; in fact, to be free . . . there was no need to shave, no hesitation about what tie he should wear, none of the fidgeting with studs and collars and links that so distracts the waking moments of civilized man. He felt like the happy people in the advertisements for shaving soap who seem to have achieved very simply that peace of mind so distant and so desirable in the early morning.

A comic gloss on Lovelace's "To Althea, from Prison," the chapter in which this passage appears has the title "Stone Walls Do Not A Prison Make"; not surprisingly, a later chapter is called "Nor Iron Bars A Cage."

As we proceed from *despite* to *because,* we move as well from a conception of the imagination as that which redeems reality to a conception of the imagination as, in the last analysis, sufficient unto itself. A clear statement of this last analysis is found in J. K. Huysmans' *À Rebours,* which develops the logic of the prison paradox into an aesthetic principle. The protagonist of that novel ingeniously devises a means by which to travel without ever having to leave his room, secure a passport, book passage, pack bags, or say farewell—without, in short, any of the inconveniences of actuality. "Travel, indeed, struck him as being a waste of time, since he believed that the imagination could provide a more-than-adequate substitute for the vulgar reality of actual experience." Two poets upon whom Elizabeth Bishop has exerted a powerful influence, James Merrill and John Ashbery, offer inspired variations on this theme of the stationary traveler. More a *récit* than a short story, Merrill's "Peru: The Landscape Game" describes a trip to the land of the Incas; the poet plans to go there, but it is his anticipation of the place that he records, a Platonic reality too good not to be true. The imagination acts, as it were, in self-defense, as it spins out an eternal possibility, proof against the disappointment Wordsworth experienced when he saw Mont Blanc:

How to find the right words for a new world?

> One way would be to begin, before ever leaving home, with some anticipatory jottings such as these. Then, even if the quetzal turns out to be extinct, if sure-footed grandmothers from Tulsa overrun the ruins, and Porfirio's baby has a harelip and there are cucarachas in the Hotel Périchole, the visitor may rest easy. Nothing can dim his first, radiant impressions.

Such "jottings," intended for perusal on the ride down to Lima, give new meaning to the idea of flight insurance.

Ashbery too would seem to subscribe to Verlaine's notion that "every landscape is a state of mind." From his vantage point in an office building more than a thousand miles away, the speaker of Ashbery's "The Instruction Manual" takes us on a guided tour of Guadalajara, "City I wanted most to see, and most did not see, in Mexico!" The task of writing "the instruction manual on the uses of a new metal" serves as the launching pad for this mental flight, this enchanted product of an imagining. "How limited, but how complete withal, has been our experience of Guadalajara!" the speaker can exclaim upon his return to the desk he never had to leave. Amusing as that statement is, it tells its sober truth about the poetic process. On paper the poet flies to Peru or Guadalajara not as places but as names, words, sounds; one arrives at "the imagination of the sound—a place." This is the conclusion reached by A. R. Ammons in his poem "Triphammer Bridge":

> *sanctuary, sanctuary,* I say it over and over and the
> word's sound is the one place to dwell: that's it, just
> the sound, and the imagination of the sound—a place.

By delineating the progression from "wanted . . . to see" to "did not see" to "I fancy I see, under the press of having to write the instruction manual," Ashbery's poem makes a further point. It is as though a condition of absence were a prerequisite for the adventurous imagination. So we are directly told in another of Ashbery's early poems, "Le Livre est sur la table":

> All beauty, resonance, integrity,
> Exist by deprivation or logic
> Of strange position.

The proposition that the imagination varies directly with deprivation and isolation, that imaginative need mothers invention, and that physical confinement is conducive to spiritual freedom, receives full treatment in Elizabeth Bishop's early and remarkably prescient short story (or *récit*), "In Prison." This account of an ideal "life-sentence" contains the seed Ashbery would cultivate in "The Instruction Manual," even as it makes the case for creative misreading, for what Harold Bloom, like Miss Bishop a mapmaker, calls "misprision":

> I understand that most prisons are now supplied with libraries and that the prisoners are expected to read the *Everyman's Library* and other books of educational tendencies. I hope I am not being too reactionary when I say that my one desire is to be given one very dull book to read, the duller the better. A book, moreover, on a subject completely foreign to me; perhaps the second volume, if the first would familiarize me too well with the terms and purpose of the work. Then I shall be able to experience with a free conscience the pleasure, perverse, I suppose, of interpreting it not at all according to its intent. Because I share with Valery's M. *Teste* the "knowledge that our thoughts are reflected back to us, too much so, through expressions made by others"; and I have resigned myself, or do I speak too frankly, to deriving what information and joy I can from this—lamentable but irremediable—state of affairs. From my detached rock-like book I shall be able to draw vast generalizations, abstractions of the grandest, most illuminating sort, like allegories or poems, and by posing fragments of it against the surroundings and conversations of my prison, I shall be able to form my own examples of surrealist art!—something I should never know how to do outside, where the sources are so bewildering. Perhaps it will be a book on the cure of a

disease, or an industrial technique,—but no, even to try to imagine the subject would be to spoil the sensation of wave-like freshness I hope to receive when it is first placed in my hands.

In Miss Bishop's later work, a quite explicit echo of this passage occurs in "The End of March" where, in a tone more wistful than whimsical, the writer describes her "proto-dream-house," a "dubious" structure that tallies in a great many particulars with her earlier version of prison as paradise:

> I'd like to retire there and do *nothing,*
> or nothing much, forever, in two bare rooms:
> look through binoculars, read boring books,
> old, long, long books, and write down useless notes,
> talk to myself, and, foggy days,
> watch the droplets slipping, heavy with light.

Indeed, for the way it prefigures attitudes and motifs that we encounter not only in *Geography III* but throughout the poet's career, "In Prison" commends itself to critical inspections over and beyond its intrinsic merits, considerable though these are. Here we find, at however ironic a remove, a defense of her "mentality," her faith in "the power of details" as momentary stays against confusion, her stance as a quiet non-conformist, whose individuality of style is something subtle enough to flourish within a regimented order. The insouciance of "One Art," the ironic process by which defeat turns into victory, is anticipated in the story; here is an initial statement of the dialectical tension between autobiographical disaster and artistic mastery, a tension central to the villanelle and one that lurks beneath the surface of the prose poem "12 O'Clock News" with its military metaphors for the act of writing. Moreover, "In Prison" contains information helpful for us to understand the painterly disposition of a poet who continually derived inspiration, as well as subject matter, from objects and apparitions, large bad pictures and tiny ones ("About the size of an old-style dollar bill"), and seascapes disguised as animated "cartoon[s] by Raphael for a tapestry for a Pope."

The strategy for reading that Miss Bishop proffers points to the governing conceit of the story, "the pleasure, perverse, I suppose, of interpreting it not at all according to its intent"—*it* standing here for prison, which willful mis-interpretation renders to mean the inner life of the imagination, the "real life" of the soul. The narrative starts with a flip reversal of Joseph K.'s predicament in *The Trial:* like Kafka's protagonist, Miss Bishop's persona has committed no crime, but there the resemblance ends. He positively wants what Joseph K. dreads; nor is it a case, as it is for the latter, of irrational guilt seeking to justify its existence. Once arrested, Joseph K. never doubts his guilt, even while ostensibly seeking to prove his innocence; Miss Bishop's nameless character runs no risk of arrest since, in order to attain the imprisonment he "can scarcely wait for," he seems prepared to do precious little and certainly nothing criminal, unless criminality be defined in the singular way attributed to Edgar Degas in "Objects & Apparitions": " 'One has to commit a painting,' said Degas, / 'the way one commits a crime.' " But if the poet adopts this position, it is without political intent or fanfare. The pun on "sentence" in the phrase "life-sentence" may get us nearer the truth; from one point of view the writer may be said to serve successive "sentences." Be that as it may, the author of "In Prison" strikes the pose of a young Hegelian, wishing literally to make a virtue of necessity. Our hero has been chosen by prison, he would say; the will is needed not to act upon this destiny but to acquiesce before it, to accept what he conceives as "necessity." Given his definition of freedom, only an attitude of passive non-resistance will do, only the passive voice will be strictly accurate. Notice the grammatical ambiguity that closes the story:

> You may say,—people have said to me—you would have been happy in the more flourishing days of the religious order, and that, I imagine, is close to the truth. But even there I hesitate, and the difference between Choice and Necessity jumps up again to confound me. "Freedom is knowledge of necessity"; I believe nothing as ardently as I do that. And I assure you that to act in this way is the only logical step for me to take. I mean, of course, to be acted *upon* in this way is the only logical step for me to take.

Justice is beside the point. It is clear we are talking metaphorically, not about guilt and punishment, but about the self and its need to make peace with the certitude of loss. To volunteer for prison is to plan a journey into the interior, confident that in the exchange of physical liberty for imaginative freedom one has, philosophically speaking, struck a good bargain, given up the apparent, embraced the real. Like Ashbery's dreary office building, prison affords both the opportunity and the motive for metaphor, but a far more urgent task also confronts the prisoner. It will be his audacious enterprise to establish an idealized dwelling place within the least likely, least congenial, of quarters; like Crusoe on his island, he will attempt to convert an alien landscape into one that responds to his humanity. It is almost as though he (or his author) were consciously designing a test for "one" art—singular, definitive of the poet's identity—an art that feeds on what might otherwise consume it, that thrives on loss, that welcomes limits in order to transcend them. We are, in sum, solidly within the walls of a conceit, a paradox regained, a cliché renewed in surprising ways. At one point at least, prison metaphorically dramatizes the situation of the writer, any writer conscious of his belatedness. Thus, referring to the "Writing on the Wall," our would-be prisoner announces his intention to "read very carefully (or try to read, since they may be partly obliterated, or in a foreign language) the inscriptions already there. Then I shall adapt my own compositions, in order that they may not conflict with those written by the prisoner before me. The voice of a new inmate will be noticeable, but there will be no contradictions or criticisms of what has already been laid down, rather a 'commentary.' I have thought of attempting a short, but immortal, poem, but I am afraid that is beyond me; I may rise to the occasion, however, once I am confronted with that stained, smeared, scribbled-on wall and feel the stub of pencil or rusty nail between my fingers." The sense of postponement here as elsewhere in the piece reinforces our impression of it as an initial statement of purpose, a warm-up for the main event yet to come, the time of confrontation, pencil stub in hand, "with that stained, smeared, scribbled-on wall" of poetic tradition.

What makes "In Prison" work so well is that, having subtly and very quickly established the figurative nature of the writing, Miss Bishop ironically becomes a literalist of the imagination, specifying the exact dimensions of the cell, describing its walls and window and the view from the window with painterly precision, ruling out such surrogates for prison as monasteries. To live, in a shabby hotel room, "as if I were in prison"? No, the narrator says, that won't do. Nor will what we now call a country-club prison, the sort of place that has temporarily housed persons of a certain class convicted of wrongdoing with relation to the Watergate burglary and cover-up. Joining the navy is likewise eliminated from consideration, though on different grounds: not so much because it would parody "my real hopes," but for the telling reason that "there is something fundamentally uncongenial about the view of the sea to a person of my mentality." Why? Because, we may infer, it is the very symbol of the lawless and limitless and as such must clash with the mentality that yearns for fixed borders; also because the sea's vastness and essential unity threaten to drown out all details, all the "slight differences" that strike the poet as inherently valuable. The sea's great expanse is a needless luxury, a point implicitly made in that portion of the story given over to a mock-review of the literature of incarceration. Oscar Wilde is rebuked for the self-pitying note that mars "The Ballad of Reading Gaol." " 'That little tent of blue, Which prisoners call the sky,' strikes me as absolute nonsense. I believe that even a keyhole of sky would be enough, in its blind, blue endlessness, to give someone, even someone who had never seen it before, an adequate idea of the sky." The "romantic tunnel-digging" of *The Count of Monte Cristo* is also rejected by this early spokesman for Miss Bishop's views, this hard-liner impatient with sentimental formulae. What is desired, after all, is not an escape from, but an escape into, the unadorned cell of consciousness.

As in "Crusoe in England," it is a persona and not the poet who does the talking in "In Prison." To make sure we realize this, Miss Bishop takes pains to distinguish the speaker's gender from her own. (He has thought of enlisting in the armed services—and of playing on the prison baseball team.) The distance thus created between writer and text sets ironies in motion, but these seem otherwise directed than at the speaker's expense. Rather, they work to effect a delicate interplay between order and chance, limitation and space, determinism and free will, the philosophical dualities that energize the story. If one's reading consist of a single book, and that a boring one, one can multiply it by a theoretically infinite number of misreadings, magical as lies. If one's view be restricted to a bare cobblestone courtyard, framed by the window so that it takes on the aspect of a painting, its boundaries severely defined, its activity therefore rescued from disorder, it is nevertheless a series of paintings in one, and within its order there is plenty of room for chance; vagaries of weather ensure the possibility of variations galore, as Monet demonstrated with his cathedrals and haystacks, products of the changing light. The confinement, then, is meant not to eliminate dealings with the external world but to circumscribe the relations and, by doing so, to put them on an aesthetic plane. What one sees becomes an ever-changing picture, what one reads, an occasion for the imagination to roam free. If, for the aesthete's ends, what barely suffices ("a keyhole of sky") is deemed better than a surfeit, that is partially because it underscores an important truth about poetic knowledge. All that we can know are parts and fragments; by the same token, each part, each detail, acts as a synecdoche, pointing to a potential whole, a design the mind must intuit or invent. "I expect to go to prison in full possession of my 'faculties,' " the speaker says. "In fact," he adds, "it is not until I am securely installed there that I expect fully to realize them." In short, the prison of his aspirations is nothing like a place of asylum, refuge from trouble, a rest cure; on the contrary, his sentence will tax, and reward, his powers of imagination. And one can go further: one can say too that he plots his prison itinerary for reasons similar to those that elsewhere impel Miss Bishop's "I" and fellow travellers to undertake journeys to unfamiliar places that call "home" into question. A fantasized excursion to prison can give rise to such "questions of travel" as Miss Bishop will pose in a memorable poem:

"Is it lack of imagination that makes us come
to imagined places, not just stay at home?
Or could Pascal have been not entirely right
about just sitting quietly in one's room?

Continent, city, country, society:
the choice is never wide and never free.
And here, or there . . . No. Should we have stayed at home,
wherever that may be?"

Such interrogations yield no answers, only suasions, and these subject to
change. "In Prison" leans one way, *Questions of Travel* the other. But
whatever the differences in their attitudes to travel, the restless geographer and the secluded inmate have an ultimate direction in common, an
ultimate task in which their opposing inclinations will equally culminate—
the making of the map of an identity.

As a theory of imagination which is necessarily a theory of absence, "In Prison" prepares us well for the projects of Miss Bishop's mature
poetry. It is remarkable how often she turns to imagery of room, cell,
cage, and box, and usually within the context of an aesthetic inquiry; she
has a penchant for illustrating her sense of art by postulating constructions
the shape of boxes or made of them. Take "The Monument," which traces
the growth of a work of art from "piled-up boxes" to "a temple of crates."
Its external appearance seems to some extent a subordinate value; it functions to safeguard "what is within," about which it is protectively reticent:

It may be solid, may be hollow.
The bones of the artist-prince may be inside
or far away on even drier soil.
But roughly but adequately it can shelter
what is within (which after all
cannot have been intended to be seen.)

A "crooked box," the dream house of "The End of March" is prison-like
in more ways than one, a rough but adequate shelter with constraints
enough to provide the stimulus, if not the necessity, for creative action.
And in "Objects & Apparitions," Miss Bishop's translation of Octavio
Paz's homage to the boxes of Joseph Cornell, the paradox of a nutshell's
infinite space is immediately articulated:

Hexahedrons of wood and glass,
scarcely bigger than a shoebox,
with room in them for night and all its lights.

Monuments to every moment,
refuse of every moment, used:
cages for infinity.

Cornell's boxes have been characterized as "monumental on a tiny scale";
the phrase is not without relevance to Miss Bishop's art. The impulse
toward this peculiar brand of monumentality combines with the conceit of
the "enormous" room most notably, perhaps, in "12 O'Clock News," in
which the writer's desk and the objects on it are magnified (and mis-
translated), seen as through the eyes of a Lilliputian, with results at once
humorous and touching.

Paradise, as Elizabeth Bishop with tongue-biting irony conceives it,
has a precedent in "The Great Good Place" Henry James described, as
these sentences from James's story make clear: "Slowly and blissfully he
read into the general wealth of his comfort all the particular absences of
which it was composed. One by one he touched, as it were, all the things
it was such rapture to be without." The tone (and much else) is different,
but the sentiment the same, in "One Art." There the disaster-prone are
advised to "Lose something every day" and then to "practice losing
farther, losing faster." The imperative seems at first purely ironic, a way to
keep anguish and dread at bay, to avoid giving in to self-pity. But the
ironist's supreme gesture is to mean just what she says, contrary to
appearances as well as expectations. Miss Bishop does, at least in one
sense, recommend that we go about losing things, not so much because
this will prepare us for the major losses inevitably to follow, but because
the experience of loss humanizes us; it shows us as we are, vulnerable,
pathetic, and yet heroic in our capacity to endure and to continue our
affirming acts amid conditions less than propitious. When Miss Bishop
talks of losing as an art she does not mean losing well; it's not a matter of
good sportsmanship or "grace under pressure." On the one hand, she
means considerably less: it isn't hard to master what comes naturally to us:
we are always losing things, from our innocence to our parents to our
house keys: that is why *lose* was the perfect syllepsis for Alexander Pope.
Yet "the art of losing" is a wonderfully ambiguous phrase, and the ability
to reconcile its two meanings—to experience loss as itself a remedy for
loss—constitutes a powerful poetic gesture, whose success may be measured by the poet's skillful handling of the villanelle's intricate form in the
face of all that militates against order and arrangement.

In "The Poet," Emerson wrote that "every thought is also a prison;
every heaven is also a prison." Not the least virtue of Elizabeth Bishop's
poetry is that, from the start, it shows us the truth that remains when
Emerson's terms are reversed.

SANDRA McPHERSON

"The Armadillo":
A Commentary

I don't know if there will be Elizabeth Bishop scholars making their living writing exegesis-after-theoretical-analysis of her poems. Because those poems seem supremely self-sufficient. Nonetheless, every year some student says, "I bought the Bishop like you said; sometime could you tell me what's so great about her?" Then I try to think back to before I knew her, so my judgment will not be colored by personal loyalty. At age 21 or 22, I felt that I needed to read EB to learn how to use *anything* as the subject of the poem or as an object in the poem. Her work said, if you like things enough they'll stay alive even in a poem, whatever their nature. And another thing: her work *didn't* say "I am a poet." In fact, the *I* was omitted from her work for pages on end, the better to show her affection for her subjects.

One can't add to "The Armadillo." It happens to be the Fourth of July and we can hear illegal noises of shock and delight. I have never seen fire balloons, though. For six stanzas we watch her guide us through them, before we come to the animals. The poem is 60% balloon, 13% owl, 13% rabbit, 13% armadillo—a strange proportion. One of her trademarks is taking time to notice details and to state them in the slowed-down wording of musing; the third through fifth lines of this passage, for instance—

> Once up against the sky it's hard
> to tell them from the stars—

From *Field: Contemporary Poetry and Poetics* 31 (Fall 1984), [pp. 14–16]. Copyright © 1984 by Oberlin College.

> planets, that is—the tinted ones;
> Venus going down, or Mars,
>
> or the pale green one.

We're glad she didn't know the name of "the pale green one." That wording makes her an observer, not an expert in an observatory. Again, when "a baby rabbit jumped out, / *short*-eared, to our surprise," she is not so startled by the flashier fire balloons that she can't save a line for both the short ears and her surprise.

In this poem she's skillful at both slow and quick portraiture. The patient portrayal of the balloons through eighteen applicable verbs; the quickly-realized sketch of the "glistening armadillo . . . / rose-flecked, head down, tail down / . . . and a weak mailed fist / clenched ignorant against the sky."

The last stanza is something I wouldn't have predicted from Miss Bishop. An outcry in italics. Every emotion (beauty, mockery, fear, panic, anger, frustration, bafflement) is highlighted and exclamation-marked. This is the conclusion to her patient lines. She began saying this was the time of year such events happen. I like this poem partly because this is the time of *life* they happen. And I fear the poem because this is the century, the administration [Reagan], in which they happen to those whose armor is weakest.

DAVID WALKER

"Filling Station":
Elizabeth Bishop and the Ordinary

To read through Elizabeth Bishop's poems, now collected under one elegant roof, is to re-experience all those qualities for which she is celebrated, not least her skills as guide to the marvelous and the arcane. As the titles of her individual volumes suggest, Bishop was fascinated by the experience of travel, the extremes of geography and the varieties of human experience. Her precise and penetrating sense of observation allows us to visit landscapes from Cape Breton to Key West, from Paris to Mexico and her tapestried, extravagant Brazil. Her taste for the extraordinary also produced poems displaced into the strange worlds of history ("Brazil, January 1, 1502"), myth ("The Gentleman of Shalott," "The Prodigal"), and literature ("Crusoe in England"). What keeps these poems from representing mere exotica or a tourist's souvenirs is that Bishop herself always remains present as a kind of balancing or qualifying element, never content simply to accept the glittering surface as given, always probing for the echo of something richer and more resonant beneath. The details of Bishop's poems are always compelling, but they are never the whole point, even in those apparently most purely "descriptive." The true subject of the travel poems is the mysterious act of perception by means of which we learn to distinguish ourselves from the peculiar landscape and the bizarre artifact, and also to discover what binds us to them.

Perhaps less often recognized is Bishop's interest in the plainly and

From *Field: Contemporary Poetry and Poetics* 31 (Fall 1984), [pp. 34–39]. Copyright © 1984 by Oberlin College.

even stubbornly ordinary. Her curiosity extends to the mundane and the banal, the universal emotion and the domestic scene, and here the process of perception is equally crucial: it is the fierce intelligence and affectionate accuracy with which such subjects are evoked that makes them seem so fully worthy of our attention. In a poem like "Filling Station," the ordinary becomes mysterious, revelatory, unique.

The first line demonstrates the sort of ambiguities from which the poem is constructed, immediately raising questions of situation, voice, and tone. (I've sometimes thought "Filling Station" would make a good exercise for acting students, given the number of different ways the first line—and much of the rest—might be stressed.) Is the opening exclamation solemn and childlike, or prissy and fastidious, or enthusiastic? All we can identify with certainty, I think, is the quality of fascination, the intent gaze on the filling station's pure oiliness. Nor is the scale on which the observation takes place very clear. Filling stations can, after all, be pretty dirty places, and yet there's something peculiar about an oiliness so deep that it turns the whole place translucent, almost into the essence of oil itself. And just how "little" is this place, anyway? Try to imagine Bishop standing across the street observing, and it doesn't work: the quizzical tone seems to miniaturize the filling station and divorce it from any context, as though its designer were Mother Goose or Walt Disney. (Or, more appropriately, Joseph Cornell, a favorite of Bishop's, and who with Edward Hopper seems to have had a hand in the poem's origins.) The sense of the miniature and the fabulatory is developed in the second stanza, where the human element is introduced in the form of a generic Father and his generic saucy sons, all cut from the same oily cloth— though the cheeriness of this is characteristically qualified if we noticed that Father's costume doesn't fit, or that Mother seems to be absent from the scene.

In the third stanza, the accumulation of details is matched by an increasing involvement on the part of the speaker. Curiosity ("Do they live in the station?") overtakes description, as she tries to probe beyond the flat, drab, objectified surface to the human meaning beneath. By this point the oiliness has become so pervasive that the "set of crushed and grease- / impregnated wickerwork" may seem like appropriate designer decor, and the "quite comfy" dirty dog sounds the detached, parodic note even more strongly. But in the next stanza the camera bores in more relentlessly, almost obsessively listing the dumb details, qualifying and repeating ("the only note of color— / of certain color," "a big doily . . . a big hirsute begonia") until it's clear that the perceiver has somehow become implicated in the scene. And the mask of detachment is shaken by the pressure of questions breaking through:

> Why the extraneous plant?
> Why the taboret?
> Why, oh why, the doily?

Clearly, much is at stake here. I'm reminded of Frost's poem "Design," which also seeks to discover a meaningful pattern in apparently random details, but whereas that poem points uncomfortably toward a sinister architecture in the world of nature, here the speaker seeks to understand a goofy "extraneous" beauty, a concern for harmony at the heart of this oil-soaked darkness. Her answer comes—and here the poem is at its most mysterious—in the final stanza, a vision of domestic attention anonymously embodied. It's a measure of the poem's richness that it's difficult to tell metaphysical or even theological implications here from a parody of them. The tone is quiet and delicate, but also bemused ("Somebody waters the plant, / or oils it, maybe"), and we're left facing the irony that the poem's final proof of "love" is a row of Esso cans. What I find most remarkable is that all these opposing elements are held in perfect balance. On repeated readings the mystery deepens rather than resolving itself: I think no other poet of Bishop's generation could manage such poignance and wit simultaneously.

J. D. McCLATCHY

"One Art": Some Notes

It is the poems you have lost, the ills
From missing dates, at which the heart expires.
Slowly the poison the whole blood stream fills.
The waste remains, the waste remains and kills.

—WILLIAM EMPSON

Bishop was not often attracted to formal patterns. The key words in various titles show her preference for the bracing leads of rhetorical conventions (exercise, anaphora, argument, conversation, letter, dream, a view) or for occasional premises (visits, arrival, going, wading, sleeping). Twenty years separate her two sestinas; her double-sonnet "The Prodigal Son" appeared in 1951, her ballad "The Burglar of Babylon" in 1964, her last poem "Sonnet" in 1979. When she did write by formula, her line stiffened toward the regularity of the pattern's grid, her tone of voice gave over its intimacy. At the same time, of course, her way with the line and her tone transfigured each of the forms she worked in—none more so, as Merrill notes, than the villanelle.

A poet's debt is her starting-point; her interest cancels it. Bishop's debt to Empson's "Missing Dates" is clear. His variations on "the consequence a life requires" are a study in slow poison. No less than Bishop's imperatives, his series of denials and definitions ("It is not . . .," "It is . . .") serves as an instruction. And his contradictory rhyme *fill/kill* sets up Bishop's similar (but, because feminine, more difficult) *master/disaster*.

From *Field: Contemporary Poetry and Poetics* 31 (Fall 1984), [pp. 10–11]. Copyright © 1984 by Oberlin College.

The exemplary poems are the grand Wordsworthian encounters—"At the Fishhouses," "The End of March"—that find their moral in their own slow pace. But I remain fascinated by those few poems—uncharacteristic, one might say, except that they are as central to an understanding of her work as anything else—that are *private* (or seem so), that defy decoding, are mysterious in their references and effect. The end of "Roosters" is such a moment, but I am thinking of whole poems that are short, their obliquity (is threatened love the lurking shape?) wrought up to a pitch of extreme lyricism. I am thinking of "Insomnia," "The Shampoo," "Varick Street," "Conversation," "Rain Towards Morning," and "O Breath." "One Art" is in this mode too. (And it looks more like a short poem as it's now printed, on one page, in *The Complete Poems* than it did, padded over two, in *Geography III*.) It is directly, even painfully autobiographical (or seems so), yet more accessible than the earlier poems. It *shares* its subject with the person who reads and not just with the person written about. Perhaps it seems more accessible because of the quality of resignation that dominates. Or perhaps it is because of the form, that does not mask the experience but strips it of the merely personal. That is to say, the form characterizes the autobiography; in the arbitrary is discovered the essential. The villanelle serves as a field to explore the self's history, but also as a vantage point above it.

It is a familiar advantage in Bishop's poems, achieved by tone rather than by form: "awful but cheerful." Over the poems in *Geography III* could hang, sampler-like, the more dire motto of "The End of March": "perfect! but impossible." The nine poems in the book all exemplify that strain in Bishop—the strain native to Frost and Stevens as well—of dark knowing. "Cold is our element and winter's air/ Brings voices as of lions coming down," says Stevens in "The Sun This March." That same element, the element bearable to no mortal, is where Bishop hears her voices. In its own way, "One Art" is their after-echo, the lyrical form a defense against extremes, against both perfection and impossibility.

Her title I take to mean "one art among others," as defense is the obverse of access. And I take "art" to mean "skill," but I want to come back to "art" in its other—primary? secondary?—meaning. What stays to puzzle is that the celebrated skill (a word we associate with *acquiring*) is for *losing*. The peculiar resonance of the phrase "the art of losing" is that the word has two meanings, transitive and intransitive. It can mean to mislay, or to fail. We hear the second meaning on the poem's first line, and the ghost of it throughout. "Lose" has other overtones: to elude, to stray, to remove, to be deprived. And etymologically (its root is to cut, loosen, divide) it's linked with pairs of terms that define the poem's emotional borders: analyze and solve, forlorn and resolve.

The catalogue of losses, from keys to continent, is a masterful sequence. The key starts a chain of being, objects to ideas, the course of a life. Much is named without being specified. When I read "Then practice losing farther, losing faster," I hear—because of the mother's watch in the next stanza—"losing *father*." Then, the watch as an emblem of time is joined with the houses' containment of space. If the cities stand for society, then the rivers and continent stand in for nature.

Before the terrible estrangement both recorded and enacted in the final stanza, there is an odd moment just ahead that cues it:

I lost two cities, lovely ones. And, vaster,
some realms I owned, two rivers, a continent.
I miss them, but it wasn't a disaster.

The rhythm is exact, low-keyed, but the diction is queer. "Vaster" strikes a discordant note, not just because it is a forced rhyme-word, but because it is the first of three "literary" words (a usage Bishop avoided). The others are "realms" and "shan't," not including the "*Write* it!" that caps the sequence. They are words that seem out of place unless accounted for by some less obvious motive. I mean a reader's, not necessarily the poet's motive: the need to interpret, to allow the poem to make sharp departures from itself, and add layers of meaning. Any poet—any reader—so surprises himself, and form, that psychopomp, leads by its exigencies.

But "realms," secure in mid-line, is a deliberate choice. Is it a deliberate allusion? Brazil *was* a kingdom—but that's not it. "Realm" is a word from books, old books, and one use of it springs immediately to mind: "Much have I travelled in the realms of gold / And many goodly states and kingdoms seen." Keats's sonnet is about acquiring—a poem, a planet; a continent, an ocean; a *power*—in much the same way (and in roughly the same locale) Bishop's Brazilian poems are, and she may be alluding to having abjured the more exotic style of poetry she wrote during her Brazilian years in favor of the sparer style of her later poetry. But "realms" is a royal trope not just for style but for poetry itself, in Keats's and (perhaps? surely!) in Bishop's reckoning here. This being so, could the poem—one of its layered meanings, that is—be about the loss of poetic power, the failure of mastery? If that were the case, then the "you" addressed in the last stanza (and no wonder her "voice" is singled out) is akin to Apollo in Keats's sonnet—say, the enabling god, or familiar muse. That the poem traces its diminishments in so rigorously lyrical, even keening, a pattern; that it must force itself at the end to do what the poet no longer can do, to *Write*—there is the poignancy of this dejection ode.

But to say these days that a poem is "about writing" is both a critical cliché and a method to dismiss. Besides, the "you" of this stanza—her "joking voice" that mocks both mastery and disaster—has all the specific gravity (and general levity) of a real person. The loss of love here is not over and thereby mastered, but threatened: a possibility brooded on, or an act being endured. How Bishop dramatizes this threatened loss is uncanny. "I shan't have lied," she claims. Under such intense emotional pressure, she shifts to the decorous "shan't," as if the better to distance and control her response to this loss, the newest and last. And again, my mind's ear often substitutes "died" for "lied." In self-defense, lying makes a moral issue out of the heart's existential dilemma; a way of speaking is a habit of being. The real moral force of the stanza comes—and this is true in many other Bishop poems—from her adverbs: *even* losing you; not *too* hard to master. These shades of emphasis are so carefully composed, so lightly sketched in, that their true dramatic power is missed by some readers.

And then that theatrical last line—how severely, how knowingly and helplessly qualified! It reminds me of that extraordinary line in "At the Fishhouses," at three removes from itself: "It is like what we imagine knowledge to be." The line here begins with a qualification ("though"), goes on to a suggestion rather than the assertion we might expect of a last line ("it may look"), then to a comparison that's doubled, stuttering ("like . . . like"), interrupted by a parenthetical injunction that is at once confession and compulsion, so that when "disaster" finally comes it sounds with a shocking finality.

The whole stanza is in danger of breaking apart, and breaking down. In this last line the poet's voice literally cracks. The villanelle—that strictest and most intractable of verse forms—can barely control the grief, yet helps the poet keep her balance. The balance of form and content, of "perfect! but impossible."

The forms themselves seem to invite [some little departure from tradition], in our age of "breakthroughs." Take the villanelle, which didn't really change from "Your eyen two wol slay me sodenly" until, say, 1950. With Empson's famous ones rigor mortis had set in, for any purposes beyond those of vers de société. Still, there were tiny signs. People began repunctuating the key lines so that, each time they recurred, the meaning would be slightly different. Was that just an extension of certain cute effects in Austin Dobson? In any case, "sodenly" Elizabeth's ravishing "One Art" came along, where the key lines seem merely to approximate themselves, and the form, awakened by a kiss, simply toddles off to a new stage in its life, under the proud eye of Mother, or the Muse.

—James Merrill

DAVID BROMWICH

Elizabeth Bishop's Dream-Houses

In a very striking passage of "Roosters,"
Elizabeth Bishop turns to address the shiny, gloating, and definitively male
creatures whose cries disturb her sleep:

> each one an active
> displacement in perspective;
> each screaming, "This is where I live!"
>
> Each screaming
> "Get up! Stop dreaming!"
> Roosters, what are you projecting?

The sleeper, as she tells us in another poem, eventually recovers from
these assaults and continues to inhabit "my proto-dream-house,/ my crypto-
dream-house, that crooked box / set up on pilings." She has taken in
enough of the roosters' admonitions to concede, "Many things about this
place are dubious." But the force of her rhetorical question—"What are
you projecting?"—suggests a reserve of personal strength. Bishop's own
poems are active displacements of perspective. They too project a warning
about where she lives, and they have the authority of dreams rather than
awakenings.

That she was praised throughout her career for a humbler kind of
success is doubtless just as well: charitable misunderstandings help an artist
to go on working quietly. Yet it is worth recalling the standard terms of
this praise, for they reveal how little had changed in the years that

From *Raritan* 4, no. 1 (Summer 1984). Copyright © 1984 by *Raritan*.

separate Bishop's first appearance from that of Emily Dickinson. Admirers of "Success is counted sweetest" (who thought it probably the work of Emerson) were replaced by encouragers of the best women poet in English. And a sure ground of appreciation for so special a performer was taken to be her "accuracy." What did that mean? Not, evidently, that she adapted the same style to different situations, and not that she changed all the time, with a relentless originality. It was an esthetic compliment, difficult to translate into English. Similarly, Bishop was prized for her "charm." In the sense of a warm sociability, she certainly was not charming, least of all when she meant to be, as in her poems about the poor. In any other sense, charm is a tedious virtue for a poet, just as accuracy is an impracticable vice. And yet, in spite of their evasiveness, both words converge on a trait which all of Bishop's readers have felt in her poems: the presence of an irresistible self-trust. To her, art is a kind of home. She makes her accommodations with an assurance that is full of risk, and, for her as for Dickinson, the domestic tenor of some poems implies a good-natured defiance of the readers she does not want. The readers she cares for, on the other hand, are not so much confided in as asked to witness her self-recoveries, which have the quality of a shared premise. Her work is a conversation which never quite takes place but whose possibility always beckons.

My point of departure in testing what this feels like in practice is an early poem, "The Monument." Bishop appears to have conceived it as an oblique eulogy for herself, and she frames it deferentially enough to suit a posthumous occasion. The poem's authority and weight have less in common with modern inventions like Joseph Cornell's boxes than they do with an older tradition of immortality—"Not marble, nor the gilded monuments/ Of princes, shall outlast this pow'rful rhyme." We are well-advised at the start not to measure a sure distance between those lines and these:

> Now can you see the monument? It is of wood
> built somewhat like a box. No. Built
> like several boxes in descending sizes
> one above the other.
> Each is turned half-way round so that
> its corners point toward the sides
> of the one below and the angles alternate.
> Then on the topmost cube is set
> a sort of fleur-de-lys of weathered wood,
> long petals of board, pierced with odd holes,
> four-sided, stiff, ecclesiastical.

Irony, in one of its meanings, is a pretense of concern in a speaker, for the sake of revising a listener's whole structure of concerns; the pretense here is that Bishop's listener, in order to cherish the monument, need only hear it described just so. She patiently adjusts the description ("It is X. No. Like several X's . . .") to anticipate any complaint, as later in the poem she will give the listener a more official embodiment by composing speeches for him. All this self-qualification is a gravely enacted farce. When it is over we will find ourselves still staring at the monument and rehearsing what she has said about it, until we see that the object of the poem was to compel our attention without giving reasons.

In the course of the one-woman narration, with its imagined interruptions, we listeners are permitted exactly four objections to the monument. These may be summarized abstractly: I don't understand what this thing is trying to be; I've never seen anything hang together like this; It's just too makeshift to succeed; and, What are you trying to prove, anyway? In short, museum-boredom ("Big deal; take me somewhere else"), which the poet meets at first with a curatorial delicacy. But her final speech, which takes up almost a third of the poem, overcomes all defensiveness and simply expands the categorical authority of her earlier statement, "It is the monument."

> It is an artifact
> of wood. Wood holds together better
> than sea or cloud or sand could by itself,
> much better than real sea or sand or cloud.
> It chose that way to grow and not to move.
> The monument's an object, yet those decorations,
> carelessly nailed, looking like nothing at all,
> give it away as having life, and wishing;
> wanting to be a monument, to cherish something.
> The crudest scroll-work says "commemorate,"
> while once each day the light goes around it
> like a prowling animal,
> or the rain falls on it, or the wind blows into it.
> It may be solid, may be hollow.
> The bones of the artist prince may be inside
> or far away on even drier soil.
> But roughly but adequately it can shelter
> what is within (which after all
> cannot have been intended to be seen).
> It is the beginning of a painting,
> a piece of sculpture, or poem, or monument,
> and all of wood. Watch it closely.

This ending allies "The Monument" with other American appeals to the power of metaphor to shape a life, particularly Frost's "A Star in a Stone-Boat" and Stevens's "Someone Puts a Pineapple Together." Even in their company, Bishop's poem keeps on growing as one thinks of it. It has perhaps less invention than they have; but then, it presumes a questioner suspicious of all that is new; and its persistent skepticism is a grace equal to any exuberance.

Earlier in the poem, still explaining the look of the monument itself, Bishop had composed a diagram of the viewer's relation to what he sees, which may also be read as a geometric proof of her own power over her readers.

> The monument is one-third set against
> a sea; two-thirds against a sky.
> The view is geared
> (that is, the view's perspective)
> so low there is no "far away,"
> and we are far away within the view.

I take the first five lines to mean that our eye is placed just above horizon-level, so that the whole sky and sea appear as a flat vertical backdrop, without depth and therefore without any far or near. But in what sense can we be said to be "far away within the view?" It must be that the view looks out at us too, as through the wrong end of a telescope, from a perspective capable of absorbing everything: it takes us in as it pleases. Indeed, the monument can contain the world, by implication. That is the sense of the listener's disturbed question, "Are we in Asia Minor,/ or in Mongolia?"—site of "Kubla Khan," where a kindred monument was decreed by imaginative fiat. So the poem says here, with the metaphor of perspective, what it says at the end by the rhetoric of conjecture: an active mind alone makes the world cohere, as "Wood holds together better/ than sea or cloud or sand could by itself,/ much better than real sea or sand or cloud." The flat declaration, "It chose that way to grow and not to move," only seems to announce a faith in the autonomy of art objects; Bishop returns us to the human bias of the thing, by her emphasis on those features of the monument which "give it away as having life, and wishing;/ wanting to be a monument, to cherish something." Before it can be, it must want to be something. And we read it for whatever spirit it communicates; we cannot do more than watch. But we are accompanied by the prowling sun which also keeps watch—a casual sublimity, the reward of the poet's discovery of a shelter uniquely right for herself. It is an image to which Bishop will return in "The End of March," where "the lion sun . . . who perhaps had batted a kite out of the sky to play with," is mysteriously connected with the wire leading out from her dream-house "to something off behind the dunes."

The monument will do for a figure of a poem, which turns out to be an allegory of what it is to *make* anything in the optative mood. A figure of a poet appears in the more straightforward allegory called "The Man-Moth." In a brief note, Bishop traces the title to a newspaper misprint for "mammoth," but the reason for its appeal to her is plain when one remembers the man-moth of Shelley's "Epipsychidion":

> Then, from the caverns of my dreamy youth
> I sprang, as one sandalled with plumes of fire,
> And towards the lodestar of my one desire,
> I flitted, like a dizzy moth, whose flight
> Is as a dead leaf's in the owlet light,
> When it would seek in Hesper's setting sphere
> A radiant death, a fiery sepulchre.

Part of Bishop's aim is to translate this image of the poet to a less radiant climate—that of the modern city—where his quest can take on the shape of an almost biological compulsion.

> Up the façades,
> his shadow dragging like a photographer's cloth behind him,
> he climbs fearfully, thinking that this time he will manage
> to push his small head through that round clean opening
> and be forced through, as from a tube, in black scrolls on the light.
> (Man, standing below him, has no such illusions.)
> But what the Man-Moth fears most he must do, although
> he fails, of course, and falls back scared but quite unhurt.

Where the monument chose a certain way to be, the Man-Moth acts without a will: his quest is merely a condition of existence. It is as if he were born knowing, *there is a creature (and you are he) who does all of this*—climbs skyscrapers because he "thinks the moon is a small hole at the top of the sky"; travels backward in underground trains, where he dreams recurrent dreams; and through all his risks, looks on mortality as "a disease he has inherited the susceptibility to." He is defined not by his activity but by the contrast he makes with man, who

> . . . does not see the moon; he observes her vast prop-
> erties, feeling the queer light on his hands, neither warm nor
> cold, of a temperature impossible to record in thermometers.

Man's shadow is no bigger than his hat; the Man-Moth's is almost palpable, trailing "like a photographer's cloth behind him"; and one is reminded that "shadow" is still our best English word for *figura* and *typus*. In a way that can be shown but not said, the Man-Moth, by being what he is, interprets man to himself. But the poem makes a lighter fable of this. Like any other second-story artist, the Man-Moth abstracts a few choice possessions from his victim and flees the scene.

How his theft may be retrieved is the subject of Bishop's final stanza, which is addressed to man, still "observing" and coldly pragmatic.

> If you catch him,
> hold up a flashlight to his eye. It's all dark pupil,
> an entire night itself, whose haired horizon tightens
> as he stares back, and closes up the eye. Then from the lids
> one tear, his only possession, like the bee's sting, slips.
> Slyly he palms it, and if you're not paying attention
> he'll swallow it. However, if you watch, he'll hand it over,
> cool as from underground springs and pure enough to drink.

The Man-Moth's eye is "an entire night itself," a complete image of that world of the earth's surface in which he seeks what is most different from himself. The object of his quest he calls a tiny hole of light; man, less interestingly, calls it the moon. To reach it would mean suffusion by the light and hence, to an eye all pupil, destruction. The Man-Moth, however, is sustained by the fantasy of an ascent through "that round clean opening," and of being forced "in black scrolls on the light." In this dream of consummation he would become his writing.

One may interpret the dream as at once expressing and concealing a hope that some principle of self will survive the dissolution of the body. Of course, the fallacy is easy to expose: immortality is not a form of health to which one can inherit a susceptibility. Yet this analysis gives no comfort to man, about whom we have heard it said that "Man, standing below, has no such illusions"; for the compliment holds in reserve a fierce irony: "Man, standing below, has no such ambitions." Nor does Bishop herself want to unbuild our illusions. She is interested in the use we make of everything the illusion-bound creature brings back from his journeyings. This is figured in the poem as hardly calculable refreshment, with the character almost of bodily secretion. The Man-Moth's "one tear, his only possession, like the bee's sting," may be his gift to us. The image comes close to a hackneyed sentiment about perfection and pain, and hovers near an allusion to Keats's "Melancholy," but slips free of both. It is hard not to read it poignantly—the reader, like the map-printer in another of Bishop's poems, "here experiencing the same excitement/ as when emotion too far exceeds its cause." But the tear is not really a possession, the light that produced it after all was man's, and both parties seem amenable to the exchange. Our acceptance of every curiosity in the poem owes something to its conscious urbanity: the opening line even gives us the "battered moonlight" of a cityscape—battered by too much jingling in the pockets of too many songwriters, but still salvageable by one poet. Elsewhere, the same word appears to evoke a larger freedom with imagery that looks worn or already found: the fish that is "battered and venerable/ and homely"; the big tin basin, "battered and shiny like the moon." "The Man-Moth" and "The Monument" go beyond the dignity of statement— the somewhat ponderous naturalism—that such diction has usually aimed to license and keep honest. They stand apart from the poems of Bishop's generation in the stubbornness with which they try ingenuity by the test of prosaic heft.

To an exceptional degree in modern poetry, Bishop's work offers resistance to any surmise about the personality of the author. One reason is that the poems themselves have been so carefully furnished with eccentric details or gestures. These may seem tokens of companionability, yet a certain way into a poem the atmosphere grows a little chill; farther in, as the conversation strolls on, one senses the force field of a protective ease. Some day, a brief chapter in a history of poetry will describe Lowell's misreading of Bishop as a voice of resonant sincerity, and his appropriation for journalistic ends of her more marked traits of syntax, punctuation, and anomalous cadence. But to the reader who returns to these poems for their own sake, the question likeliest to recur is: what are they concealing? It helps, I think, to frame this as a question about a difficult passage—for example, about the pathos of some lines near the end of "Crusoe in England," in which Crusoe describes the objects that recall his years of solitude.

> The knife there on the shelf—
> it reeked of meaning, like a crucifix.
> It lived. How many years did I
> beg it, implore it, not to break?
> I knew each nick and scratch by heart,
> the bluish blade, the broken tip,
> the lines of wood-grain on the handle . . .
> Now it won't look at me at all.

Like many comparable passages of her work, the description is weirdly circumstantial. What does it mean for a poet who is a woman to write, as a man, of an object so nearly linked with masculine assertion, with this mingling of tenderness, pity, and regret?

The poetic answer, which has to do with the cost of art to life, does not exclude the sexual one, which has to do with an ambivalent femininity. The poet's own weapons in art as in life have been more dear to her than she can easily confess. The punishment for deserting them is that they refuse to return her gaze; they lose their aura, and she ceases to be a poet. A similar recognition is implied in other poems, where a wish to conquer or dominate—resisted at first, then acted on—darkens the celebration of having come through every challenge. Thus, "The Armadillo" moves from horror of a creature, quite distinct from the poet, to wonder at the same creature, which in the meantime has been implicitly identified with her. She devotes a poem to the armadillo because it is a survivor, forearmed against any catastrophe. Like her, it watches in safety a dangerous and beautiful spectacle, the drifting of the "frail, illegal fire balloons" which at any moment may splatter "like an egg of fire/ against the cliff." As for the poet herself, the poem is proof of her armor. In the same way, in "Roosters" she is a second and unmentioned crier of the morning; the poem, with its "horrible insistence" three notes at a time, announces exactly where she lives.

These identifications go deep. Such poems are not, in fact, animal-morality pieces, in the vein of Marianne Moore. They more nearly resemble Lawrence's "Fish," "The Ass," "Tortoise Shell," and "Tortoise Family Connections"—protestant inquests concerning the powers of the self, which have the incidental form of free-verse chants about animals. Bishop writes without Lawrence's spontaneous humor, and without his weakness for quick vindications. Indeed, there is something like self-reproach in a line that begins the final movement of "Roosters": "how could the night have come to grief?" By a trick of context, this phrase opens up an ambiguity in the cliché. It warns us that there has been matter for grieving during the night, before the first rooster crowed, at a scene of passion which was also a betrayal. "The Armadillo" too reveals the complicity of love with strife, in its italicized last stanza; here the last line and a half is a chiasmus, in which strength is surrounded by a yielding vulnerability.

> *Too pretty, dreamlike mimicry!*
> *O falling fire and piercing cry*
> *and panic, and a weak mailed fist*
> *clenched ignorant against the sky!*

"Weak" and "ignorant" are meant to temper the surprise of the "mailed fist clenched," and they cast doubt on those three central words: the fist, emblem of contest, is defended by weakness and ignorance, its only outward fortifications. The gesture of defiance, however, becomes all the more persuasive with this glimpse of a possible defeat. The way "The

Armadillo" comes to rest has felt tentative to some readers, and yet the only question it asks is rhetorical: "See how adequately I shelter my victory?" In other poems just as surely, an elaborate craft gives away the poet as always present, at a scene she has painted as uninhabitable. The repeated line in a very late poem, "One Art," will declare her control by rhyming "disaster" with "The art of losing isn't hard to master"; as if we could expect her endurance to be taxing of course, but no more doubtful than her ability to pair the words for a villanelle.

Sexuality is the most elusive feature of Bishop's temperament— before writing any of the poems in *North & South,* she had learned to allegorize it subtly—and the reticence of her critics alone makes its existence worth noting. Like other habitual concerns, it interests her as it joins a care for what she sometimes calls the soul. This is an argument carried on from poem to poem, but its first appearance, in "The Imaginary Iceberg," is startling.

> Icebergs behoove the soul
> (both being self-made from elements least visible)
> to see them so: fleshed, fair, erected indivisible.

Until these concluding lines the poem has been a light entertainment, a "Convergence of the Twain" told from the iceberg's point of view. The lines shift our perspective on everything that came before—in effect, they translate a poem which did not seem to need translation. "Fleshed, fair, erected indivisible": the words, we see at once, belong to the human body rather than the soul. They are monstrously beautiful because they are a lie. For in the metaphor about the soul which has been perfectly built up, the comparison rightly demands instead: cold, white, immense, indestructible. This yields a pleasant description of an iceberg which, when we ponder it, is replaced by a sublime representation of the soul.

It is characteristic of Bishop's wit that she should have begun the same poem fancifully: "We'd rather have the iceberg than the ship,/ although it meant the end of travel." Translating, as the poem suggests we do, this becomes: "We'd rather have the soul than the body,/ although it meant the end of life." Yet for Bishop travel is not a chance metaphor. It stands for all that can divert the soul from its prospects. To hold fast to what it knows may mean for the soul to remain always "stock-still like cloudy rock"; or like a mariner, curled asleep at the top of a mast or seated with his eyes closed tight, untouchable by the charms of the voyage. This is the condition of "the unbeliever" in the poem of that title: believing only in himself, he knows "The sea is hard as diamonds; it wants to destroy us all." With his intensity perhaps, the soul may be equal to the imaginary iceberg which "cuts its facets from within./ Like jewelry from a grave/ it saves itself and adorns/ only itself." The phrase "from a grave," as it finally seems, is not fanciful at all but descriptive. It says that a guarding of the soul's integrity may also be a defense against death. And the sense in which this is especially true for a poet is the sense that matters to Bishop.

The titles of three of Bishop's volumes (*North & South, Questions of Travel, Geography III*) show how far she accepted—at times rather flatly—the common opinion that travel was her distinctive subject. Yet few readers are likely to know even a single region as intimately as she knew two hemispheres; and to make her geography poems interesting we have to read them as poems about something else. With this need of ours, a whole tract of her writing refuses to cooperate; poems about squatters and other half-cherished neighbors—efforts of self-conscious whimsy (like "Manuelzinho") or of awkward condescension (like "Filling Station"). I think these are the only poems Bishop ever wrote that dwindle as one comes to see them more more clearly. One has to move away from these in order to learn what must have been clear to her from the first: that geography carries interest as a figure of the soul's encounter with fate (or as she puts it, with "what we imagine knowledge to be"). Occasionally, in the terms she proposed for this encounter, Bishop echoes the hero of Stevens's "The Comedian as the Letter C," who sought

> an elemental fate,
> And elemental potencies and pangs,
> And beautiful barenesses as yet unseen,
> Making the most of savagery.

But the poems I have in mind all end in a distrust of these things. In them, the dream of freedom, under the aspect of a perpetual self-renewal, is interpreted as a helpless revolt against the conditions of experience. The poet, however, offers no hope that we shall ever escape the enchantment of the dream.

"Brazil, January 1, 1502" marks the conquistadors' first step into a trap, a vast mesh of circumstance disguised as a jungle, and cozily misnamed "the new world." The poem starts off, innocuously, with an epigraph from Sir Kenneth Clark, "embroidered nature . . . tapestried landscape."

> Januaries, Nature greets our eyes
> exactly as she must have greeted theirs:
> every square inch filling in with foliage—
> big leaves, little leaves, and giant leaves,

> blue, blue-green and olive,
> with occasional lighter veins and edges,
> or a satin underleaf turned over.

It is all, she goes on to say (confirming her epigraph) "solid but airy; fresh as if just finished/ and taken off the frame." Courteously artful, we are like the conquistadors in supposing that we can make Nature over in a language we know—for them, the language of tapestry, for us that of naturalistic description. In either case we reproduce the nature prized by a Western connoisseur of art; and the poem is about how we cannot ever effect the conversion without loss. Nature will always take its revenge by drawing us still farther in, and suspending our knowledge of the thing that claims our pursuit.

So, in the next stanza, the tapestry is described as "a simple web"—a moral text, its foreground occupied by "Sin:/ five sooty dragons near some massy rocks." Even after these have been naturalized as lizards, Bishop tells us "all eyes/ are on the smaller, female one, back to,/ her wicked tail straight up and over,/ red as a red-hot wire." Between then and now, the allegorical and the natural, the poem admits no disparity— none, anyway, to compete with the similarity implied by such imperial habits of seeing. Hence the appropriateness of the poem's grammatical structure, its "As then, so now." This structure is completed only in the third and last stanza, which reverses the order of the comparison. As we find it now, not unfamiliar,

> Just so the Christians, hard as nails,
> tiny as nails, and glinting,
> in creaking armor, came and found it all,
> not unfamiliar:
> no lovers' walks, no bowers,
> no cherries to be picked, no lute music,
> but corresponding, nevertheless,
> to an old dream of wealth and luxury
> already out of style when they left home—
> wealth plus a brand-new pleasure.
> Directly after Mass, humming perhaps
> L'Homme armé or some such tune,
> they ripped away into the hanging fabric,
> each out to catch an Indian for himself—
> those maddening little women who kept calling,
> calling to each other (or had the birds waked up?)
> and retreating, always retreating behind it.

In the light of this ending, the poem may be read as a colonial dream of all that seems infinitely disposable in the colonized.

But it is also about something that evades our grasp in every object that appeals to the human love of conquest. The Indian women, "those maddening little women who kept calling, calling to each other"—but not to their pursuers—only repeat the attraction of the female lizard, "her wicked tail straight up and over,/ red as a red-hot wire." Both alike appear to beckon from behind the tapestry of the jungle fabric. They entice, and bind their spell. Another retreat will always be possible to them, since the jungle has gone opaque to the men hunting them, who believe at every point that it is transparent. This is another way of saying that the invaders have become victims of their own conquering perspective. They recreate here "an old dream of wealth and luxury"; yet the dream was "already out of style when they left home"; and the new place, as disclosed to other eyes, has seemed far from homelike. In the end their crossing of this threshold, "hard as nails,/ tiny as nails," says most about their sense of home, which was equally marked by a failure of knowledge. What they take to be an act of possession is not, therefore, even a successful repossession, but the enactment of a familiar ritual of self-seduction.

This poem shows Bishop moving well outside the limits of the travel sketch. By itself, it is almost enough to persuade us that she exploits the genre elsewhere chiefly to break with it, from an impulse comparable to Dickinson's in revising the poem of "home thoughts." At any rate, the sketch that goes furthest to appease the worldly taste of her readers carries a suspicious title, "Over 2,000 Illustrations and a Complete Concordance," and the steady mystification of its narrative seems bent on protracting our suspicion. The poem, with an unsettling confidence, treats worldliness as a form of literal reading that is death—but the title is worth pausing over. What is a concordance? A system of reference to all the uses of every important word in the Bible, or for that matter in any sacred book, including the work of a great poet. The illustrations accompanying it may be pictures—the picture-postcard atmosphere of much of the poem will toy with this—yet they are as likely to be passages longer than a phrase, which give a fuller context for the entries. When reading a concordance, we do not look at individual words to be sure of their reference, but to satisfy ourselves of a fateful pattern of choice. From the sum of an author's repetitions, we may learn a tact for whatever is irreducible in his character. "Over 2000 Illustrations" owes its force to the propriety with which one can substitute both "reader" and "traveller" for "author," and view a place in the world as denoting a locus in a text.

The thought that troubles Bishop at the start is that the book of nature and history may not be either a clean text or an already canonical one, whether Bible or secular fiction, but something more like just such a concordance, with occasional glimpses into its depths coming from the illustrations alone.

> Thus should have been our travels:
> serious, engravable.
> The Seven Wonders of the World are tired
> and a touch familiar, but the other scenes,
> innumerable, though equally sad and still,
> are foreign. Often the squatting Arab,
> or group of Arabs, plotting, probably,
> against our Christian Empire,
> while one apart, with outstretched arm and hand
> points to the Tomb, the Pit, the Sepulcher.
> The branches of the date-palms look like files.
> The cobbled courtyard, where the Well is dry,
> is like a diagram, the brickwork conduits
> are vast and obvious, the human figure
> far gone in history or theology,
> gone with its camel or its faithful horse.
> Always the silence, the gesture, the specks of birds
> suspended on invisible threads above the Site,
> or the smoke rising solemnly, pulled by threads.

The broken, randomly spliced rhythm of this opening, the discreteness of its sentences, as well as the words "often" and "always," suggest the episodic quality of the moments chronicled in the illustrations. They tell a story, apparently senseless, and in no particular order, which the poem later names the story of "God's spreading fingerprint." Only the Christians in the illustrations make a connection from place to place; and in the margin, everywhere, are faintly sinister Arabs, plotting or "looking on amused": together, these figures give it the unity it has. But as the account moves on, it grows still more oddly inconsequential: "In Mexico the dead man lay/ in the blue arcade; the dead volcanoes/ glistened like Easter lilies./ The jukebox went on playing 'Ay, Jalisco!' " The blare of the jukebox comes in when the story's meaning appears to have been surely lost, and it signals a transition. Now, the tone of the illustrations (which somehow have become cheap guidebook images) drifts toward the hallucinatory:

> And in the brothels of Marrakesh
> the little pockmarked prostitutes
> balanced their tea-trays on their heads
> and did their belly dances; flung themselves
> naked and giggling against our knees,
> asking for cigarettes. It was somewhere near there

> I saw what frightened me most of all:
> A holy grave, not looking particularly holy,
> one of a group under a keyhole-arched stone baldaquin
> open to every wind from the pink desert.

By the first five lines of this passage, every worldly fact has been rendered exchangeable with every other, and the loss is of nothing less than the history and the pathos of the things one may come to know.

Bishop is frightened "most of all" by the suddenly exposed grave in the desert because it reminds her of a life emptied of causes and consequences, with "Everything only connected by 'and' and 'and.' " The conclusion of the poem brings together author, reader, and traveller a last time, and envisions a sort of text that would return attention to something beyond it.

> Everything only connected by "and" and "and."
> Open the book. (The gilt rubs off the edges
> of the pages and pollinates the fingertips.)
> Open the heavy book. Why couldn't we have seen
> this old Nativity while we were at it?
> —the dark ajar, the rocks breaking with light,
> an undisturbed, unbreathing flame,
> colorless, sparkless, freely fed on straw,
> and, lulled within, a family with pets,
> —and looked and looked our infant sight away.

Much less than everything is restored by this ending. Though the holy book, once opened, confronts us with an ideal representation of our origins, we have to read it uninnocently. We know how thoroughly we have revised it already by our later imaginings, by every arrangement which makes the end of a life or work distort its beginning. To deny our remoteness from the scene would be to cancel the very experience which permits us to pass through "the dark ajar." Thus, we stand with the poet, both in the scene and outside it, uncertain whether pleasure is the name for what we feel. Her wishfully innocent question—"Why couldn't we have seen / this old Nativity while we were at it?"—has the tone of a child's pleading, "Why couldn't we *stay* there?"—said of a home, or a place that has grown sufficiently like home. Some time or other we say that about childhood itself. The book, then, is hard to open because it is hard to admit the strength of such a plea; harder still, to hear it for what it says about our relationship to ourselves. Any place we live in, savage or homely, dream-house or rough shelter, we ourselves have been the making of. And yet, once made, it is to be inherited forever. Everything may be connected by "because" and "therefore," and every connection will be provisional. The last line accordingly yields an ambiguous truth about nostalgia: to look our sight away is to gaze our fill, but also to look until we see differently—until, in our original terms, we do not see at all. The line, however, warrants a more general remark about Bishop's interest in the eye. In common with Wordsworth, she takes the metaphor of sight to imply the activity of all the senses, and these in turn to represent every possibility of conscious being. Sight is reliable because it can give no account of itself. We make it mean only when we look again, with "that inward eye/ Which is the bliss of solitude" (words, incidentally, which the hero of "Crusoe in England" tries reciting to himself on the island, but can remember only after his rescue). It is the same poem that Wordsworth says of the daffodils, "I gazed—and gazed"; and the action of "The Fish" turns on this single concentrated act: "I stared and stared," and the colors of the boat changed to "rainbow, rainbow, rainbow," and she let the fish go.

In passing from sight to vision, or to "what is within (which after all/ cannot have been intended to be seen)," Bishop always respects the claims of unbelievers different from herself. Her mood is almost always optative, in its readiness to inquire into not-yet-habitable truths; and I want to conclude with an especially full expression of that mood, from "Love Lies Sleeping." She writes there of a dawn in a city, with eleven lines of a soft introductory cadence, good enough for the opening bars of a Gershwin tune; with a memory of the waning night and its "neon shapes/ that float and swell and glare"; with a panoramic view and a long tracking view that ends in the window of one dwelling, where the poet asks the "queer cupids of all persons getting up" to be mild with their captives:

> for always to one, or several, morning comes
> whose head has fallen over the edge of his bed,
>   whose face is turned
>   so that the image of
>
> the city grows down into his open eyes
> inverted and distorted. No. I mean
>   distorted and revealed,
>   if he sees it at all.

The words are as serious and engravable as an epitaph. At the same time, with a doubt exactly the size of a comma, they point to a revelation that may have occurred, and, for the sake of its distortion as well as its truth, keep it living in surmise.

JOANNE FEIT DIEHL

At Home With Loss:
Elizabeth Bishop and the
American Sublime

In a wryly discursive letter to Anne
Stevenson, her first biographer, Elizabeth Bishop comments directly upon
her relationship to the American literary tradition. "But I also feel," she
writes, "that Cal (Lowell) and I in very different ways are both descen-
dants from the Transcendentalists—but you may not agree." Bishop,
despite the characteristic demurral, thus acknowledges that her work
derives from that early manifestation of American self-consciousness known
as transcendentalism. The particular slant she takes toward American
Romanticism, her swerve from Emerson and his heirs (different as it is
from Lowell's) substantially depends upon her gender, upon the fact of
Bishop's being a woman. In what follows I sketch the outlines of a reading
of Elizabeth Bishop that attempts to account both for the influence of
gender and the importance of tradition in her work, her awareness of
origins and the origins of her difference. That Bishop continues to define
herself in terms of the American Romantic imagination is perhaps less a
conscious decision than an unavoidable burden affecting all our poets,
male and female, who cannot, of course, evade their literary predecessors.
Yet a consideration of the relationship between eros and poetics suggests
the possibility that the woman poet can win a certain measure of freedom
from literary indebtedness and thus acquire, in the very weakening of those
traditional ties, a restitution born of loss.

If, as Wittgenstein writes, "to imagine a language means to imagine a form of life," then contemporary women poets are inventing, through their poems, new forms of constitutive identity; in remaking language, they strive to re-invent themselves. The impetus for this reinvention derives from the woman poet's need to reassert authority over experience, establishing an unmediated relationship with the natural world and, beyond it, with the powers of the word. Dickinson is the first woman poet to attempt such a transformation, and, although Bishop expresses a certain disdain for the self-pity she perceives in Dickinson's poems, she acknowledges not only her forebear's genius but her historical significance as well. "I particularly admire her having dared to do it all alone," Bishop remarks. And the relationship between Dickinson and herself may be closer than the urbanely disingenuous Bishop might reveal. In any case, I preface this discussion with a brief excursus into an earlier struggle for origins in order to delineate an alternative poetic tradition which begins with Dickinson and finds its most powerful contemporary display in the works of Elizabeth Bishop.

In her response to Emerson's vision of the poet as central man, Dickinson provides the groundwork of an alternative poetics for future women who would stake out a new territory for the Sublime as she engages the fundamental issues that characterize the psychodynamics of the poet's quest for authority over experience. How Dickinson conceptualizes the American Sublime and her strategies for dealing with its imminent manifestations in terms of her struggle with her forebears thus becomes the primary, compelling instance of the ambitious nineteenth-century woman poet fighting for her poetic authority. In the Romantic pattern of the Sublime which Dickinson inherits, the process of inspiration is inseparable from the drama of poetic influence, for at the sublime moment, an external power floods into the poet, causing the self momentarily to fall away, thus creating an intense, if temporary, anxiety on the part of the subject alleviated solely by the foreknowledge that the infusing power shares its fundamental identity with the experiential self, an identity chiefly expressed in terms of gender, or, in the dynamics of the family romance, as a paternal relationship. Dickinson, as woman poet, experiences no prior assurance either that this male-identified influx of power shares her identity or that the Sublime encounter, once completed, will not render her vanquished—sexual anxiety shadowing, as it must, the poetic encounter. If there is no recognizable continuity between the patriarchal power and the female experiential self, then the poet may be unable to resolve the conflict between ravishing other and receptive self, thereby rendering her unable to retrieve the requisite power to write the

Sublime poem. Instead, she responds to his power with a grim version of Emersonian compensation:

> Your Riches—taught me—Poverty.
> Myself—a Millionaire
> In little Wealths, as Girls could boast
> Till broad as Buenos Ayre—
>
> You drifted your Dominions—
> A Different Peru—
> And I esteemed All Poverty
> For Life's Estate with you—
>
> (299)

The priceless gift proves just that—no compensation can make up for the sense of indebtedness the speaker experiences. The gift becomes a potentially debilitating one because it demonstrates that as woman and as poet, Dickinson cannot make this wealth her own, nor can she preserve (once transgressed) her former illusion of self-sufficiency. In terms of poetic influence, then, the lack of a recognizable continuity between the patriarchal power and the female experiential self renders the poet unable to resolve the conflict between the ravishing other and the receptive self in her favor, thereby potentially barring the poet from retrieving the power to write the Sublime poem.

Consequently, Dickinson and the women poets who follow her witness a profound discontinuity when faced with the masculine-identified experiential sublime, their ontogenetic development as poets, and more to the point here, their poems, reflecting this discontinuity. In the wake of such discontinuity, Dickinson conceives of the process of poetic influence in both homo- and heterosexual terms, and this transference of gender identity serves as a measure of the extent to which she envisions the masculine as imposing a threat while the feminine offers, if only intermittently, a vision of poetic influence freed from a possibly crippling anxiety. When Dickinson confronts her inherited male power, the poems incorporate a defense against the potentially catastrophic nature of these encounters by responding to the necessity of receiving such an influx, by privileging the process of abstention, by making renunciation the foundation of her counter-sublime. With an aplomb that checks desperation, Dickinson asserts, "Art thou the thing I wanted? / Begone—my Tooth has grown!" Only when Dickinson envisions the workings of poetic inspiration in terms of a female-to-female transference as in poem 593, "I think I was enchanted," does one witness the abatement of anxiety and the celebration of poetic renewal. Yet there are in Dickinson's poems no more than a few instances that describe such a benign process; more characteristic of the poems that deal explicitly with the process of influence are those which describe it in agonistic terms, where the poet fights for her/his very life. Dickinson's legacy of the counter-sublime might best be summarized as a tactical audacity that, in its confrontations with an emergent and potentially dangerous Emersonianism, challenges the very tenets of syntax, the development of a poetics that fractures so as to bestow meaning. By thus obscuring her meaning, Dickinson rehabilitates the subversive thoughts she might otherwise be forced, because of internal and external strictures, to suppress.

Separated as she is from Dickinson both by time and temperament, Elizabeth Bishop nonetheless faces an allied if somewhat extenuated version of the Emersonian Sublime, and, once again, the crux of the poetic problem relates to gender. But Bishop, even more than Dickinson, defends against the challenge to her poetic autonomy by ursurping the very terms in which it is made. In other words, Bishop compensates for the recognition of her loss of poetic authority in Emersonian terms by an erasure of the sexual dialectic upon which his vision fundamentally depends. Although Dickinson experiments with a similar strategy, substituting the male for the expected female pronoun or referring to her youthful self as a boy, she moves beyond gender only at intervals; it remains for Bishop to provide a sustained rhetoric of asexuality in order to find an adequate defense against the secondariness to which the American Sublime would sentence her. What distinguishes Bishop's work from the canonical American Sublime, I would suggest, is a loss equivalent to restitution, the enactment of Bishop's "I" as the eye of the traveller or the child, able to recapture an innocence that only apparently evades intimate sexuality or the assertion of gender. One finds in Bishop's poems a map of language where sexuality appears to yield to an asexual self, making possible a poetry that deceptively frees her from the gender-determined role into which she would be cast as a female descendant of the American Sublime. Bishop evades being diminished, exiled, or isolated from the tradition by sidestepping the distinctions imposed by Emerson and his agonistic disciples. Her poems' prevailing absence of the overtly sexual Whitmanian self, the apparent dismissal of heterosexuality, becomes a means of reestablishing woman's unmediated relationship to the world she would make her own. Thus, her poems are a kind of brilliant compensation, a dazzling dismissal of the very distinctions that might otherwise stifle her.

In her late poem, "One Art" (whose title conveys the implicit suggestion that the mastery sought over loss in love is intimately related to the control she maintains in her poetry), Bishop articulates the tension between discipline in life and the force of circumstance. The poem speaks in the tones of the survivor:

> the art of losing isn't hard to master;
> so many things seem filled with the intent
> to be lost that their loss is no disaster.

Renunciation, as for Dickinson, becomes the way for the poet to acquire a tentative mastery over Emerson's fatal vision. By articulating the control such renunciatory self-sufficiency implies, the poem wrests its essential individuating authority. From its opening line, with its echo of a folk prescription such as "an apple a day," the poem leads into the specifics of daily loss—of keys, or time—the syntactic parallelism suggesting an evaluative equation of what we immediately recognize as hardly equal realities. Such parallelism, by providing a temporary distraction that draws the reader away from the cumulative force building in the poem, functions as a disarming form of humor that undercuts the self-pity otherwise latent in the poem's subject.

> Lose something every day. Accept the fluster
> of lost keys, the hour badly spent.
> The art of losing isn't hard to master.

The poem presents a series of losses as if to reassure both author and reader that control is possible—an ironic gesture that forces upon us the tallying of experience cast in the guise of reassurance. By embracing loss, as Emerson had that Beautiful Necessity, Fate, Bishop casts the illusion of authority over the inexorable series of losses she must master.

> Then practice losing farther, losing faster:
> places, and names, and where it was you meant
> to travel. None of these will bring disaster.

The race continues between "disaster" and "master" as the losses span her mother's watch, houses, cities, two rivers, a continent, and perhaps, in the future, an intimate friend whom, breaking out of the pattern of inanimate objects, the poem directly addresses:

> —Even losing you (the joking voice, a gesture
> I love) I shan't have lied. It's evident
> the art of losing's not too hard to master
> though it may look like (*Write* it!) like disaster.

Here conflict explodes as the verbal deviations from previously established word patterns reflect the price of the speaker's remaining true to her initial assertion that the experience of loss can yield to mastery. In this deceptively direct poem, with a directness that comes to predominate in Bishop's late work, she delineates the relationship between the will and the world. Note the split of "a gesture / I love" across two lines, the profession standing by itself as well as turning back to the beloved gesture, as syntax reveals the pain that the poem has been fighting, since its beginnings, to suppress.

Determined upon a course of truth-telling that will cover all contingencies, the thought of losing "you" triggers an anxiety with which the poem must wrestle to its final lines. This last time, the refrain varies its form by assuming an evidential structure which challenges as it expresses what has hitherto been taken as a fact known from within the poet's consciousness. Coupled with the addition of "It's evident" is the adverbial "too" (It's evident / the art of losing's not too hard to master") which increases the growing tension within the desire to repeat her credo while admitting growing doubts about its accuracy. In the end, the pressure to recapitulate the by-now-threatened refrain betrays itself in the sudden interruption of the closing lines by an italicized hand that enforces the completion of the "master" / "disaster" couplet that the poem itself has made, through its formal demands, an inevitable resolution: "the art of losing's not too hard to master / though it may look like (*Write* it!) like disaster." The repetition of "like" postpones ever so fleetingly the final word which hurts all the more. "Disaster's" inevitability ironically recalls the fatalism of such childhood rituals as "he loves me; he loves me not"—in which the child's first words, "he loves me," and the number of petals on the flower determine the game's (and the prophecy's) outcome. In its earlier evocation of folk ritual and in its tight rhyme scheme, where prescribed verbal patterns determine the "disaster" with which the poem concludes, "One Art" reveals an ironic playfulness that works in conjunction with a high seriousness, a strategy that proliferates in Bishop's poems. With its reiterated assertion of the ability to control loss, the poem rushes headlong into increasingly intimate occasions, until, by the end, the italicized "write it" forces the poet to acknowledge disaster—to write is *to redeem* that loss.

The "you" "One Art" fears to lose is not sexually identified, and this identification, of course, makes little difference. But in "Crusoe in England," another poem of loss from the stark territory Bishop called *Geography III*, the issues of same-sex friendship and life on an island, where biological reproduction proves impossible, receive more direct treatment, as Bishop seeks to compensate for Crusoe's severely privative circumstances by the power of an informing eye and the reproductive workings of the fertile imagination. Bishop's Crusoe is essentially a survivor, returned now to that other island, the England from which he feels even more deeply estranged. Reflecting on his earlier life amid a terrain at once forbidding and unique, hence no longer discoverable or nameable ("none of the books has ever got it right"), Crusoe describes a surrealistic landscape domesticated by the powers of the isolated imagination, where conventional assumptions about biology give way before the uncanny and the strange. Here, oddly, even with a certain delirium, the imagination re-makes its self-made world. On his island Crusoe witnesses a world where procreative doublings are denied:

> The sun set in the sea; the same odd sun
> rose from the sea;
> and there was one of it and one of me.
> The island had one kind of everything!

If Coleridgean echoes evoke a world of trance-like stasis, what distinguishes Crusoe's island is its profound sexual as well as geographical isolation. Drunk on home-made brew, playing his home-made flute (recall the tunes of Thoreau's solitary instrument), Crusoe whoops and dances among the goats, crying, "Home-made, home-made! But aren't we all?" And with the question he simultaneously implicates us in his world as he forces us to measure our distance from it.

When the grotesque, inebriated bard quotes Wordsworth to his audience of snail shells metamorphosed by the desperate imagination into iris beds, he forgets the final word: " 'They flash upon that inward eye, / Which is the bliss . . .' The bliss of what?" "One of the first things that I did / When I got back was look it up." The word, of course, is "solitude," and with its ironically unspoken inclusion, the poem witnesses Wordsworthian consolation transformed into the burden of repressed memory. Carried to the edge of a madness that includes the nightmare of accidentally slitting a baby's throat, "of islands / islands spawning islands, like frogs' eggs turning into polliwogs / of islands" (regeneration become hopeless replication), Crusoe blesses Friday's arrival with a simplicity that belies as it asserts the sexual burden of his description.

> Friday was nice
> Friday was nice, and we were friends.
> If only he had been a woman!
> I wanted to propagate my kind,
> and so did he, I think, poor boy.
> . . . .
> Pretty to watch; he had a pretty body.

Crusoe breaks off, silent on the details of his relationship with Friday until the poem's close, where, examining the relics of his island experience, he finds them useless—all except the haunting memory of his friend: "And Friday, my dear Friday, died of measles / seventeen years ago come March." The plaintive, arcane "come" with its forward thrust, assures one that Friday's memory, rather than fading with time, will, in Crusoe's imagination, expand through it. "A boy with a pretty body," he dies of a childhood disease, neither able to produce new life nor himself to live. Such a recollection of lost friendship is finally the best Crusoe as survivor can do, invoking through his reminiscence a homemade world where, in the midst of stark privation, the stranded, exiled imagination philosophizes, dances, and sings. The hallucinatory quality of Crusoe's experience reveals a desperately fertile mind struggling for its very life.

In tones of wry and bitter humor, in language deceptively innocent yet expressive of deep feeling, "Crusoe in England" articulates an extenuating quality which parallels that of Bishop's own poetics. Through the narrative transposition of female to male voice, a voice that describes an asexual world in which the self longs to sustain its imaginative life, Bishop evokes a homoerotic desire equivalent to that which informs her own linguistic imagination. Spoken in the naive tongue of the masculine voyager, what Crusoe's words ironically veil is the plaint of a self questing beyond the hierarchies of the heterosexual, an imagination creating a homeground in exile. Through his conversion of the harshest of geographic regions, Crusoe bizarrely celebrates the powers of the solipsistic imagination transforming the truths of isolation. Although Bishop's carefully modulated ironies and cool reserve distance her from Crusoe's desperate creativity, what her vision shares with her daemonic persona's is a desire to convert such isolation into a region that allows her to reconstitute the relationship between self, words, and world—to identify, solely in her own terms, an island made new for both poetry and friendship. The eye of the traveller and the innocence of the voice combine here to test the wild freedom of privation as well as to acknowledge the pain of its irretrievable loss.

As Bishop writes in "Santarém," a poem from the last year of her life (1979):

> Even if one were tempted
> to literary interpretation
> such as: life/birth, right/wrong, male/female
> —such notions would have resolved, dissolved, straight off
> in that watery, dazzling dialectic.

The alluvial dialectic we witness in Santarém is created not by divergence but by the confluence of the Tapajós and Amazon rivers. In her attempt to free herself from the Emersonian tradition, Bishop, as she states here, eschews the hieratic distinctions of Self-Other which are its foundation. Her literary dialectic, akin to the merging rivers which she so admires and does not want to leave, converts her ground of loss, of deprivation based on gender, into a source of strength. Through this redefinition, Bishop tests the very origins of literary sexual difference by trying on a comparison between Santarém and Eden, the canonical genesis of guilt related to gender. The distinction between these two sacred scenes depends, for Bishop, on the difference between divergence and union. "Two rivers. Hadn't two rivers sprung / from the Garden of Eden?" "No, that was four / and they'd diverged. Here only two and coming together." Arriving at the place where she "really wanted to go no farther," Bishop describes an alternative Eden, one that rejects the patriarchal, Judaeo-Christian origins of sexual differentiation for a fusion that draws all power into the observing self. This engrossing self differs from Emerson's imperial "I" in its very disavowal of a dualism founded upon sexual differentiation; Bishop's "I" evades by eliding the gender distinctions so pervasive in Emerson's rhetorical world view. Nor is this an instance of androgynous merging; instead, the very terms of the observing self reject the premises of gender identification.

Turning from this moment in "Santarém" when Bishop delineates the conditions that surround the Sublime moment (an experience she typically defines through travel, presence, and observation—the lapidary radicalism that informs Bishop's best poems), I want to consider a text vastly different in tone, but which treats rather directly, if with characteristic archness, the issue of sexual transference. Aware of the ontological ambiguities behind the apparently innocent activity of "Exchanging Hats," Bishop writes:

> Unfunny uncles who insist
> in trying on a lady's hat,
> —oh, even if the joke falls flat,
> we share your slight transvestite twist
> in spite of our embarrassment.

The acknowledgment of shared interest in sexual shifts, the "slight transvestite twist," is not unrelated to a plural self, as the poem's "we" at once playfully dissociates the speaker from the poet and simultaneously suggests her multiple identities. The provisional status of costume itself becomes an issue as it prods the fictive imagination: "Costume and custom are complex. / The headgear of the other sex / inspires us to experiment." Mysteries, Bishop informs us, are revealed as much as they are hidden by such awkward experimentation. Tawdry as the "unfunny uncle" seems, he may still be hiding "stars inside" his "black fedora." And the "aunt exemplary and slim," (at once an ideal and an exemplum) becomes, through her "avernal" eyes, at once hellishly male and female and, through the auditory associations of the adjective, "vernal," springlike, embodying change and rebirth. Bishop underscores this second reading by speaking of change:

> Aunt exemplary and slim,
> with avernal eyes, we wonder
> what slow changes they see under
> their vast, shady, turned-down brim.

Bishop's play on "avernal" recalls, then, the abyssal eyes of her aunt and the vernal mix of opposites, the equinoctial experience of night and day as analogous to a male/female equivalency that remains a mystery both apparently to itself and to the observer. The brim of the aunt's hat, like the uncle's fedora, withholds knowledge from view as it ambiguously protects one's identity from a too intense scrutiny.

Such a blurring of distinctions and the implications of crossing over through costume reappear in the late poem, "Pink Dog," where the poor animal is dangerously exposed (her vulnerability the result of her nakedness). The subject of Bishop's poem, a rather sickly, depilated bitch, must disguise herself so that she avoids being an object of scorn or ridicule; she must don a costume to survive the continuing "celebration" of life known as Carnival. Despite a vast difference in tone, "Pink Dog" is related to Wallace Stevens's "The American Sublime," for both poems address what one needs to survive in a place of deception. Stevens, seeking what will suffice, poses the question, "How does one stand / To behold the sublime, / To confront the mockers, / The mickey mockers / And plated pairs?" His provisional answer is a stripping away of the external self so that all that remains is "The spirit and space, / The empty spirit / In vacant space." What can such a spirit draw upon for sustenance? Stevens poses this question in sacramental terms, asking where one can find a sustaining faith. "What wine does one drink? / What bread does one eat?", lines Bishop will parodically echo at the close of her poem. "Pink Dog" similarly confronts a world of disguise and advocates a necessary defense, not, however, a stripping away but the armor of costume. And the difference in response, I suggest, is related to the dog's color, to her femaleness, to the biological embarrassments of being a nursing mother with scabies (a disease caused by an insect that gets under the skin and causes intense itching). Her discomfort, then, is related to a once external, now internalized agent, a discomfort that can be masked but not cured by disguise.

Immediately following the poem's opening, "The sun is blazing and the sky is blue," with its echo of another Stevens poem about transformation, "The house was quiet, and the world was calm," we meet the hairless dog. Afraid of contagion, the crowds "draw back and stare" with us.

> Of course they're mortally afraid of rabies.
> you are not mad; you have a case of scabies
> but look intelligent. Where are your babies?

The dog's raw, pink skin and her hanging teats need a defense that can only come through the use of intelligence operating as disguise. Bishop rhymes teats and wits with an apparently effortless, desperado humor, an associative gesture so assured that the identification seems, as it frequently does in her poems, to carry all the circumstantiality of truth.

> (A nursing mother, by those hanging teats.)
> In what slum have you hidden them, poor bitch
> while you go begging, living by your wits?

Unless the "poor bitch" can now redirect her wits in aid of disguise, she will join those "idiots, paralytics, parasites" thrown into nearby tidal rivers. The practical solution, explains the level-headed sardonic voice of the poem, is to wear a "fantasia," a carnival costume: the time for penance, for suffering, "Ash Wednesday'll come but Carnival is here." The only way to merge with the present and save oneself is through disguise. With a stunning irony that borders on parody, Bishop's "What sambas can you dance? What will you wear?" echoes Stevens's "What wine does one drink? / What bread does one eat?", converting his sacramental question into a *danse macabre*, where deceit becomes (albeit with a playful gesture toward the pathos of the subject and the speaker's common-sensical tone) the only means for survival. With the Ecclesiastical "all is vanity" lurking behind the question of dress, costume here is granted the importance of survival through Bishop's sardonic parody. At this moment, however, the poem pulls back as the now-generalizing voice belittles all attacks on "Carnival" to speak with a crowd's boosterism (thus intensifying the pressure on the pink dog by increasing her isolation and extenuating her anomalous status):

> Carnival is always wonderful!
> A depilated dog would not look well.
> Dress up! Dress up and dance at Carnival!

Such a dance would, of course, be a living lie performed in order to win the guarantee of life's continuation. The voice that proffers this advice is at once sympathetic and admonitory, insisting that the necessity of costume in such a situation is self-evident.

The issue here, as in Huizinga's descriptions of medieval dances, is one of death and the flesh; only external form can control and thus insure the pink dog's safety. Though the doubly enforcing distance of species and consciousness separates the woman and the dog, the fact that the poem's speaker gives her advice with such assurance suggests that their situations, while apparently dissimilar enough for the speaker to adopt a peremptory tone, nonetheless reflect the need for similar action. The two are related by their exposure, their gender, and, perhaps, their vulnerability. Wit alone can protect each of them—a wit the poet practices so as to disguise and preserve her identity. Rarely does Bishop confront masking so directly, although throughout her poems, the need for protection is met by the courage of a self willing to insure the risk of exposure. In fact, the predicament of the isolated, exiled, anomolous self, whether in "Man-Moth" or "Giant Toad," keeps reappearing because it is related to Bishop's sense of herself as poet, particularly as woman poet in relation to the tradition.

Compensation (as Emerson himself came to recognize) is not only a boon in nature, but may be a significant human activity as well. In her creation of a poetics that seeks to disrupt the fixities of our inherited understanding, Bishop strives not simply to turn the world upside down (as in her poem "Insomnia," where the expression of true feeling is articulated by an imagined visual inversion of the real image), but, more subtly, to assign the human map of comprehension a less rigid set of directions, an alternative geography based not upon polarities of difference but upon the dictates of the poet / geographer's painterlike understanding freed of disabling divisions: "More delicate than the historian's are the map-makers' colors." Inherited historical distinctions fade before this more vivid rendering of personal aesthetics. Bishop's eye thus evades (as it questions the distinctions of both geography and gender, envisioning in their stead a world that invites a freer conception of sexual identity and a highly particular sense of place—the dissolution of all externally imposed hieratic distinctions. Such an alternative mapping creates, as in "Santarém," another version of the Sublime, one that develops from an inherited sense of loss and discontinuity, that with dazzling restraint reconstitutes the world according to its and the world's priorities. With all the audacity of Emerson, albeit disguised by a tact made necessary by the radicalism of her vision, Bishop's poems aim at nothing short of freedom from the inherently dualistic tradition that lies not only at the foundations of the American Sublime, but at the very heart of the Western literary tradition itself.

Bishop alters her stance *vis à vis* the Emersonian Sublime by denying her secondariness in relation to the central poet. In her rejection of Emerson's assigning woman to subordination, she herself also disavows an overt sexual presence without sacrificing erotic intensity. Bishop thus manages a more complete and, in some ways, a more extreme self-metamorphosis than even Emerson achieves. By incorporating the male Not Me into the female Me and so creating a transsexual self-as-poet, Bishop does not simply present an impersonal or asexual poetic voice, but rather substitutes a comprehensiveness that extends her authority over experience. There is no depersonalization here; instead, by so eradicating the dialectical terms in which Emerson, the frustrated monist, had been forced to face his world, Bishop rejects the debilitation of the woman poet at the moment of Sublime infusion of power into the Self. Imagining that incursive power as neither male nor female and experiencing her self as beyond gender, Bishop defuses the Oedipal struggle by desexualizing it. Nor does she simply play the role of passive observer in this transformation. In fact, her imaginative gestures, as in "One Art" and "The Fish," are often those of active relinquishment, the compensatory work of the imagination we call poetry. Finally, it is in the act of reconstitution, of a moment recaptured—a moose's sudden appearance, loss of a sense of self while waiting for her aunt at the dentist's office, the death of an intimate friend—that Bishop recovers herself as center of a self-made world as independent as Dickinson's. Such sacrificial compensation may seem more severe than Emerson's, yet the extremity proves a necessary defense on the part of a woman poet who would face the Romantic imagination's insistence upon the poet as central man. Even when she is most carefully describing the world before her, Bishop meticulously celebrates departure, loss becoming a precondition for poetic entitlement. This tendency, though akin to an extreme solipsism, is for Bishop, if not always for Dickinson, a relinquishment that includes an acceptance of the world as it is, an imaginative vision that constitutes an act of generosity, extending to the world, through the poet's precise descriptive powers, its own inviolable autonomy.

If, for Bishop, the Sublime poem must begin and end in loss, hers is a loss equivalent to restitution—no intrusive self but a world as minutely observed as it is tellingly rendered; for, between the brackets of loss stands the witness of the poem, as in "Crusoe in England," the making of a homeground so distinctive Robert Lowell once remarked of Bishop's work, "She's gotten a world, not just a way of writing." Bishop imagines a form of life where circumstantiality merges into art, where the rivers of Santarém run together, where breathtakingly subtle modulations of language replace Dickinson's encoded poetics. The costume so necessary to the "pink dog's" survival becomes, for its creator, a highly articulate speech that distances as it draws us ever closer to the anomolous, isolated, yet sublimely defiant territory Bishop calls home.

Chronology

1911	Born February 8 in Worcester, Massachusetts, daughter of William Thomas Bishop and Gertrude Bulmer Bishop, both of Canadian families. Poet's father dies when she is eight months old.
1916	Insanity of poet's mother becomes permanent after several previous breakdowns. Separation of daughter from mother, never to meet again. Miss Bishop subsequently raised by maternal grandparents in Nova Scotia.
1927	Enters boarding school in Natick, Massachusetts.
1930–34	Attends Vassar College. First meeting with poet Marianne Moore in 1934.
1935–38	Travels in France, England, North Africa, Spain, Ireland, and Italy.
1939	Moves to Key West.
1943	Lives in Mexico.
1945	Houghton Mifflin Poetry Award.
1946	*North & South*, first book, published.
1949–50	Consultant in Poetry, Library of Congress.
1951	First visit to Brazil; decision to live there.
1955	*Poems: North & South—A Cold Spring.*
1956	Pulitzer Prize.
1957	*The Diary of "Helena Morley."*
1965	*Questions of Travel.*
1969	*The Complete Poems.* Becomes Poet-in-Residence at Harvard.
1970	National Book Award.
1976	*Geography III.* National Book Critics Circle Award.
1979	Dies on October 6.
1983	*The Complete Poems 1927–1979.*
1984	*The Collected Prose.*

Contributors

HAROLD BLOOM, Sterling Professor of the Humanities at Yale University, is the author of *The Anxiety of Influence, Poetry and Repression* and many other volumes of literary criticism. His forthcoming study, *Freud: Transference and Authority*, attempts a full-scale reading of all of Freud's major writings. A MacArthur Prize Fellow, he is general editor of five series of literary criticism published by Chelsea House.

JOHN ASHBERY is one of the most distinguished of living poets. His volumes include *The Double Dream of Spring, Houseboat Days* and *A Wave*.

JAN B. GORDON, who teaches at the State University of New York, Buffalo, has published many articles on the poetry and criticism of the last century.

RICHARD HOWARD is widely acclaimed as poet, critic, and translator. His best known books are *Untitled Subjects*, a volume of verse monologues by eminent Victorians, and *Alone With America*, a study of contemporary American poetry.

JEROME MAZZARO, Professor of English at the State University of New York, Buffalo, has written widely upon both Renaissance and modern poetry.

DAVID KALSTONE is Professor of English at Rutgers University. He is editing the letters of Elizabeth Bishop, and has published extensively upon poets from Sir Philip Sidney to James Merrill and John Ashbery.

JOHN HOLLANDER is Director of Graduate Studies in English at Yale University, where he is Poet-in-Residence. His books include the critical study, *The Figure of Echo*, and *Powers of Thirteen*, a poetic sequence.

HELEN VENDLER teaches both at Boston University and at Harvard. Her books include studies of Yeats, Stevens, George Herbert, and Keats.

WILLARD SPIEGELMAN teaches at Southern Methodist University, where he edits *Southwest Review*. His many articles on Romantic and contemporary poetry include several studies of James Merrill.

ANNE R. NEWMAN teaches at the University of North Carolina, Charlotte, and writes on contemporary poetry.

PENELOPE LAURANS is Associate Editor of the *Yale Review*.

DAVID LEHMAN, poet and critic, is a book reviewer for *Newsweek*. He has edited critical volumes on the poetry of Ashbery and of Merrill.

SANDRA MCPHERSON's volumes of poetry include *Elegies for the Hot Season* and *Patron Happiness*.

DAVID WALKER teaches at Oberlin, and is the author of *The Transparent Lyric*, a study of Stevens and W. C. Williams.

J. D. MCCLATCHY teaches at Princeton. His poetry includes *Scenes from Another Life*; his criticism includes several essays upon the work of James Merrill.

DAVID BROMWICH is Associate Professor of English at Princeton University. He is the author of *Hazlitt: The Mind of the Critic*, and of many essays on contemporary poetry.

JOANNE FEIT DIEHL is Associate Professor of English at the University of California, Davis. She is the author of a study of Emily Dickinson, and of several articles on nineteenth and twentieth century American poetry.

Bibliography

Alvarez, A. "Imagism and Poetesses." *Kenyon Review* 19 (Spring 1957): 321.

Ashbery, John. "The Complete Poems." *The New York Times Book Review* 118 (June 1, 1969): 8.

Bishop, Elizabeth. *North and South.* Boston: Houghton Mifflin, 1946.

———. *Poems: North and South—A Cold Spring.* Boston: Houghton Mifflin, 1955.

———. *Poems.* London: Chatto and Windus, 1956.

———. *Brazil.* New York: Time-Life World Library, 1962.

———. *The Diary of Helena Morley,* translated by Elizabeth Bishop. New York: Farrar, Strauss and Giroux, 1965.

———. *Questions of Travel.* New York: Farrar, Straus and Giroux, 1967.

———. *The Ballad of the Burglar of Babylon.* New York: Farrar, Straus and Giroux, 1969.

———. *The Complete Poems.* New York: Farrar, Straus and Giroux, 1969.

———. *Geography III.* New York: Farrar, Straus and Giroux, 1976.

———. *The Complete Poems 1927–1979.* New York: Farrar, Straus and Giroux, 1983.

———. *The Complete Prose.* New York: Farrar, Straus and Giroux, 1984.

Bishop, Elizabeth, and Brasil, Emanuel, eds. *An Anthology of Twentieth Century Brazilian Poetry.* Middletown, Conn.: Wesleyan University Press, 1972.

Bloom, Harold. "The Necessity of Misreading." *Georgia Review* 29 (Summer 1975): 267.

———. "Books Considered." *The New Republic* 176 (Feb. 5, 1977): 29.

Bogan, Louise. "On 'North and South'." *The New Yorker* 22 (Oct. 5, 1946): 121.

Booth, Philip. "The Poet as Voyager." *The Christian Science Monitor* 58 (Jan. 6, 1966): 10.

Bromwich, David. "Verse Chronicle." *The Hudson Review* 30 (Summer 1977): 279.

———. "The Retreat from Romanticism." *Times Literary Supplement* (July 8, 1977): 831.

Brown, Ashley. "Elizabeth Bishop." *Dictionary of Literary Biography.* Detroit: Gayle Research, 1980.

———. "Elizabeth Bishop in Brazil." *Southern Review* 13 (Oct. 1977): 688.

Davison, Peter. "The Gilt Edge of Reputation." *The Atlantic Monthly* 217 (Jan. 1966): 82.

Dodsworth, Martin. "The Human Note." *The Listener* 78 (Nov. 30, 1967): 720.

Ehrenpreis, Irvin. "Solitude and Isolation." *Virginia Quarterly Review* 42 (Spring 1966): 163.

———. "Loitering Between Dream and Experience." *Times Literary Supplement* (Jan. 18, 1968): 61.

———. "Viewpoint." *Times Literary Supplement* (Feb. 8, 1974): 132.

Estess, Sybil P. "The Delicate Art of Map Making." *Southern Review* 13 (Oct. 1977): 705.

———. "Shelters for 'What is Within': Meditation and Epiphany in the Poetry of Elizabeth Bishop." *Modern Poetry Studies* 8 (Spring 1977): 50.

Fowlie, Wallace. "Poetry of Silence." *Commonweal* 65 (Feb. 15, 1957): 514.

Frankenberg, Lloyd. *Pleasure Dome.* Boston: Houghton Mifflin, 1949.

———. "Meaning in Modern Poetry." *Saturday Review* 29 (March 23, 1946): 5.

Garrigue, Jean. "Elizabeth Bishop's School." *The New Leader* 48 (Dec. 6, 1965): 22.

Gibbs, Barbara. "A Just Vision." *Poetry* 69 (Jan. 1947): 228.

Goldensohn, Lorrie. "Elizabeth Bishop's Originality." *American Poetry Review* 7 (March/April 1978): 18.

Hamilton, Ian. "Women's-Eye Views." *The Observer* (Dec. 31, 1967): 20.

Hollander, John. "Elizabeth Bishop's Mappings of Life." *Parnassus* 5 (Spring/ Summer 1977): 359.

Jarrell, Randall. "Fifty Years of American Poetry." *Third Book of Criticism.* New York: Farrar, Straus and Giroux, 1969.

———. *Poetry and the Age.* New York: Farrar, Straus and Giroux, 1969.

Kalstone, David. "All Eye." *Partisan Review* 37 (Spring 1970): 310.

———. "Conjuring with Nature: Some Twentieth-Century Readings of Pastoral." *Twentieth Century Literature In Retrospect*, edited by Reuben Brower. Cambridge: Harvard University Press, 1971.

Liebowitz, Herbert. "The Elegant Maps of Elizabeth Bishop." *The New York Times Book Review* 126 (Feb. 6, 1977): 7.

Lowell, Robert. "For Elizabeth Bishop 1–4." *History.* New York: Farrar, Straus and Giroux, 1973.

———. "Thomas, Bishop, and Williams." *Sewanee Review* 55 (Summer 1947): 493.

Mazzoco, Robert. "A Poet of Landscape." *The New York Review of Books* 9 (Oct. 12, 1967): 4.

McNally, Nancy L. "Elizabeth Bishop: The Discipline of Description." *Twentieth Century Literature* 11 (Jan. 1966): 189.

Merrill, James. "Elizabeth Bishop, 1911–1979." *The New York Review of Books* 26 (Dec. 6, 1979): 6.

Moore, Marianne. "Archaically New." *Trial Balances*, edited by Ann Winslow. New York: Macmillan, 1935.

———. "A Modest Expert." *Nation* 163 (Sept. 28, 1946): 354.

Moss, Howard. "All Praise." *Kenyon Review* 28 (March 1966): 255.

Nemerov, Howard. "The Poems of Elizabeth Bishop." *Poetry* 87 (Dec. 1955): 179.

Perloff, Marjorie. "The Course of a Particular." *Modern Poetry Studies* 8 (Winter 1977): 177.

Pinsky, Robert. "Elizabeth Bishop, 1911–1979." *The New Republic* 181 (Nov. 10, 1979): 32.

———. "The Idiom of a Self: Elizabeth Bishop and Wordsworth." *American Poetry Review* 9 (Jan./Feb. 1980): 6.

Rizza, Peggy. "Another Side of This Life: Women as Poets." *American Poetry Since 1960: Some Critical Perspectives,* edited by Robert B. Shaw. London: Carcanet, 1973.

———. "Elizabeth Bishop, 1911–1979." *The Real Paper* (Oct. 20, 1979).

Schwartz, Lloyd. "Elizabeth Bishop, 1911–1979." *The Boston Phoenix* (Oct. 16, 1979).

———. "One Art: The Poetry of Elizabeth Bishop, 1971–1976." *Ploughshares* 3 (Spring 1977).

Schwartz, Lloyd, and Estess, Sybil P., eds. *Elizabeth Bishop and Her Art.* Ann Arbor: University of Michigan Press, 1983.

Shore, Jane. "Elizabeth Bishop: The Art of Changing Your Mind." *Ploughshares* 5 (1979).

Smith, William Jay. "Geographical Questions: The Recent Poetry of Elizabeth Bishop." *Hollins Critic* 14 (Feb. 1977): 1.

Spiegelman, Willard. "Elizabeth Bishop's 'Natural Heroism'." *Centennial Review* 22 (Winter 1978): 28.

———. "Landscape and Knowledge: The Poetry of Elizabeth Bishop." *Modern Poetry Studies* 6 (Winter 1975): 203.

Wilbur, Richard. "Elizabeth Bishop: A Memorial Tribute." *Ploughshares* 6 (1980).

Williams, Oscar. "North But South." *The New Republic* 115 (Oct. 21, 1946): 525.

Acknowledgments

"Introduction" by Harold Bloom from *Elizabeth Bishop and Her Art*, edited by Lloyd Schwartz and Sybil P. Estess, copyright © 1983 by Harold Bloom. Reprinted by permission.

"The Complete Poems" by John Ashbery from *The New York Times Book Review* (June 1, 1969), copyright © 1969 by *The New York Times*. Reprinted by permission.

"Days and Distances: The Cartographic Imagination of Elizabeth Bishop" by Jan B. Gordon from *Salmagundi* (1973), copyright © 1973 by Skidmore College. Reprinted by permission of Jan B. Gordon.

" 'In the Waiting Room' " by Richard Howard from *Preferences* by Richard Howard, copyright © 1974 by Richard Howard. Reprinted by permission.

"The Poetics of Impediment" by Jerome Mazzaro from *Postmodern American Poetry* by Jerome Mazzaro, copyright © 1980 by the Board of Trustees of the University of Illinois. Reprinted by permission of The University of Illinois Press.

"Questions of Memory, Questions of Travel" by David Kalstone from *Five Temperaments* by David Kalstone, copyright © 1977 by David Kalstone. Reprinted by permission.

"Elizabeth Bishop's Mappings of Life" by John Hollander from *Parnassus* (Fall 1977), copyright © 1977 by Poetry in Review Foundation. Reprinted by permission.

"Domestication, Domesticity and the Otherworldly" by Helen Vendler from *Part of Nature, Part of Us: Modern American Poets*, copyright © 1980 by The President and Fellows of Harvard College. Reprinted by permission of Harvard University Press.

"Elizabeth Bishop's 'Natural Heroism' " by Willard Spiegelman from *Centennial Review* 22 (Winter 1978), copyright © 1978 by *Centennial Review*. Reprinted by permission of Willard Spiegelman and *Centennial Review*.

"Elizabeth Bishop's 'Roosters' " by Anne R. Newman from *Pebble: A Book of Rereadings in Recent American Poetry*, no. 18–19–20 (1980), copyright ©

1979 by Greg Kuzma. Reprinted by permission of Greg Kuzma and The Best Cellar Press.

" 'Old Correspondences': Prosodic Transformations" by Penelope Laurans from *Elizabeth Bishop and Her Art*, edited by Lloyd Schwartz and Sybil P. Estess, copyright © 1983 by The University of Michigan. Reprinted by permission of The University of Michigan Press.

" 'In Prison': A Paradox Regained" by David Lehman from *Elizabeth Bishop and Her Art*, edited by Lloyd Schwartz and Sybil P. Estess, copyright © 1983 by The University of Michigan. Reprinted by permission of The University of Michigan Press.

" 'The Armadillo': A Commentary" by Sandra McPherson from *Field: Contemporary Poetry and Poetics* 31 (Fall 1984), copyright © 1984 by Oberlin College. Reprinted by permission.

" 'Filling Station': Elizabeth Bishop and the Ordinary" by David Walker from *Field: Contemporary Poetry and Poetics* 31 (Fall 1984), copyright © 1984 by Oberlin College. Reprinted by permission.

" 'One Art': Some Notes" by J.D. McClatchy from *Field: Contemporary Poetry and Poetics* 31 (Fall 1984), copyright © 1984 by Oberlin College. Reprinted by permission.

"Elizabeth Bishop's Dream-Houses" by David Bromwich from *Raritan* 4, no. 1 (Summer 1984), copyright © 1984 by *Raritan*. Reprinted by permission.

"At Home With Loss: Elizabeth Bishop and the American Sublime" by Joanne Feit Diehl, printed for the first time in this volume, copyright © 1984 by Joanne Feit Diehl. Printed by permission.

Index

Modern Critical Views